Sacha Guitry:

THE LAST BOULEVARDIER

By the same author:

SAINT-SAËNS AND HIS CIRCLE
THE DUKE OF WELLINGTON

Sacha Guitry:

THE LAST BOULEVARDIER

by James Harding

> Women are an inexhaustible cause of worry and discord. And therefore a continual inspiration for plays.
>
> SACHA GUITRY

CHARLES SCRIBNER'S SONS · NEW YORK

FOR GILL

de tout coeur

❧ Acknowledgments

The late Jean Cocteau and the late René Fauchois, who had known Sacha intimately since his youth, gave generously of their personal reminiscences to help me write this book. I am also grateful to the late Alex Madis, Sacha's friend and biographer; to Gilbert Renault, who is better known as Colonel Rémy, the distinguished Secret Service agent of World War II; to Madame Fernande Choisel, who was Sacha's secretary for some twenty years; to Clément Duhour, who was Sacha's co-producer on some of the later films; and to the musicologist, Rollo Myers, who once knew the alarming experience of having as his immediate neighbors Sacha's current wife, mother-in-law, and mistress. Miss Ellaline Terriss (Lady Seymour Hicks), Miss Heather Thatcher, and Mr. Austin Trevor told me of their acting experiences with Sacha in Paris and London. I am further indebted to Jacques Guignard, curator of the Bibliothèque de l'Arsenal, for permission to work on the extensive Rondel collection there; to Madame Sylvie Chevalley, archivist of the Comédie-Française; to Jean-Louis Sarthe, curator of the Musée de Luchon; and to J. M. Dent & Co., London, for permission to reproduce the photograph of Lucien, Sacha, and Yvonne Printemps. The following organizations offered most helpful co-operation: The British Film Institute (Ernest Lindgren, director, and Miss Brenda Davies, librarian); the Cinémathèque Français (Henri Langlois, director); the Société des Auteurs et Compositeurs Dramatiques; and United Music Publishers (Mrs. Pauline W. Wood, managing director). My thanks are also due to Madame André Lanardonne, Madame de Zogheb, Yves Leroux, and Elliot Henderson.

The lips of Sacha's surviving widows were, understandably, sealed.

Contents

Lever de rideau 3

Chapter 1 7

Chapter 2 17

Chapter 3 25

Chapter 4 32

Chapter 5 45

Chapter 6 51

Chapter 7 71

Chapter 8 96

Chapter 9 116

Chapter 10 139

Chapter 11 160

Chapter 12 177

Chapter 13 197

Chapter 14 215

Chapter 15 228

Chapter 16 245

Baisser de rideau 253

PUBLISHED WORKS OF SACHA GUITRY 255

PLAYS OF SACHA GUITRY 257

FILMS OF SACHA GUITRY—with principal players 263

BIBLIOGRAPHY 266

INDEX 269

List of Illustrations

1. Sacha Guitry
2. The young Sacha
3. Lucien Guitry
4. Sacha with Tristan Bernard and Jules Renard
5. Alphonse Allais, the melancholy humorist
6. Sacha aged 28, with his first wife, Charlotte Lysès
7. A famous trio: Lucien, Yvonne Printemps, and Sacha
8. Introducing Sarah Bernhardt in *Ceux de chez nous*
9, 10. Two of Sacha's friends: Paul Léautaud and Raimu
11, 12. Inside the house at 18, avenue Élisée-Reclus
13. Sacha takes the lead in *le Roman d'un tricheur*
14. Sacha with Jacqueline Delubac in *Bonne Chance*
15. Sacha with Lana Marconi in *N'écoutez pas, Mesdames!*
16. Sacha's sketch of his father
17. A page from the manuscript of *Quadrille*
18. Sacha as Talleyrand in *le Diable boiteux*
19. Sacha with Claudette Colbert in *Si Versailles m'était conté*
20. Sacha on the film set

Sacha Guitry:

THE LAST BOULEVARDIER

Lever de rideau

$\mathcal{T}$he day of the boulevard has long since vanished. It flourished during the nineteen-hundreds in an area bounded to the north by the Madeleine and the rue Royale, and to the south by the boulevard Montmartre. Along the boulevards de la Madeleine, des Capucines, and des Italiens were to be found the haunts frequented by the men who created a minor literature and who added a brief chapter to social history. Many of the landmarks remain. Maxim's restaurant still keeps watch close to the place de la Concorde. The attractive absurdity of the Opéra's wedding-cake design is as fresh as ever. And the Théâtre des Variétés, where Offenbach once reigned, preserves its Empire facade intact. The boulevardiers themselves came from the ranks of journalists, playwrights, novelists, and dandies. Most of their writing was done at marble-topped tables amid the haze and chatter of crowded cafés. Their raffish legacy was an instantly recognizable form of wit. They were impertinent and worldly. They were cynical and disrespectful. They would sacrifice everything for the sake of an epigram.

The last of the race was Sacha Guitry. His father was Lucien Guitry, France's greatest actor at the time. He was born into the theater and made his first stage appearance at the age of five. He grew up in the shadow of Sarah Bernhardt. His mentors were Jules Renard and Octave Mirbeau. His closest friends were Jean Cocteau, Tristan Bernard, and Claude Monet. Sacha had his first play performed when he was sixteen. By the time he was twenty he had become the idol of Paris. An idol he remained for over half a century except for that brief period in 1944 when jealousy found a way of blackening his name and, temporarily, managed to silence a rival whose success was bitterly envied.

In his time Sacha wrote and produced more than a hundred and twenty plays. The leading role he usually acted himself and his current wife would appear opposite him. (He had five wives in all. "Most men have had as many women in their life," he said. "I marry them.") Often there were several plays of his in the Paris theaters at the same time, for he worked at tremendous speed and quickly tired of the boredom of long runs. A Sacha Guitry first night, somebody once remarked, was ". . . the most typically Parisian thing in the world of the theatre—clear, lightly moving, brilliant, like the air of Paris itself, filled with the cynical but still happy tolerance of the author, and with the confident readiness of the audience to be amused and charmed."

The only formula Sacha could offer for his success was a negative one; he always sought to avoid boring people, he said. Like Molière, he aimed to make people think without letting them know he was doing so. With the lightest of touches he drew a moral that was far more telling than the grimmest existential drama. Anyone can write a passable tragedy. It is quite a different matter to write an effective comedy.

The invention of the sound film opened up a still greater

audience for Sacha to conquer. Among the thirty-two films he wrote and directed there are at least three classics of the French cinema. The world came to recognize in him the incarnation of Parisian wit and elegance. Playwright, actor, poet, novelist, sculptor, artist, and superb raconteur, he was throughout his life an avid collector of fine art and of beautiful women. His famous home, which stood in a fashionable avenue not far from the Eiffel Tower, was more like a museum than a private house. He filled it with art treasures and lovely objects. There and on the stage he led the existence he had chosen in the setting which he had himself created with exquisite detail. Few people can have distilled so much enjoyment out of life—or, it may be added, have given so much enjoyment to others.

For Sacha was the complete hedonist. He pursued happiness with imperious exuberance and he was rarely disappointed. His circle was a small one, but he observed it shrewdly and with the same relish as had his equally prolific forerunners, the Italian Goldoni and the Spaniard Lope de Vega. It is true that he did not speculate on the nature of the universe. Neither can it be denied that he failed to give us the benefit of his reflections on the destiny of man. Molière, also a working actor, was guilty of this oversight.

Sacha had style and he had wit. Much may be forgiven the possessor of those rare qualities. His plays and films live on in frequent revivals. The grandchildren of his earliest admirers continue to acclaim the freshness and vivacity of work that in some cases was written as much as fifty years ago. When Sacha died in 1957, there died with him a brilliant world of which he was partly a creator and certainly the last representative.

Chapter 1

Women, I adore you—as one adores a first edition, with all its misprints.

SACHA GUITRY

*T*he abbé de Choisy was born, by some chronological oversight, into the seventeenth rather than the eighteenth century. He is perhaps the only dean of Bayeux Cathedral to have spent his life dressed as a woman. In a blaze of diamonds and rich embroideries, he was a regular patron both of the gaming tables and of the Académie Française, where his literary reputation was sustained by an eleven-volume history of the Church, meditations on the psalms, and dialogues on the immortality of the soul. He was much favored by Louis XIV, who sent him as French Ambassador to Siam. When he was appointed delegate to a Papal Conclave no one seemed to mind very much his habit of dressing his mistresses, among whom was Bossuet's sister-in-law, as boys.

But the engaging abbé, as Kipling would have said, is another story; he appears here as one of the earliest chroniclers to mention the Guitry family. His memoirs, which move gracefully from the

7

pulpit to the court and to the bed, tell of a certain Guy de Chaumont, marquis de Guitry, who was Grand Master of the Wardrobe to Louis XIV and a councillor of state. Guitry had intervened on behalf of Madame de Montespan, the current royal mistress, who was being insolently treated by another member of Louis' entourage. The offender was clapped into prison for ten years, just after Sacha's gallant ancestor had perished in one of the king's wars. Saint-Simon also mentions the incident. The family was already a long-established one, the first Seigneur de Guitry having been active during the eleventh century. Like Sacha, who owned both a town house and three country houses, he had a mania for building which he assuaged by constructing a church in 1020 and spending the rest of his time restoring his château. Sacha had the superstition of the typical actor and never mentioned that the ancestral fiefs included a property called Guitry-Fours, since *four* is theatrical slang for a "a flop."

Sacha's paternal grandfather was born in Merlerault, Normandy. He had all the usual Norman characteristics. A certain hardness, a deep reserve, and a reluctance to talk very much were what his son, Lucien, chiefly remembered about him. He detested sentimentality and only revealed his feelings to those who had known him for years and could appreciate his fund of sincerity and tenderness. His sons he always addressed as *"mes amis,"* and his relationship with them was comradely rather than patriarchal. Each year after his death Lucien would travel, alone, to Merlerault and lay a wreath on his grave. This little village in Normandy had been his father's birthplace and it was here that the family, though long since settled in Paris, had come regularly to spend their summer holidays. Lucien would arrive in the morning and leave in the evening, having made a solitary pilgrimage through the streets and lanes where he had played as a child sixty years before.

In 1847 Sacha's grandfather took over a small cutlery business in the Palais Royal at 139, Galerie de Valois. It had been founded in 1817 by a Monsieur Aubril, who soon became prosperous on the strength of a patent razor sharpener of his own invention. It was a flat object, about the size of a lipstick, wrapped in silver paper and selling at a franc. In return for an annuity of fifteen hundred francs, Monsieur Aubril sold his lease and the secret of his invention. He also, unwittingly, gave his successor his name, for although the face had changed Sacha's grandfather was inevitably addressed by customers for the rest of his life as "Monsieur Aubril."

Little is known of grandmother Guitry except that her resemblance to Queen Victoria tended to chill the infant Sacha. She was a noble-looking woman with strong features and a generous mouth. There was, Sacha thought, a strange similarity between her and Lucien. "I realize now that it was not only her glance that impressed us: it was the same commanding attitude, that same gift of wearing any garment with an air, that same ability to remain a long time motionless, and that same pleasure in remaining silent." It is clear that Lucien inherited from his mother some of his most notable traits as an actor.

The Guitrys had four children. The first, Edmond, was born with unquenchable good humor and wit. He followed his father and sold the razor sharpener and shaving soap, in the service of which his talents must have been persuasive. To the customer who queried whether the soap would live up to his promise he would blandly reply: "For thirty years I have used no other," and no one ever thought of remarking upon the luxuriant beard he wore. His sister Adèle was a born spinster. When she grew up she lived with a monkey as her sole companion. Even though it once bit her ferociously she did not refer to the incident and considered any mention of it by a third party as the height of bad taste. She never went out visiting, never received, and spent her Sundays on a bench in the garden of the Palais Royal. The third child, Valentine, was a talented pianist who won a first prize at the Conservatoire in 1867. She enjoyed a hearty old age and answered enquiries after her health with: "I've got quite enough for my age, thank you." Valentine was a piano teacher all her life and old habits died hard. Once, bidding farewell to a little boy, she bent down to kiss him and murmured absent-mindedly: "Goodbye, little girl, and don't forget to bring your fourth finger down hard."

Lucien Guitry was born on December 13, 1860, at 27, rue de Valois. He had chosen an appropriate setting for his birth. Nearby is the rue de Richelieu where Molière's son was born, a few doors down from the friend who lent the dramatist his dressing gown and nightcap to play Argan at the first night of *le Malade imaginaire*. Even more fitting was the presence of the Comédie-Française itself at the junction of the rue de Richelieu and the rue de Rivoli. Had Lucien arrived four months earlier he would have been able to call Normandy his birthplace, for that was where the family, as usual, had passed their summer holidays. As it happened, the city of his birth added a Parisian gloss to the flint of his Norman ancestry.

At the age of nine Lucien was attacked by a bout of typhoid so severe that he lost his memory. It became necessary for him to start his education all over again, and in the process, by some strange psychological quirk, his memory, which had until then been no more than ordinary, suddenly became abnormally re-tentive. It was to stay so for the rest of his life and it explains why he remained word-perfect in dozens of roles many years after he had first acted them. His father, too, had an excellent memory, and this brings us to the one topic which would arouse him from his usual taciturnity. The old man was incurably stage-struck, and so was his wife. He had more than fifty plays of every kind off by heart and could recite all the parts in them. The family home resounded to the tirades of Corneille and Racine, and one day even the cook was to be heard declaiming the imprecations of Camille in the middle of her washing-up. Around seven o'clock in the evening, by which time the box-office at the

Comédie-Française had decided whether or not there was going to be a full house, it often happened that doorkeepers were sent along the galleries of the Palais Royal distributing complimentary tickets to the shopkeepers. Even a "paper" house was preferred to empty seats at the Maison de Molière, and Lucien's father was delighted to help keep up appearances. If his wife could not go with him he took one of the children, the girls dressing as boys when their turn came so that they could be admitted to the pit.

When Lucien started school he proved, as his son was to do after him, a poor pupil. His exercise books were badly kept and, worse still, seemed to indicate that he rarely went to lessons. Confronted with his father's natural curiosity, he was fertile in excuses but unable to conceal that he was spending whole days in a public reading room. There he studied plays which he was learning by heart. It is hardly necessary to say that Guitry *père* was thrilled and took the logical step of sending him to drama lessons. Lucien's first teacher was Monrose, a retired actor from the Comédie-Française where he had maintained a father-son tradition of playing comic servants in the classic comedies. He was plump, bushy-browed, and enveloped in a roomy dressing-gown whence peeped forth Turkish slippers. "I want to learn how to act," announced Lucien. Glancing at the schoolboy's satchel Monrose growled: "You'd do better pulling up cabbages." This, as Lucien afterwards said, was the first piece of advice Monrose gave and the only one he did not follow. "What do you know?" the old actor enquired.

"Everything!"

"You're a fool . . . you don't know everything. You don't know *le Philosophe marié.*"

Whereupon Lucien obliged with a long extract.

"That's enough. You don't know *les Fourberies de Scapin.*"

But Lucien knew his Molière as well. He also knew his Corneille, his Racine, and all the other dramatists his interrogator could think of. Monrose give up and, peering over his gold-rimmed spectacles, said simply: "I prefer you in the comic parts." Then he drew forth a huge register, wrote down Lucien's name and address, and asked how old he was. The boy told him. "And what the devil do you think you'll ever do at the age of thirteen?!" roared Monrose angrily. Nevertheless, he calmed down enough to write an authorization for Lucien to attend his classes at the Conservatoire.

Two years later the precocious actor was old enough to be accepted as a full pupil at the Conservatoire. He showed exceptional ability. At the age of fifteen he looked nineteen, and this maturity revealed itself in his work. He became bored with lessons. He wanted a live audience, footlights and the sound of applause, and he wanted them as quickly as possible. All he asked of life—except for women—was the theater, and if, for some terrible reason, he had had to choose between the two he would, after a moment's struggle, have given up the former. Many years afterwards, when he had achieved everything that fame and money could bring, he was asked what was his greatest happiness in life. Without hesitation he replied: "The moment when I prepare to open the door of a stage set." It was this total absorption in his art which inspired his father to hire a theater for him. On a Sunday in January 1877, Lucien made his first public appearance at the age of seventeen playing Don César de Bazan in Hugo's piece of romantic bravura, *Ruy Blas*. The cast of this production at the Théâtre Saint-Denis was made up of fellow pupils at the Conservatoire who each received a fee of ten francs from Guitry *père*. Other performances were given at the Théâtre d'Étampes outside Paris where they arrived at six in the evening, were fed on sandwiches by Lucien's father while they made up in their dressing rooms, and then caught the train back after the show. Thanks to paternal generosity, Lucien was able in this way to serve a practical apprenticeship in the classic roles. It must be added that on occasion he gave imitations of Coquelin, Mounet-Sully, Brasseur, and other famous actors, and—the record is sadly firm on this point—even danced in a vaudeville one night.

The following year Lucien emerged from his examinations at the Conservatoire with second prizes in Tragedy and Comedy. The jury was presided over by the composer Ambroise Thomas, who had by that time completed his sixty-seventh year and his nineteenth opera. Other members were the dramatists Émile Augier, Alexandre Dumas, Victorien Sardou (the Anouilh of his day), the popular but now forgotten novelist Octave Feuillet, and those inseparable comic authors Meilhac and Halévy. The ordeal was made all the more nerve-racking in that it was public and was attended by drama critics of the leading Paris newspapers. They would invariably begin their reviews next morning: "The examination was neither worse nor better than the previous one . . ." The fact that he had not won a first prize did not worry Lucien, for he regarded that "laughable dump," which was how he described the Conservatoire, as a boring formality. "You will, I hope," he told a later generation of students, "consider the teaching you get there as of little importance compared with what you will hasten to learn by yourselves."

But the Conservatoire had not done with him yet. The contract he had signed on entering gave the Comédie-Française first call on his services. The administrator, Émile Perrin, decided to take up the option and ruled that Lucien should spend one more year at the Conservatoire before going on stage at the Français. Lucien was outraged. For the clause with which Perrin was threatening him had long since fallen into disuse. He was determined, however, to make an example. Lucien had also taken his decision. He marched straight out of Perrin's office to the director of the Théâtre du Gymnase and signed a three-year contract with him. The court gave judgment to Perrin, and while the young man was carrying out his first professional engagement he must often have wondered how on earth he was to pay a fine of ten thousand francs, when his annual salary amounted to just over half that sum. Moreover, the new contract was much harder than anything Perrin had ever suggested. Under its terms he was to be at the orders of the director at all times, if necessary to act in two theaters on the same day, and if he fell ill he was to receive no salary at all. He did not care. He had shown his contempt for the "laughable dump" and for a State theater which he looked upon as a haven of security for mediocre actors. At the age of eighteen he was magnificently confident in his destiny. Most important of all, he was now really acting.

During his years of near slavery at the Gymnase, Lucien established himself as an actor of promise and attracted the attention of Sarah Bernhardt. She was then at the beginning of her glory. The illegitimate daughter of a French lawyer and a Dutch-Jewish cocotte, she had been helped into the theater by the duc de Morny, one of her mother's more influential lovers.*
As a junior member of the Comédie-Française, she had swept out of its corridors angrily refusing to apologize for baiting the theater manager. Then she had gained her first real success in François Coppée's little fantasy, *le Passant,* where Venetian costume had shown her long slim legs to exquisite advantage. Reconciled with the Maison de Molière, she triumphed during a six-week season in London which brought receipts of nearly half a million francs. When she finally broke with the Comédie-Française, in a career which was more than usually littered with lawsuits, she was fined a hundred thousand francs which she paid off by irregular instalments from the takings of her foreign tours.

Much has been written about Sarah. We have heard in detail of the generous assortment of lovers ranging from the Prince de Ligne, by whom she had a son, to King Edward VII. We have been told of her menagerie of boa constrictors, cheetahs, crocodiles, and wolf hounds. We have seen pictures of the human skull,

---

* Accounts of Sarah's birth and parentage vary enormously—she had a fertile imagination.

autographed by Hugo, which she used as an ink-well; of the rosewood coffin, lined with satin and old love letters, in which she slept; and of her statuary, for she was a clever sculptor who excelled in full-breasted art-nouveau torsos. We have admired that extravagant flair for publicity which caused an exasperated author to write *"All about Sarah 'Barnum' Bernhardt, her loveys, her doveys, her capers and her funniments,"* after her riotous American tour. And we have savored the ferocity which nourished her vendettas against rival actresses. ("She's done for, poor woman. Why do they let her go on acting? Look at those cords standing out on her neck—ropes, they are. Somebody ought to tear them out and strangle her with them.") Photographs of Sarah give little idea of her strange beauty, black-eyed and pallid-faced, or of the power that bewitched audiences for over half a century. The fabulous "golden voice," emerging painfully from old cylinders and primitive gramophone records, ends as a strangulated croak. If, after nearly fifty years in the grave, she can still excite the imagination so vividly, what must she have been like when alive? The drama critic Maurice Baring supplied a fair answer when, speaking of other actresses in roles which Sarah had made her own, he wrote: ". . . one longed in vain for those haunting, thirsty eyes that sent an electric current through the whole theatre, for that voice that made you think the words were being spoken for the first time; for those gestures which were too swift to analyze, for that harmony and rhythm in utterance, movement, speech and silence, crescendo and diminuendo, speed and pause and delay. . . ."

For Lucien, who traveled to London in June 1882, as a member of Sarah's company, there was no doubt at all. "Sarah," he apostrophized her, "an incomparable splendor . . . a monster sublime with grace, power and nobility . . . Sarah, whom we named 'Sarah' when we talked about her and whom we called 'Madame' when we talked to her—yes, 'My Lady,' for she was truly Our Lady of the Theater." He played Armand Duval to

Sarah's Marguerite Gautier in *la Dame aux camélias,* that venerable tear-jerker which few French actresses have been able to resist. He was also in Hugo's *Hernani* and Legouvé and Scribe's
Adrienne Lecouvreur. Sarah was by now a familiar visitor to London, where her annual appearances were a major event of the
season and where she was royally welcomed by Irving and Ellen
Terry. She adored London and its squares, the bustle of Hyde
Park and the gaiety of Rotten Row. The city also had sentimental
memories for her. The previous year, at St. Andrew's Church off
Oxford Street, a flustered curate had solemnized her marriage to
the ineffectual drug addict who became her legal husband. This
time she was to assist at a similar occasion, though in a supporting
role, as witness to Lucien's marriage at St. Martin-in-the-Fields.
His bride was a twenty-year-old beauty called Renée de Pont-Jest,
whom he had abducted against her father's wishes. It was a sort
of poetic justice, for the gay blade himself was untypically strait-
laced where his only child was concerned. They were married on
Wednesday, June 10. "Ah, that first trip to London, where I
arrived on Saturday evening at six o'clock," Lucien remembered.
"Everything was shut! And the next day was Sunday! The day
after was Whit Monday! Tuesday was the Queen's birthday! On
Wednesday, fortunately, I found something to do . . ."

Chapter 2

Deception, betrayal, yes, they're awful—but remaining faithful is cruel too, because it means chaining down the other.

SACHA GUITRY

Lucien's involuntary father-in-law, René de Pont-Jest, was a noted dandy, wit, duelist, and boulevardier. He dutifully neglected his wife to spend all his evenings and many of his nights at the tables of the Press Club, where he eventually ruined himself elaborating an infallible system of playing the squares around zero. (His grandson Sacha inherited this doomed propensity for the neighborhood of zero and was convinced it would one day win him the bank at Monte Carlo, chandeliers, carpets and all.) Pont-Jest's razor-sharp mustache, ubiquitous monocle, check trousers, and snow-white spats were familiar in all the boulevard cafés and newspaper offices. He was a prolific journalist who wrote many gossip columns and started a vogue for "eye-witness" reports of fashionable court cases. As a young Marine officer he had traveled and adventured in China. By the end of his long Parisian career he was the hero of twelve duels in the Bois de Boulogne.

Besides his journalism, René de Pont-Jest wrote over forty books—now totally forgotten. *Le Fire Fly,* though, is still readable as an exotic account of travels in the Far East. Most of his output consisted of "daring" novels, often running to three large volumes after initial publication as newspaper serials. He was a universal provider of detective stories and tales of high life in St. Petersburg or of low life among opera singers and artists' models.

Though Pont-Jest had been fiercely opposed to his daughter's marrying an actor, when the couple returned from London he was apparently resigned to the situation. Soon a baby was expected, and Lucien, at the age of twenty-two and with a family to support, signed a contract for nine consecutive winter seasons at the Mikhailovsky Theater in St. Petersburg. There he served another arduous apprenticeship. A new play was mounted every week throughout the season, and during the period of his contract he must have played at least fifty roles, from Shakespeare and Hugo to adaptations of novels by Zola and Daudet. On special occasions Alexander III and his court would honor the troupe with their attendance, and once, as Lucien never forgot, asked for the company to be presented. "Expressions were strained and smiles anxious. I was on the far end at the left next to an old actress who had been playing at the Mikhailovsky Theater for twenty years. The Emperor took three steps in her direction. This intimidated my neighbor so much that her stomach began at first to rumble, to complain, to make an unbelievable uproar, like the noise of an overloaded dustcart. Then there came a dripping sound and a wail from her innards, suddenly followed by something like the prolonged tearing of several yards of silk. It was extremely painful for me to think that the Tsar might attribute to my personal entrails the extraordinary characteristics of the lady's inside, so I moved away a couple of steps."

The Guitry firstborn, a boy, only survived a few days. A second son, Jean, was born in Russia on March 5, 1884. The third son, also born during a winter season at the Mikhailovsky Theater, came into the world at No. 12, Nevsky Prospekt, on February 21, 1885. His parents looked at him in horror and exchanged a sad look. "He's a monster," said Lucien comfortingly, "but never mind. We'll love him just the same." The boy was christened Alexandre Georges Pierre, and his first name was soon shortened to the diminutive, Sacha, by his Russian nurse. A fourth son, born in France, did not survive.

During the first five years of their lives, the Guitry brothers spent their winters in Russia and their summers in France, their father traveling back and forth to fulfill his engagement with the Imperial Theaters. As many women later found, existence with Lucien was apt to be bad on the nerves, and soon the daughter of René de Pont-Jest was suing him for divorce. While the action was being prepared, Jean and Sacha lived with their mother, who returned to her father's house again. Lucien came to see them on Sundays, and on one particular visiting day—he wore a check overcoat and cape, Sacha remembered—he embraced them both, took a long look at them, and said: "I know that Jean hasn't been a good boy this week, so it's Sacha I shall take with me to buy the cakes for dessert." Holding a proud Sacha by the hand, he led him to an open cab that waited by the door. At the first cake shop they passed, the little boy excitedly pointed it out. "No, not that one," said Lucien. Five minutes later they passed another. "No, the cakes aren't very good there, either. There's a better one farther on." To calm his perplexity, Lucien added: "You'll get your cakes, never fear." After another quarter of an hour's drive they arrived at a railway station where Lucien paid off the driver and bundled Sacha under the folds of his cape. The innocent trip for cakes had become a kidnap. As the train steamed on toward Russia, the realization dawned upon an agitated household in Paris, and while an infuriated René de Pont-Jest demanded Lucien's arrest and sent dramatic telegrams to all the towns on the route, Sacha lay wrapped in a blanket under the carriage-seat quivering with terror at every frontier they crossed.

Thus Sacha accompanied Lucien on his last winter season in St. Petersburg. "Of course, what he did was horribly cruel," noted Sacha, "since my mother was to go eight months without seeing me again. But let no one ask me to regret having been during those months the best loved, most spoilt and cherished child that ever lived."

Lucien had copies made of some of his theater costumes and Sacha paraded up and down the drawing room showing off Louis XI's cloak or Hamlet's doublet and hose. He stood his toy Punch behind a towel rack, dubbed him Polonius, and killed him so often that he ended by destroying him. Grown-ups listened with amusement as the child bellowed ranting speeches from old melodramas. "How like his father he looks!" they cried. Sacha, too, was convinced of the resemblance and had long ago made up his mind to do what Lucien did when he grew up—but he was not at all sure what this was. The dinner-table conversation did not help. "I nearly died laughing at Hittemans in Two . . ." Lucien would recall the day's work. "Lina Munte is doing well now, but she's been hamming it up over the past few days . . . As for Lorteur, he's terrified he'll dry up on Tuesday." There was, it seemed, something very special about Tuesday, which Sacha later learned was opening night of the week at the Mikhailovsky. On these evenings Lucien dined nervously and hurriedly, and Sacha, looking up from his plate, would be transfixed by a thick-browed frown and told: "Monsieur le Marquis, you are a nobleman and I am but a commoner, yet I dare tell you that any man who insults a woman is a coward!" Then, in a loud voice, Lucien would accuse himself of the most abominable crimes—in front of the servants, too, Sacha worried. Suddenly, his threatening glare melting into unbelievable gentleness, he would coo at his astonished son: "Clementine, I would give my life for a kiss from your lips." Sacha went to bed puzzled and curious. "Where is papa going this evening?" he asked his nurse as she tucked him up. "He's going to work and earn some money for you." Seeing his surprise, she added: "Well, he's going to play this evening." He fell asleep with the notion that you could earn money by playing, and for the rest of his life he believed that play was a synonym for work.

Sacha always revered clowns of genius. Grock, Little Tich, and Charlie Chaplin were among his heroes. His admiration dated from an afternoon when he sat in the front row of the Ciniselli circus and saw the great Russian clown Douroff for the first time. The moment Douroff tumbled into the ring with his tame bear and performing geese, his flour-white face with the crooked eyebrows, one up, one down, and his glittering multicolored costume, Sacha's heart began to thump. And how was it that Douroff knew so much about him? Pointing a finger at the little boy, he would cackle in French with a comic English accent: "There's a young fellow who didn't eat his supper last night!" Those mischievous black eyes must see everything, thought Sacha. (Sometimes, among his father's guests at home, there was a gentle, fat, melancholy man with eyes like Douroff's. Rightly, the adults left Sacha with his illusions.) He decided he had found his vocation: he would be a clown, he who enjoyed making people laugh so much.

Yet it was not as a clown that Sacha made his first stage appearance, but as a Pierrot. His father had organized a little pantomime which they performed with the Russian actor Davidoff at the Imperial Palace before Alexander III. The year was 1890 and Sacha was five. After the performance they took supper with the Tsar. Sacha had been strictly drilled beforehand not to leave anything on his plate. Helping himself to cheese, he moved so awkwardly that a huge lump of Gruyère toppled onto his plate. The servant was about to help him when the Tsar nudged his elbow and he left Sacha to his ordeal. Lifting his eyes, the boy met Lucien's pitiless stare and resignedly attacked his portion in a dreadful silence. At the fifth heroic mouthful the Tsar burst into laughter and ended his torture. From that time onward his table manners were of the most exquisite.

When he could tear himself away from play-acting, Sacha absorbed the sights and sound of the Imperial capital, ". . . the swift and silent sledges, the coachmen who seemed to have such fat bottoms because of their fur-lined coats, tightly belted at the waist and flaring out at the hips." He remembered the skaters on the River Neva, ". . . their light silhouettes that the wind seemed to bend first to the left, then to the right, like pendulums . . . I remember most of all the astonishing silence that reigned in the streets, disturbed only from time to time by the muffled trot of horses' hoofs and made deeper still as they went off into the distance. I see the Nevsky Prospekt and the passers-by, their fur collars pulled up to their ears and fur hats jammed down over their eyes, hands deep in pockets, feet in high boots, mouths shut and noses red. I see the Emperor's palace, the Kazan Cathedral, the Alexander Bridge. The city is completely white, the pavements have vanished under snow which falls so gradually that it seems to come from not very far above, and falls for hours and hours until it has rounded every angle—falling like the light itself on bronze statues, and in the same place too, so that all the statues look as if they are lit from above."

After the St. Petersburg season had ended Sacha returned to Paris, his brother Jean and his mother again. The divorce was now final and Madame Guitry had custody of the children. They were aware that something important had happened but they did not know quite what. "How like your father you look already!" said his mother one day, repeating a comment Sacha was frequently to hear. "Oh," replied Sacha, "do you know Daddy, then?"

While they were domiciled with their mother, the boys followed a strict routine of visits to their various relatives. On Sundays they went to see their paternal grandmother who continued to live in the Palais Royal after her husband's death. Two chairs awaited them beside the card table on which she laid out endless games of patience. Enthroned in her armchair, she put them through a catechism which they both knew by heart and to which they invariably replied with the same answers. Later in the evening the whole family assembled for dinner and she made her ceremonial progress, escorted by her eldest son and walking with difficulty, from drawing room to dining room. There she delayed the meal, secretly hoping that Lucien, her favorite son, would turn up—and although she knew he never would, as Sunday is a working day in the French theater, she always began her soup with a disappointed air. But Lucien Guitry was aware of her feeling for him, and one day—it was her birthday—he asked to lunch alone with her. It was the eve of one of his most important first nights and he had brought the manuscript of the play with him. When the plates had been cleared away he took it out and acted the whole piece to her, performing all the parts and managing the effects himself, for she was too infirm ever to see him again on stage.

As a man, Sacha used to say: "I had two parents and adored them both—but separately. As for a family, what other people call a family, I just don't know what it means." After her divorce Lucien's wife took the name of Pontry and went on the stage herself, playing a number of small parts and understudying. There were no family excursions or treats on Sundays, for with a matinée and an evening performance to do it was the busiest day of the week for the two parents. Sacha and Jean spent Sunday evenings after dinner in the wings of the theater where their father was acting. "The first thing we did on arriving there was to go and 'kiss Madame Sarah.' Madame Sarah Bernhardt played a very great part in our lives. After our father and mother she was certainly, in our eyes, the most important person in the world—and it was always to her house that we went first at Christmas, New Year's Day, and Easter. The Christmas tree at Madame Sarah's was marvelous. In the middle of her studio there rose up this immense tree lit by a thousand candles and hung with fifty toys—for there were a good fifty children in her home that day. Each toy was numbered, and when the time came to distribute them Madame Sarah held out to us a large velvet bag from which every child drew a number, by chance. But somehow chance always arranged things so well that the prettiest toy fell to her little granddaughter . . . We went to 'kiss Madame Sarah' every Sunday for ten years, just as other people go to Mass—piously. For us she was a being at once fabled and familiar. We always walked into her room with a bouquet of roses or violets in our hands. We knew of course that she was not a queen, but we understood that she was a sovereign."

In 1891, when he had reached his sixth year, Sacha was plunged into what he soon discovered, apart from the incidents of 1944, was the most uncongenial experience of his life. His brother Jean was already subjected to the disagreeable necessity of school and it was with great reluctance that Sacha followed suit. His record was not without distinction. In all, he was to be an unwilling student at twelve schools. And at each of them he was never to progress beyond the first class.

Chapter 3

*Schools: establishments where children are taught what it is
essential for them to know to become teachers themselves.*

SACHA GUITRY

Knowledge is sometimes defined as being of two kinds:
we know a subject ourselves, or we know where we can find
information about it. Sacha always advocated the latter sort of
knowledge. Why, he demanded, waste time in memorizing lists
of facts? When you want to address a letter and ask your friends
in which county Florac is, somebody will tell you Auvergne and
somebody else Ardèche. So you look it up and find it's in Lozère.
"That's where you should have begun. Everything's in the dictionary. And, anyway, you should know how to read between
the lines . . . It's less tiring for the eyes."

Sacha's first school was in the Ternes district. The teacher, a
gentle, melancholy man, persisted in asking his pupils questions.
". . . I got it into my head that he could not possibly know or
remember anything. He asked us: 'What do two and two make?'
'Four!' we used to reply in chorus. And I thought: That's three
days together that we've told him. He's forgotten again." Grand-

25

father Pont-Jest, anxious to check the boy's progress in reading, thrust a newspaper in front of him and told him to read out the title. "L, e, le . . . F, i, Fi . . . g, a, ga . . . r, o, ro," Sacha spelled laboriously. "Which says?" "I don't know." So he did it again. "Which says?" "Le Gaulois!" replied Sacha, happily guessing.

Next year, deeply worried by the family's repeated assurance that school would do him good, he went as a boarder to the Lycée Janson de Sailly. Here the headmaster's reign of terror caused him to reflect: "Don't they love their profession, those people? Don't they understand it? Obviously they don't understand that it could be the finest in the world. They prefer to make themselves feared rather than loved. It's more quickly done, and easier. But school ought to be a true paradise. The very idea of gathering children together in order to educate them and make social beings of them is a beautiful one." His classmates dubbed him "Pasha," a nickname that was to remain with him for the rest of his schooldays, and that night, sleeping with fifty other boys in the dormitory, he felt that he was sleeping alone for the first time in his life.

Expelled for incapacity, Sacha then found himself in a Catholic school at Neuilly. "I was sluggish and absent-minded, not discernibly intelligent, and my extreme gentleness must have been taken for a slight air of hypocrisy—and that, probably, is why a friend of my mother's had planted in her mind the idea that I was 'just the sort of child' to enter the Church, and why, too, people were careful to say things in my presence calculated to awaken the religious vocation in me. Yet in those days I was still without faith. I did not achieve this until much later, when I had known several atheists." The atmosphere was happier at this school, where as prize-day approached the staff racked their brains to ensure that every pupil was rewarded on some ground or other. Sacha presented difficulties. It was hard to think of a suitable prize for a boy who was not only two classes behind but who also was lazy and disobedient. When the day arrived his family joined the other parents and pupils in the school hall, curious to see how the problem had been resolved. First came one of the oldest boys who had won seven prizes. ("How he was applauded," wrote Sacha. "I remember that he could recite by heart twelve pages of the *De viris illustribus urbis Romae*. That boy is now a hairdresser.") Soon it was the turn of Sacha's class, and upon his disbelieving ears fell the announcement: "Sacha Guitry: second prize for gymnastics." His teachers' ingenuity had not been defeated. Scarcely daring to breathe, he walked on trembling legs to the platform and mounted the first three steps. At the fourth he slipped and tumbled down to the floor amid shouts of laughter. It was a novel way of proving his gymnastic ability.

After a brief interval in another Catholic school at Arcueil, where he had quite a lot of trouble in getting himself expelled, Sacha joined Jean at a crammer's institution run by an alcoholic German who occasionally lightened their evenings by reeling about in a night shirt and top hat. They acted in the classrooms, refused to go to bed, and locked themselves into their studies. It was here that Sacha evolved an excellent method of doing arithmetic. He rushed into the nearby store and said: "I'd like four kilograms of sugar at seventy-five centimes a kilo; two hundred and fifty grams of lentils at two francs a kilo; a hundred and twenty-five grams of salt at fifty centimes a kilo; and three and a half pounds of flour at eighty centimes a kilo."

"Certainly, Master Sacha."

"How much does it come to?"

"Five francs, five centimes," answered the storekeeper after working it out on a piece of paper. "Thank you," shouted Sacha, running back to school with the answer to his homework.

Then came three months at the École Lacordaire, a month at the Lycée de Chambéry—"a penal colony for children," Sacha recalled with a shudder—and forty-eight hours at another crammer's. The ninth school was an English establishment at Passy which at least offered better food and a proprietor who conveniently died soon after Sacha arrived. The proprietor's son, an enterprising boy, inherited the school and wrote to all the parents saying that his uncle would be taking over. He then dismissed the staff. The pupils spent several glorious months of parties, feasts, and outings which they paid for with the fees their parents had sent, but it was not long before the game was up and the nomadic scholar was on his way again. His next school was notable for two reasons, the first being his new acquaintance with a charming bird brain called Paul Dufrény, who was later Sarah Bernhardt's secretary. In time he became Sacha's and contributed to the gaiety of the household by absent-mindedly setting the chimney afire, or by ignoring what he had been asked to do and doing the opposite. The other important event was that here, in the Institution Mariaud, at the age of sixteen, Sacha wrote his first play. "What obstinacy!" his teacher would sigh as he caught him writing and had to punish him yet again.

The eleventh school was certainly of a nature to inspire a boulevard playwright. It was graced by a French mistress who also served the proprietor in that capacity. The fact that she knew little French was the least of her crimes in the eyes of this gentleman's wife, and the pupils watched enthralled as she daily stalked into the classroom to tax her husband with his infidelities, brandishing a letter or a woman's handkerchief she had found in his pockets. Yet all good things must come to an end, and Sacha moved on to his twelfth and last school. The headmaster put up with him for several months until, in desperation, he went and tackled Lucien in his dressing room. "Monsieur," he announced, "I have decided to expel your son . . . but unfortunately I cannot."

"Why not? If you can't keep him, I'm sorry. Just throw him out."

"I can't, Monsieur. It's impossible for me to get rid of him—
he hasn't been in the place for the past five days.''

So, without ever having really begun it, Sacha finished his
education. He bore no ill will toward the men who had made
his schooldays so unrewarding. In 1934 the Lycée Janson de Sailly
celebrated its fiftieth anniversary and invited him as guest of
honor. His address reminded the gathering that he still did not
know the names of the counties of France. He had spent only a
short time at the Lycée, he said, because he was in a hurry to get
on with his other eleven schools—and how unjust fate was, since
the perfect scholar who had only attended one school was entitled
to just one banquet each year, whereas he, the deplorable example,
could reasonably claim twelve. Why had he been chosen to speak?
Perhaps, as the idler among the busy bees, he was thought to be
the exception that proved the rule. He remembered how his
teacher had told him to leave the classroom and not to return
until he had written a hundred lines. Well, beamed Sacha on the
hundredth line of his address, here they are, forty years late.

His extra-mural progress during the school years was equally
unsuccessful. At the age of thirteen he fell desperately in love
with the wife of one of Lucien's dramatist friends. Not to have
loved such a beautiful woman, he felt, would have been monstrous, criminal even, and it was his duty to do so. But he would
have died rather than tell her. So he laboriously saved up all his
pocket money until he had enough to buy her some flowers. With
his eight francs he bought an enormous bouquet of violets, so big
that he had to hold it in both hands. She was just putting on her
hat to go out as he entered her dressing room bearing his tribute.
"Oh," said she, "what beautiful flowers!" Sacha stepped exultantly
forward, the game as good as won. "*Do* thank your Daddy for
me," she added.

A little later, he joined forces with a schoolmate and aspired
to ask a pretty actress to supper. Their overtures were met with

amusement, so they went off to the Moulin Rouge hoping to find easier prey. Those were the days of La Goulue and Jane Avril, when the Moulin Rouge was not the neon-lit cinema of today, but a vulgar, boisterous music hall. In between dances Sacha persuaded one of the performers to dine with them. At one in the morning the quaint little party crossed the place Blanche to the private room of a restaurant. "But our joy was somewhat confined," reported Sacha. "Our conquest was lugubrious. High cheekbones. Big, magnificent eyes with dark shadows beneath them. Eyes that burned up her face. She was a perfect Toulouse-Lautrec—in fact, he immortalized her in his pictures. The conversation was dull and she avoided taking any part in it. We drank champagne, *demi-sec,* and ate ham." The two boys chattered on and Sacha's friend suggested Sacha should ask his father for tickets at next Sunday's matinée. "Is your father on the stage?" she asked idly.

"Yes," replied Sacha.

"What's his name?"

"Lucien Guitry."

She jumped in astonishment. "What are you up to, out at this hour of the night . . . ? Aren't you at school?"

"Yes, but we skipped out."

"And you pick up the first woman you come across at the Moulin Rouge, without even knowing her? Don't you know the risk you're running? To think that parents take such trouble to bring up their children properly . . . and this is what happens!" And within a few minutes she had bundled the pair of them back to the more tranquil surroundings of the Institution Mariaud.

At last Sacha was rewarded in his quest for knowledge. He became a regular caller at a flat in the rue de Chazelles where there lived a ravishing young woman whose habit it was to wear nothing but a fur coat. She claimed that it simplified discussion enormously. One day Sacha was tracked there by his suspicious headmaster who promptly informed the family. Wearing his best top hat and carrying his most elegant cane, René de Pont-Jest presented himself in the rue de Chazelles. "Will you be kind enough to tell Mademoiselle X that Duval *père* is here?" he said to the maid who opened the door. He was shown into the boudoir of her bewildered mistress. "I am Duval *père*," he declaimed from the doorway. "You understand, don't you, Marguerite?" She whose name was Odette confessed that she did not. René de Pont-Jest explained. "In the third act of *la Dame aux camélias*, Monsieur Duval calls on the mistress of his son Armand to ask her to break off her affair with the young man." He went on to inform her of his relationship to her schoolboy lover. He pointed out the danger into which she was leading the youth. He drew a moving picture of innocence blemished and of purity corrupted. He spoke, as always, as if he were writing one of his novels. Two hours later Sacha looked in and found Mademoiselle X awaiting him, in bed, a smile on her face. Pointing toward the empty place beside her, she said: "Guess who's just got out of here."

We should not forget the important part which this thoughtful grandfather played in Sacha's education. Strolling in the rue Royale one evening they came upon a blind beggar. Pont-Jest gave Sacha some coins to put in the man's bowl and they walked on. "You ought to have touched your cap to him," said his grandfather.

"To him? Why?" asked Sacha.

"You should always touch your cap to beggars when you give them something."

"But not this one—he's blind," riposted Sacha triumphantly.

"Never mind," was the reply. "He may be an impostor."

Chapter 4

An admirer: "Tell me, Monsieur Guitry, do you find acting difficult?"
Lucien Guitry: "No, Madame, I find it impossible."

By the time he was thirty-five Lucien Guitry had gained a reputation as one of the most brilliant actors on the French stage. With the young Rumanian Édouard de Max, he was the outstanding attraction of Sarah Bernhardt's seasons at the Théâtre du Gymnase.

The styles of her two leading men were quite different. De Max had a habit of starting his speeches in a low monotone which gradually loudened into a piercing shriek, only to fade away into a softer utterance broken by sighs and a heavy Rumanian accent. He was absurd, affected, and magnificent. At rehearsal his battles with Sarah became legendary. One day they quarreled for good. In the nineteen-twenties a friend sought to reconcile them. "Ah! Little de Max, show him up. It's all forgotten now. It was years ago," said Sarah. When de Max entered her dressing room she was sitting at the mirror, her back to the door and a gauze veil covering her own ravaged features to the eyes. Without turning

32

round she straightened up and, pointing a dramatic finger at de Max's reflection, she cried pathetically: "De Max! How you've aged! Go, go—all I wish to remember of you is the image of your youth!" Sarah never forgot an old score.

Lucien, both on stage and off, was the opposite of de Max. His gestures were rare. Unlike Réjane, whose trademark was fiddling with her handkerchief, or Mounet-Sully, who sometimes appeared to be playing an invisible harp, or Antoine, who frequently seemed to be shaking his hands after washing them, Lucien had no recognizable mannerisms. He was tall, handsome like a Roman emperor, and deep-voiced. His speech was low and even, and he gained his effects by subtly grouping and building up phrases more or less in the same tone, a complex artifice which gave the most complete illusion of truth. Like the old Greek sculptors, he knew how to express more than was being said and to create an impression of vast inner depths. His "silences" were as telling as the words he pronounced. It seems impossible that an actor many yards away from the spectators could dominate them with his eyes, but that was the overriding sensation his audiences experienced. They have recorded how his look seemed to speak every emotion, how his massive immobility lent irresistible power to his quiet voice, and how his magnetism—there is no other word for it—sent a shiver through them the moment he appeared. He never tore a passion to tatters and always aimed to be master of himself and of his audience. He introduced a new style of naturalistic acting which sounded the knell of the declamatory boulevard manner which had flourished when he entered the theater. "I have an audience of three," he said. "One is deaf as a post, the other is blind as a mole, and the third is the most intelligent man in the world, cultured, sensitive, and appreciative beyond all expectation . . . only he doesn't understand French. My job as an actor is to convince all three of them."

The theater was his life and he never stopped acting. "I have always acted," he said, "everywhere, in every place, at every minute—always, always! I can't imagine it ever having been otherwise the whole of my life . . . When I ask for bread in a restaurant I am acting. When I inquire after a friend's wife I am acting. And he, too, is acting in my opinion by replying, and I judge him as I judge an actor who gives me my cue . . ." An unusual face glimpsed in the street sent him rushing home to create a make-up based on it. He would then have himself photographed and, a few days later, would carefully file the proofs, remarking: "It'll come in handy for a play some time." His wardrobes were packed with costumes and a selection of sixty wigs. When he was not at the theater he spent hours dressing up and planning effective entrances around the house. While preparing a new role he carried his script everywhere, even though he already knew it by heart, until he had decided exactly how he was going to act it. (His exceptional memory enabled him to keep a permanent repertory of more than twenty tragedies, over a hundred comedies, and all of Hugo's dramas, besides complete chapters from books and thousands of lines of poetry.) For a fortnight, to occupy his hands, he held his script in his right hand, his walking stick in the left, and read the words over and over again, repeating every speech of every character hundreds of times. Nothing was left to chance. As a mnemonic exercise he spoke his part in various regional accents, a practice he found useful when the author had been too liberal with plosives or sibilants. These exhaustive preparations stood him in good stead. Once, when his partner dried up, Lucien placed himself in front of him, his back to the audience, and, imitating the other's voice, acted both parts himself without anyone realizing what had happened. There was, though, one famous time when his memory failed him. Called upon to give the name of the character he was playing so that his leading lady could introduce him to a new arrival on the stage, he suddenly found that for some inexplicable reason he could not think of it. "What's your name?" hissed the actress desperately. Very quickly, in a voice not to be heard by the audience, he flashed back: "Lucien Guitry!"

Paradoxically enough, like many actors he was basically a shy man and suffered horribly from stage fright. "With every new play I'm a beginner all over again," he said. It cost him a great effort to enter a restaurant, a theater foyer, or any public place at all, and it was torment for him to know he was being looked at. Some of his power as an actor came from this marked reserve since he was forced to overcome it in his determination always to be master of himself.

Over the years he had educated himself in the arts and took a special interest in zoology and botany. His own practical knowledge enabled him extensively to re-write many of the plays he appeared in, notably the dramatizations of Anatole France's novels. He was also the author of two plays, only one of which he allowed to be produced, and of short stories and sketches. One of his two novels, *Mademoiselle Carrière de l'Odéon*, features a heroine who has to choose between her stage career and her lover. As to be expected of an author-actor who believed his profession to be the finest in the world, Lucien arranges for the stage to win, and as he tells the story he gives many authentic glimpses of the theatrical world he knew so well. His other novel, *Risquetou*, takes place in the countryside. The treatment and imagery often recall the techniques of his friend Jules Renard, though his feeling for animals and landscapes is genuinely idyllic.

His wife, Sacha's mother, died of bronchitis at the age of forty-two about ten years after they were divorced. His leading ladies had long since taken her place—the most famous of them being Marthe Brandès—and the amount of time they spent in his household was directly related to the length of the run of the play in which they were appearing together. He earned millions of francs as a percentage of receipts and did not bother to invest a centime. The moment he signed a contract he spent, or mortgaged, his fee on a picture or a piece of furniture, preferably in the style of Louis XIV. After seeing *Kismet* in London he mounted it at his own expense in the Théâtre Sarah Bernhardt, traveled to the Orient to get the documentation right, rebuilt the stage to include a lake, and was sublimely untroubled by the fact that even if he had a full house every night he would never cover the costs. All that mattered to Lucien was beautiful spectacle. It was in keeping with his reply to an impresario who tried to engage him for a mediocre play: "I'm not used to traveling second class." And again: "The time and the moment should never be allowed to pass without seizing the best of what they offer. I only regret what I haven't done."

Though Lucien's manners were those of a grand seigneur, he could not stand bores. "I speak as I think," declared one of them. "Yes," was the rejoinder, "but more often." His witticisms benefited from perfect timing. One day, as he was selecting hats in the company of his mistress, the latter disapproved of one as being too small. "Too small," echoed Lucien, passing it back to the assistant. The next was judged too big. "Too big," repeated Lucien. A third was tried. "Ugh! it makes you look like a pimp!" Lucien swiftly handed it over: "Not this one . . . it ages me."

With the days of success he took a lavish apartment at 15, rue Rossini. Then he moved into a still more sumptuous apartment at the top of a block overlooking, on one corner, the rue de la Paix, at number 26 in the place Vendôme. At the far end were the bedrooms of Sacha and Jean, next to a large drawing room that separated them from Lucien's own suite. Then came a smaller drawing room, the paternal dressing room, and finally a vast hall with two windows looking on to the place Vendôme. It was hung with elaborate tapestries and filled with choice Louis XIV furniture. Here Lucien entertained his friends who were the most fashionable writers and dramatists of the time. From the conversation that went on for hours around the long Russian dining table Sacha learned the secrets of an effective "curtain" and how to tailor a line, how to build up a character and how to prepare for a denouement. On one historic occasion he was there when Edmond Rostand gave the preliminary reading of *l'Aiglon*. Three years before, the wildly triumphant first night of *Cyrano de Bergerac*—which the management esteemed so little that they mounted it with second-hand scenery and invited Rostand to help with production costs—had brought him a fame only rivaled in its suddenness and extent by that of Byron's earlier in the century. Through the elaborate versifying there glinted streaks of poetry which showed Rostand to be the only French writer with a claim to succeed Hugo in the lyric line. For his next subject he had chosen Napoleon's ill-starred son, the duc de Reichstadt, whom he showed dreaming of glory in captivity at Schönbrunn. Sarah made of it one of her most famous parts, and opinion is still divided on whether she was best as Hamlet or as l'Aiglon. One day toward noon in Lucien's drawing room, seated on a Louis XIV tabouret upholstered in red velvet, Rostand read the first act to his host—a little nervously, for Sarah had ordered him to get Lucien for the part of Flambeau, a character who does not appear until the second act. "It was perhaps the most dazzling first act he had ever written," said Sacha, "and my father was delighted with it. The second act also produced a great effect on him. Indeed, Rostand didn't read his play, he acted it. He imitated Sarah Bernhardt a little and acted it admirably. He knew the play by heart and even forgot sometimes to turn the pages. Everything about him was attractive—his recent fame, his sensitive face, his pleasing voice . . . 'Magnificent,' said my father, 'magnificent.' 'Well?' asked Rostand. 'Well . . . yes . . . I don't see anything to prevent me doing this play.' But Rostand fully realized what could prevent Lucien doing it. The reason lay in the following acts: the scene of the ball and of Wagram, and the last act, in which Flambeau does not appear. It's bad enough not to be in the first act; but to die before the last one! . . ." Rostand gave up and they adjourned with Sacha for lunch at Prunier's. Eventually, for Sarah's sake, Lucien agreed. The manner in which the great *monstre sacré* conducted rehearsals was unique. They lasted for nearly six months and were confined to the afternoons. Lucien was the first to arrive at half-past two, followed by Rostand at three. Sarah was accustomed to make her entry at four o'clock, when everyone stood up and the gentlemen removed their hats to kiss her hand, a ceremony which took at least half an hour. Sarah then changed and rehearsed until five, which was the hour for tea. This she took surrounded by a respectful cast of more than sixty. The only member of the company to remain proof against her charm was a singularly placid horse, hired for the Wagram scene.

In *l'Aiglon* Sarah also gave a display of resourcefulness which has passed into French theatrical lore. There is a couplet which runs:

> Ne frappez pas la table avec colère,
> Vous avez fait tomber le glaive consulaire.

One evening she began absent-mindedly:

> Ne frappez pas la table avec violence . . .

and realized, too late, that she had set a trap for herself. An actor who "dries up" in a prose speech can easily camouflage his error, but the demands of poetry are inexorable. Sarah desperately racked her brains for a suitable rhyme for *-ence* in the second line. After a moment's reflection, and so quickly that no one in the audience perceived her dilemma, she triumphantly continued:

> Vous avez fait tomber le sabre d'ordonnance!

Under his father's roof Sacha spent his most impressionable years in an atmosphere where the only sin was to lack wit and the only grace was to possess it. As Lucien once said of a caller: "The fellow's a miser, a liar, and indiscreet into the bargain . . . but he's witty—show him in." Of all the famous visitors who came to see him, Lucien preferred his three closest friends—Jules

Renard, Alfred Capus, and Tristan Bernard. They spent as much time as possible together and formed a sort of brotherhood which they nicknamed *les mousquetaires*. Honorary membership was later granted to Octave Mirbeau and Alphonse Allais, while from time to time anarchic spirits such as Georges Courteline were also admitted.

With typical dryness, Somerset Maugham has written of Jules Renard: "He died in 1910 and there are few people still alive who knew him. The two or three I have met were agreed that, though brilliantly witty, he was detestable. It is at least to his credit that he never made an attempt to show himself better than he was." The secret of Renard's bitter character is to be found in his best-known book, *Poil de carotte,* which recounts a childhood made unhappy by the sadism of a tyrannical mother. Yet like certain other artists, he owed the urge for self-expression to this unhappy childhood. Every line he wrote came straight from his own experience and from intimate observation. He divined, with the ruthless self-knowledge that few can achieve, that he was no creator. He therefore concentrated on depicting what he knew with faithful realism. Aware that he could afford to waste nothing of his slender output, he began turning his books into plays. Guitry encouraged him to finish an original one-acter he had started, and later appeared in his *le Pain de ménage.* Drawing as usual on his own experience, Renard took his theme from a brief flirtation he had once carried on with Edmond Rostand's wife. It is not difficult to understand why Rostand declined an invitation to the first night.

"Guitry has a very rich character," Renard decided. "One feels rather a poor wretch beside him . . . He has given me far more than I've given back . . . I owe him a tremendous amount, but what does he owe me? Practically nothing. I'm not rich and neither do I shine. But perhaps he owes me this: that people were surprised at my friendship for him." From which it may be gathered that although Renard was in some respects a most unlikeable person, he was blessed with a humility that saints might have envied. As a boy he was ugly, sullen, and brutal in his habits. As a man he remained physically unattractive, with carrotty red hair, blotchy skin, and an acrid wit that kept people at a distance. Had his childhood been more sympathetic he might have been happier, but he certainly would not have produced two minor classics of French literature. Tristan Bernard's son, Jean-Jacques, remembered that his little button eyes seemed to look right through you and strip your soul bare. This unsettling stare was not one of curiosity but of defense. In every new acquaintance he saw his terrifying mother ready to strike him down. It was a long time before anyone could overcome Renard's ingrained distrust. Lucien Guitry was one of the few to offer him genuine friendship, and he accepted it with a devotion that was real and unforced.

The third *mousquetaire* possessed a very different character. Alfred Capus was born in Provence, and a southern accent favored the witticisms he negligently let fall. He had been educated at the École des Mines, but his route each day through the boulevards on the way to his studies had proved too great a temptation and he went into journalism, became editor of *le Figaro*, and wrote several dozen plays.

The man who had introduced Capus to Lucien Guitry was Tristan Bernard, the fourth *mousquetaire*. His beard was probably the biggest and blackest Paris had ever seen, and while it is difficult to imagine anyone calling Renard by his Christian name, Tristan was a jovial humorist for whom any other form of address seemed pompous. ("Christian" name is not quite right. He was Jewish and died in 1947, his end hastened by the indignities which the Nazis reserved for those of his race.) His native town was Besançon. "I was born in the same street as Victor Hugo, but the great poet came into the world at Number 138, while I, more modestly, first saw the light of day at Number 23 . . . Commemorative plaques have been put on both buildings. Mine, alas, was put there by the Gas Company." Four years after his birth, the child was hastily carried away in his mother's arms before the invading Prussian armies. Seventy years later the wheel had turned full circle and as an old man he had to flee from the same conquerors.

When the Bernard family settled in Paris, Tristan did particularly well in his law studies. During his military service an army order was issued forbidding dragoons to cut their beards. He respected it so scrupulously that from that day onward he never shaved, and the credit for a famous Parisian landmark may therefore be given to the notorious General Boulanger who was Minister of War at the time. After a happy marriage, primarily of convenience but also, as it turned out, of love, Tristan decided against law as a career, and turned to writing plays.

Although a streak of cruelty sometimes appears in Feydeau, and the glitter of well-polished mechanism may occasionally distract in Labiche, with Tristan Bernard, the last member of that great trinity of farce writers, the humor is always natural and genial. When he strays into satire his smile remains affectionate and his optimism refuses to be soured by men's foolishness. ("Have you noticed the progress ignorance is making these days?" he once asked Sacha.) His writings and his personality made him one of the best-liked men in Paris, and his witticisms were eagerly seized upon. Being an above-average man himself, he was able to express to perfection the average man's view: "Pascal used to fight his headaches with problems in geometry, whereas I wrestle with geometry by pretending to have headaches." He wrote a great deal of poetry, not all of it published, which includes the dedication to a woman:

> *Chacun de ses beaux yeux était un tel prodige*
> *Que le plus grand prodige était qu'ils fussent deux.*

and the more famous quatrain:

> *L'Amazone passait. Sur le bord de la route*
> *Un Centaure y pensait, des plus visiblement . . .*
> *Mais l'Amazone, triste et qu'assiège un doute:*
> *'Est-ce à moi qu'il en veut ou bien à ma jument?'*

But the cost of being a professional humorist is high. "I've been told you're very amusing," said one of the Rothschilds, anticipating Diaghilev's remark to Cocteau; "will you be good enough to amuse me?"

"I've been told you're very rich," replied Tristan, "will you be good enough to lend me 200,000 francs, Monsieur le Baron?" He bore his success with resignation. "Every morning I open my paper and I'm delighted to see the witty remarks I never made."

Lurking behind the amateur of the French horn and the indefatigable compiler of crossword puzzles there was a sensitive philosopher. This comes through in Bernard's plays. Somebody once observed that he must have been a sad man to keep joking all his life. It is true that he regarded his comic mask as "a formidable implement, since it is sometimes invaluable for hiding a face contorted with emotion." His humor, like Molière's, often reaches a point where it becomes a profound commentary on human existence, as in the following remark: "I had an awful nightmare last night. I'd done something very wicked and had to confess to my parents. I loved them deeply and I could imagine their distress. It was so painful that I woke up. Suddenly I realized it was only a dream. But of course, I thought, they're dead . . . what a joy!"

From time to time the *mousquetaires* left Paris and vacationed in one of Lucien's country houses. He had an establishment at Saint-Tropez where he never spent more than a fortnight each year, preferring a spacious mansion he had bought at Le Breuil, near Honfleur. (It is now a hotel, and one of Sacha's later ambitions was to go there and stay in his old room as a paying guest.) Landscapes gave him ideas for scenery, farm-laborers' expressions suggested new make-ups, and in the great park attached to the house he could rehearse his latest role. He paid the countryside the honor of dressing the part and wore a chic peasant's blouse made-to-measure, with gaiters built by his Parisian bootmaker. Guests drove in to a chorus of welcome from twenty barking dogs and tactfully admired the prize-winning cattle shown off by the proud squire. They climbed into his luxurious motor car and were taken for long rides in the course of which Renard corrected the traditional view of rural charm—"The countryman is perhaps the only man who doesn't like the country and never looks at it"—or Tristan hailed a passing hearse—"Are you free, driver?"—or Lucien delighted them with his description of the cockerel "running about with his hands in his pockets." Their conversations took the form of a battle for supremacy, always conducted with the best of humor, until in mock despair Renard asked Lucien: "Which of us three—Bernard, Capus and me—do you think is the most egoistic?"

"I am," replied Lucien promptly.

Renard: "No . . . can it be true?"

Lucien: "As true as there's a God."

Renard, triumphantly: "You're weakening!"

Lucien: "No, I'm lying."

Each of the *mousquetaires* had his own room at Le Breuil, and another was kept permanently at the disposal of Alphonse Allais, that melancholy humorist whose sallies, which he offered with the impassiveness of a Buster Keaton, provided a counterpoint to Tristan's exuberance. Allais's writings amount to several thousand stories and essays, together with a few plays he collaborated on with Sacha and others. A master of the "shaggy dog" story and an equal of O. Henry for surprise endings, Allais punctuated his comedy with macabre episodes which are the expression of a deep-seated nihilism.

Allais's chronic melancholia set his jokes in sharper relief and gave a dazzling clarity to the distorting glasses through which he viewed life. It may also have been responsible for the compulsive word-play and elaborate puns to which he was addicted. One need not know French to appreciate his humor. At Le Breuil, where he found much to admire in Lucien's choice of livestock—an eagle, exotic birds, and a chimpanzee which used to join the guests for dinner—he gave Renard plenty of material for his *Journal*. "Allais asks for a postage stamp, blue and in a good fast color: 'It's got a long way to go,' he says . . . 'We're going to make a few adjustments to Capus' play,' says Guitry. 'Splendid,' says Allais. 'I haven't read the play but it's sorely in need of them.' " Renard put Allais far above Mark Twain and was charmed with such phrases as: "Night was falling. I bent down to pick it up." Meeting Allais for the first time, he congratulated him on one of his books. "It is a masterpiece," said Allais phlegmatically.

The last word must go to Sacha. "One morning Alphonse Allais and I were walking along the road from Honfleur to Pont Audemer. We were passing by Saint Sauveur railway station, a tiny, quite pretty little place where one train stopped in the morning and another, perhaps, the same, came up from the opposite direction and stopped in the evening. Allais said to me: 'Let's go and say hello to the stationmaster. He must be very lonely.' 'Do you know him?' 'Not in the least.' We went in. There we saw a man, alone indeed, strolling up and down the platform, his hands behind his back. We went up to him.

" 'Are you the stationmaster, Monsieur?' asked Allais.

" 'I am, Monsieur.'

" 'I congratulate you. You have a charming station here, charming. But it's not in a very good position. Now, if you had it in Paris you'd make a mint of money.'

"A few days later, in Toulon, when the *mistral* was blowing strongly, Allais sat wrapped in his customary gloom outside a café. 'Waiter,' he called, 'two vermouths and a little less wind, please.' "

Chapter 5

I talked to Cochran about Eleanora Duse who only wanted to act three times a week in London. Can you imagine anyone not wanting to act three times a day? What else is there to do, apart from acting?

LUCIEN GUITRY

In the early days of this century respectable families did not consider the stage to be a suitable career for their sons. An eminent actor might also have been excused for taking a similar view, though for different reasons. If you have made a great name for yourself you are naturally diffident at the prospect of your son tarnishing it. Lucien did not react warmly to Sacha's idea of going on the stage. His reply, sent from Dieppe where he was playing a summer season, lacked enthusiasm. For the time being Sacha had to content himself with a newly discovered talent for drawing. He earned pocket money with sketches and caricatures of celebrities of the day. His impressions of people like Anatole France, Réjane, and Aristide Bruant sold quite well. Occasionally, as an encouragement to hesitant purchasers, he would add the name of a famous artist to his drawings. That is why the owners of Forain collections may often unwittingly possess a number of Sacha originals. *Le Taureau, le veau* . . . is the name of a volume of caricatures he later published in book form. These are mordant studies of human types observed as the animals they most closely resemble. It is not difficult in the course of a day to identify the bull, the calf, the ladybird, and the toad among the people we meet.

Like Sarah Bernhardt, Sacha had a gift for sculpting. He produced at least one fine piece, a head of Jules Renard, which captures the author's distrustful look. Oil painting was another medium for experiment, and among Sacha's earliest subjects was a young actor of his own age called René Fauchois. He had been introduced to Sacha by Lucien in the wings of the Théâtre Sarah Bernhardt, just before Lucien made his entry as Flambeau in *l'Aiglon*. Fauchois had recently come, on foot, from his native town of Rouen to take Paris by storm. So far he had succeeded in getting a "walk-on" role in Rostand's play. As Sacha argued, even if you have only one line to speak to Sarah Bernhardt, that line becomes a part. Within a very few years Fauchois made himself a prosperous boulevard playwright. Sarah was his leading lady when he played the title role in his own *Rossini*. Beerbohm Tree mounted his *Beethoven* during a lavish season at His Majesty's Theatre, in London, and his plays about Mozart and Liszt (*Rêves d'amour*, inevitably) enjoyed a vogue. He deserves a footnote in musical history as the author of opera libretti for Hahn and Fauré, and as the contributor of the spoken preludes to the Opéra production of Rameau's *les Indes galantes*. More in his usual line are *Boudu sauvé des eaux*, later turned into a delightful Renoir film with Michel Simon giving one of his best performances, and *Prenez garde à la peinture*, which Emlyn Williams adapted for the stage as *The Late Christopher Bean*.

Sacha gradually began to realize that he would never make his fortune as an artist. He drew too quickly and was always in a hurry to finish, believing that when he had scribbled his flamboyant signature at the bottom the thing was done. This hastiness was characteristic. He would often in later years rush through the end of a play in time to act it for a friend who was coming to lunch. As a change from drawing, which he now found a bore, Sacha wrote a one-act play. Despite grandfather Pont-Jest's advice to leave it in his bottom drawer, he showed it to the dramatist Francis de Croisset. Croisset passed it on to Marguerite Deval, proprietor of the Théâtre des Mathurins, who accepted it. Madame Deval actually lived in the theater, where her boudoir was her dressing room. In those spacious days when audiences wore tails, the evening performance was like a private social function where she "received." She decided that Sacha's little verse play must be turned into an *opéra-bouffe*, and *le Page*, with music, was put on a few weeks after his seventeenth birthday. It has never been revived nor printed, for the very good reason that thirty years afterwards a well-meaning friend happened to show the author his original manuscript.

The ten francs apiece that Sacha's drawings brought in, together with the several hundred from *le Page*, were still not enough to keep him going, so he risked his father's displeasure by accepting an acting engagement. It was in a production of *Hernani* at Versailles. The result was disastrous. "I certainly won't pay you your fee," shouted the irate producer, "and I'll be damned if you ever act again in Versailles!" He was right. Sacha never played Versailles again.

Perhaps because he felt guilty for not having helped his son more, Lucien took Sacha with him on a tour of Holland. Their companion was Eugène Demolder, the Symbolist writer and art critic, who was responsible for encouraging Sacha's love of art. "Demolder knew the importance that painting can and should have in a man's life," wrote Sacha. "He knew that at certain unhappy moments in one's existence the remembrance of a face by Memling can be as comforting and soothing as ten lines of Ronsard murmured under one's breath. He only showed us three or four masterpieces a day, but he showed us them so intelligently that we learned them by heart and never forgot them. And it is because I know so well all those pictures he showed us that I go back to Holland every year." On their return to Paris, Sacha spent a month with Demolder at his suburban home near the latter's friend Alfred Jarry. The author of *Ubu-Roi*, who has recently become the object of a posthumous cult, was a founding father of surrealism. His play created the usual scandal when it was first performed. The most remarkable feature of it was the way in which his own pathological creation, the monstrous Ubu, ended by taking possession of Jarry completely. He adopted the voice, the obscenities, and the blasphemies of Ubu until his short life became a hallucination itself, and he died in a pauper's ward of alcoholism and a generous admixture of *fin-de-siècle* vices.

Jarry lived in a disused livery stable. It had, by Sacha's reckoning, ". . . four walls, a roof of doubtful waterproof-tightness, and no flooring, only beaten earth. The door, which had no lock, swung to and fro and did not reach the ground. Inside there was a commode—which was scarcely commodious since it had neither top, nor drawers, nor bottom. His desk was a plank laid across two clothes-horses. His bed was a pallet covered with old clothes beneath which he slid to sleep at night. His bicycle hung from the ceiling by a cord and pulley. 'Otherwise the rats would eat my tires,' he explained . . . I once asked him about the color of his hair. 'It turned green when I drank a gallon of textile dye just before I was due for a military medical. I thought it might help to get me rejected for service!' he replied." Jarry's humor usually took the form of schoolboy pranks and what his English contemporaries would have called "japes," but he did make a few witticisms worth preserving. He was a marksman with bow and pea-shooter, often practising his aim at the apples in his neighbor's garden. "Stop that!" shouted the owner of the garden, "you'll kill my children!" "Never mind, Madame," replied Jarry, "I'll give you others." Jarry's anarchy appealed to the young Sacha and for many years he carefully preserved in his collection the original *maquette* of *Ubu-Roi* which the author had given him.

Another unconventional personality whose friendship he enjoyed, despite Lucien's disapproval of the company he kept, was the poet Laurent Tailhade. This extraordinarily erudite writer owed his learning to a youthful habit of committing to memory twenty lines of French and Latin verse each morning while cleaning his teeth. In the time taken to brush his lower set he had memorized the Latin verse. When he started work on his upper molars he switched to French alexandrines, after which the combing of his abundant hair allowed him a few moments to run over some Greek hexameters. His early poetry reeks of incense, damp crypts, and preoccupation with the mysteries of the Catholic rite. Soon he found a distinctive manner with verse that reads like a mixture of Rabelais, Villon, and Petronius. It is full of ingenious Latinical words and biting references to popular writers of the day, usually in medieval verse forms such as the *ballade*, of which he was a skilled manipulator. He came to Paris and existed on a legacy, enlivening the cafés with his bullfighter's cape, arrogant manners, and insolent retorts. There he became a member of Verlaine's court, privileged to assist at the *"coucher de Verlaine."* This event was as ceremonious as any invented by Louis XIV, and involved supporting the drunken poet under the armpits through the empty streets to his slum and into bed. In 1892 Tailhade gained a notoriety which extended far beyond the literary salons. Asked his opinion of a bomb outrage perpetrated by a crazed young anarchist at the Chambre des Députés, he had replied, echoing Nietzsche: "What do the deaths of vague nonentities matter, provided the gesture is a beautiful one?" Two years later, in the restaurant Foyot, he was himself the victim of a similar outrage, being severely wounded and losing an eye as a result. Then an article he wrote against the Franco-Russian pact brought him a prison sentence. Sacha drew a caricature of him as a frontispiece to one of his books. It shows him white-haired and wearing thick glasses, the features no longer those of an insolently youthful Antonine whose misfortunes had delighted the "dish-washers of the press."

Not long after Tailhade's imprisonment, Lucien Guitry called Sacha to his room and proposed something that would keep him out of mischief. This was the offer of a small part in a play he was putting on. Sacha was to appear under the name of Lorcey since Lucien did not wish to take any chances with his own reputation. The precaution was justified. One evening Sacha stayed late at a friend's home engrossed in a book. Suddenly he realized he should have been at the theater twenty minutes before. The play was a costume piece, and in the rush he forgot to put on his wig. When he made his entry before an impatient audience, his head crowned with a voluminous helmet that covered his eyes and ears, the rest of the players were unable to speak their lines for laughter. Lucien was furious. When Sacha came off-stage he saw on the call-board: "Monsieur Lorcey, fined one hundred francs for arriving twenty minutes late and for having gone on without a wig in order to make his colleagues laugh." Sacha protested that the fine was out of all proportion, since he was only earning ten francs a day. "You can take it or leave it," snapped Lucien. Sacha chose to leave it. That was in 1904. They were not to see or speak to each other for thirteen years.

Chapter 6

Since I have never been a father I have always remained a son.

SACHA GUITRY

*A*fter the quarrel with Lucien, Sacha quickly packed his bags and left the flat in the place Vendôme to his father and his brother Jean. He took a room at the Hôtel du Canada which he shared with his friend René Fauchois. The two young men were full of ideas and projects. Fauchois had already written five acts of a verse tragedy and was hatching plans for a literary review. Sacha nurtured vague aspirations for a life of fame and riches. Meanwhile they exercised their wits at living permanently on credit and parrying the demands of an impatient hotel manager.

In their modest little room at the Hôtel du Canada Sacha began to catch up with all the literature he had missed at school. Hitherto he had had little taste for the classics. "I had been punished too often because of them. How illogical you were, my dear teachers. You kept me in after class because I hadn't learnt such and such a fable by La Fontaine, and when I didn't know where Bermuda was you told me to copy out *Le Chêne et le roseau* twenty times! In French class it was a crime not to know the fable; in geography it was a punishment to copy it out. I do think you ought to have made your minds up." His first masters were Jules Renard and Tailhade, whose influence could be seen in the articles he wrote for newspapers. Unlike most people, whose education begins at the beginning, Sacha started with contemporary writers. They, in turn, led him back to La Fontaine, Montaigne, and especially the poets, whose verse he got into the habit of memorizing at length.

An engagement to play in the 1905 summer season at St. Valéry-en-Caux, near Dieppe, seemed yet again to prove that Lucien's son would never rival his father. A pair of shrunken trousers, a mustache that came adrift in the first act, and a property window that was never intended to be opened, were the features of this unhappy period. Sacha fell ill into the bargain and was visited by a doctor whose senility did not inspire confidence. After dredging up from his uncertain memory the names of drugs to be prescribed, the aged practitioner scrawled the dosage: 30 centigrams—and then, with a shaking hand, he turned the 3 into an 8. Although Sacha had already decided not to follow this lethal prescription, he thought he might as well get value for his money by chatting with the old gentleman, who, it turned out, was a native of Rouen. "An admirable town," said Sacha, "and I can understand why they call it the birthplace of great men . . . Corneille . . . Fontenelle . . . Flaubert . . ." "Flaubert? I knew him!" exclaimed the doctor. Delightedly, Sacha urged him to sit down, and plied him with questions about the author of *Madame Bovary*. Was he as irritable in private life as people claimed? What sort of clothes did he wear? Did he drink a lot? For over an hour the doctor gave Sacha the benefit of his reminiscences. And then: "I also had the pleasure on one or two occasions of meeting his brother Gustave, the literary man. . . ."

The season at St. Valéry-en-Caux was not entirely disastrous. The repertory included two plays that had a great influence on

Sacha's later development. The first of these was *Amoureuse,* the most notable work of Georges de Porto-Riche. The famous boulevard playwright had become known as "the Jewish Racine" because his specialty was the corroding effects of love. This descendant of Italian moneychangers and shipbuilders started life in a bank, where his custom of reciting Hugo's verse to an audience of dusty ledgers brought him the sack. Then he toured the land of his ancestors and met Renan, who, on asking him his name, received the proud reply: "Forgive me, Monsieur, but I haven't made one yet." (His son was later to carry on the tradition by introducing himself as: "The son of the author of *Amoureuse.*") Success in the theater came quickly. Porto-Riche's plays were written in his vast studio whose four tall windows overlooked the Faubourg St.-Honoré. The place was crammed with the Renaissance furniture, pictures, and tapestries which he loved to collect. His other interest was women, whom he collected with a similar taste and enthusiasm to such effect that his life was as crowded as were his rooms. "If I ever become very old, infirm, and condemned to immobility," he used to say, "let me be put in front of a window opening onto some busy spot where women pass by. The sight of them walking about will be enough to keep me happy and alive." *Amoureuse* is certainly one of the period's best plays, as a revival a few years ago showed. Lucien Guitry produced it several times with himself in the role of the man who feels himself being gradually stifled by the jealous, overpossessive love of his wife. "What misery it is to love!" exclaims the wife. "What torture it is to be loved!" retorts the husband. Forced to write his letters in a café and to walk the streets in order to be free for an hour or so of her continual absorption in him, he encourages her to have an affair with a friend of his— and then, illogical like all men, angrily reproaches her. She, on the other hand, has had her revenge for his indifference, but is just as unhappy as before. When the curtain falls they are still together. "We've torn each other to pieces like two enemies," she says, "and we've said unforgivable things. I've misunderstood you, you've deceived me, and here I stay. It's as if we're chained together by all the wrongs we've done each other and all the horrible things we've said." The pungent dialogue and the subtle handling of incident build up a picture of love as the enemy of ambition and as an incubus that stunts growth.

The other revelation of St. Valéry-en-Caux was Henri Becque's *la Parisienne*. Becque was a strange and often pitiable figure. His misanthropy fed on a conviction that every man's hand was against him. He ran up huge debts in legal actions to punish theater managers who, he believed, were boycotting his plays. Women had a morbid fascination for him and he expressed his misogyny with such rancorous wit that fashionable ladies were always inviting him to their dinner tables for the thrill of his brutal conversation. When the evening was done he would leave their elegant homes for his lonely little room. There he meditated his grim aphorisms—"As you get older you realize that vengeance is always the surest form of justice"—and would continually revise his somber dramas. *Les Corbeaux* is a remorseless study in the decline of a family after the father has died. The first act presents a happy and united family, and so genuine is the feeling that one suspects the author's gruffness to have concealed a secret wish for a contented domestic life. At the father's death the shadows move in with lawyers, officials, and creditors. Business partners turn out to be swindlers and moneylenders barter for young daughters in marriage. "What are you worried about?" somebody asks the distressed widow. "If you searched for the origin of every fortune in France today, there wouldn't be a hundred, not fifty even, that would stand up to careful scrutiny." After five years of trailing his play around theaters, Becque had finally seen it produced at the Comédie-Française in the 1880's. He then decided to write a comedy, though only a pessimist would have described the result as such. From scenes of bourgeois rapaciousness he had moved on to high society. In *la Parisienne* the heroine deceives her lover and her husband, unknown to them both, so that the former may get promotion to a better job. Dramatic irony is invoked with the lightest of touch, and there is irresistible malice in the way Becque depicts the hypocrisy of the men and the ruthlessness of the woman. Yet although she handles men with skill, the perverse Clotilde is driven to cry: "Men are very accommodating in order to gain our favors and very severe when we have granted them." It was a line that Réjane knew how to deliver with bitter force. The success of his two plays gave the tormented Becque little happiness. His death was typical of an existence marred by aimless misfortune. He fell asleep in bed, a cigar smoldering between his fingers, and the burns proved fatal. "Becque could never smile," wrote Louis Jouvet, "he persisted in a sort of voluntary disfavor . . . he never had any luck because he neglected luck's first law, which is to trust in it, smile upon it and hope for it."

His reading of Becque and Porto-Riche left Sacha in a thoughtful mood. He studied the way they constructed their plays and how they filled in character. Then he himself wrote, in an hour, a one-act piece of humorous nonsense called *le Kwtz*. The title, he helpfully explained, was pronounced as written. It was accepted by Michel Mortier, proprietor of the charming little Théâtre des Capucines, and paired in a double bill with a one-acter by Francis de Croisset who had earlier helped Sacha to get *le Page* into a theater. Mortier believed firmly in the policy of "all-star" casts and thought nothing of bringing together all the leading actors and actresses in Paris for a single play. His tactic paid off, since full houses at a box-office capacity of two thousand francs rarely failed to meet overheads which on average stood at eight-hundred. He loved his theater and was permanently on view there, welcoming his audience as they arrived in the foyer, questioning them about the play during the interval, and bidding them goodnight as they left. In 1910, on that famous occasion when the River Seine overflowed and caused the theaters to shut, he was playing to capacity. "To think that anyone could do this to *me!*" he groaned with endearing egoism. Rehearsals of *le Kwtz* were put in hand and one of them was attended by Jeanne Granier, the star of Croisset's play. She had with her an elderly woman whose whispered criticisms of the actors so annoyed Sacha that at last he was obliged to rebuke her. "I see I shall have to introduce you," said Jeanne Granier. "Monsieur Sacha Guitry, Madame Hortense Schneider." Which was how Sacha first met Offenbach's heroine and the living incarnation of the Second Empire.

Le Kwtz ran its modest course and is distinguished only for an incident that could have happened to no one but Mortier. Granier was yet another of the actresses who has been linked with Edward VII, and having learnt that he was staying in Paris at the time she persuaded him to visit the Capucines. This would send receipts up to the limit and, naturally, increase her own percentage of the takings. Mortier nearly went berserk. The tiny auditorium was draped with the Union Jack and the Tricolor, a Royal Box was improvised, and a band was engaged to play the British national anthem. On the night, at the appointed time, a tall gentleman with a white beard walked regally into the foyer. "But . . . it's not *you!*" babbled Mortier to an astonished King of the Belgians. A few minutes later Edward VII quickly slipped in. Shouts of *"Vive le Roi!"* and the confused strains of *God Save the King* added to the perplexity of the monarch who had got in first. And there, in the smallest theater in Paris, sat two Royal Majesties, a record perhaps unequaled by any other impresario. "I've got *two* kings!" shouted Mortier, skipping through the corridors and broadcasting his glee to the world.

One day shortly before this, his creditors being more than usually pressing, Sacha had decided it was time to raise funds by selling some caricatures. He bought drawing paper and pencils and sat down to think of a subject. Soon he had sketched Jules

Renard, Alfred Capus, Tristan Bernard, Lucien Guitry . . . and
the thought of his father suddenly gave him the idea of writing
a play. He folded his drawing paper in eight and found himself
scribbling a violent scene between a man and the mistress he was
trying to cast off. It was the sort of thing he had heard so often
in his childhood between Lucien and his companion of the moment. In a couple of hours the scene was completed and he read
it to a friend. "Isn't this a play in three acts?" his friend asked.
"Yes," Sacha replied mendaciously. "Then you must go on and
write acts two and three." "Naturally," Sacha agreed, not having
had until then the slightest intention of doing so. The remaining
acts were completed within a couple of days, and *Nono* started
going the rounds of the producers.

The plot of *Nono*, like all good plots, can be written in a
sentence. It is about a young man who has tired of a jealous mistress older than himself and gets rid of her. "How difficult it is
to break off," Robert laments. "I should have married her. We'd
have been separated ages ago by now." His friend commiserates:
"Poor old chap, you're stuck with her until your death." "No," he
replies, "until hers." Robert's manservant, Jules, who is suffering
from the same trouble, observes: "Women like that have their
good points. They look after you wonderfully when you're ill.
But you can't be ill all the time." Jules is the traditional comic
servant type, the Figaro who recurs in French classical comedy
and who is a mouthpiece for Sacha's own youthful impertinence.
His *marivaudage* when he attempts to seduce Robert's simple but
shrewd maid is characteristic. "When two people are together,
nine times out of ten one of them loves and the other doesn't.
You've noticed it yourself. Which is the happier of the two? The
one who doesn't love, the one who doesn't suffer because there's
no jealousy involved. So if, giving way to my wish, you made
love with me, you'd have nothing but pleasure. You wouldn't even
have to worry about being deceived, because, on your part, there

wouldn't have been any desire." The maid neatly rebuts this sophistical arrangement, but the debate is an eternal one that has endless variations which it amused Sacha to explore.

The dialogue is written in everyday language, brief and idiomatic, with short speeches designed to keep up a cracking speed and quite different from the lumbering pace at which boulevard comedy was then played. In fact, although they have little else in common except for style, Sacha was already doing what Noël Coward was to do twenty years later in the English theater. *Nono* brought a new and unmistakeable trend to the stage, one of verve and freshness, a heady air in which conventions are ignored, sins are excused for the sake of an epigram, and the thinnest of thin ice is skated over with the utmost grace. Whereas, though, it had been easy to find a theater for *le Kwtz*, no one seemed interested in producing *Nono* or in reading this three-act piece by a youth of twenty. Even when a management had agreed to put it on there were casting difficulties. Few leading ladies are averse to playing mistresses; they usually draw the line at playing old ones. A well-known actress of mature years, when offered the part, angrily dismissed Sacha from her presence: "It's bad enough that you should have had the nerve to write a play about my private life," she exclaimed, "but to dare to ask me to act in it! You must be mad!"

Nono was first performed at the Théâtre des Mathurins on December 6, 1905, with Victor Boucher and Blanche Toutain in the leading parts. Dazzled by its gaiety and nonchalant wit, the audience realized they were in the presence of a sensational success long before the curtain fell. Immediately after the play they crowded behind the scenes to pay their tribute to the new idol of Paris, then scarcely out of his teens. Among them were Jules Renard, his beady eye twinkling with excitement, Tristan Bernard, and Octave Mirbeau. "Last night, at the Mathurins, *Nono,* three acts which are a revelation," Renard noted in his *Journal.* "It's Guitry himself giving birth to a playwright. Youth, wit, daring, and never a moment of stupidity. We were all delighted and impressed. If the play had been the work of Capus or Donnay, it would still have seemed good to us, and Sacha will be astonishingly successful." Surrounded by a throng of admirers, most of them his father's friends who were twice his age, Sacha could not help thinking of Lucien, the one person who would have completed his triumph. Both had their pride and neither was ready to make the first move by seizing this opportunity for a reconciliation.

The man who gave Sacha the advice his father might have given him was Octave Mirbeau. With the impetuousness that marked all his actions, he fell on Sacha's neck and made him swear to settle for a dramatist's career. Mirbeau never did anything by halves, and the volcanic enthusiasm with which he acclaimed Sacha had few dissentients on this occasion. Usually it was different. He had been an impassioned champion of Monet, van Gogh, and Cézanne when most people dismissed them as triflers, and he had defended Rodin in the face of jeering opposition. He was a big man who saw everything three times life-size. A friend once threw a lighted match into a puddle and remarked that the hiss it made was a pleasing noise. "It's the most beautiful noise of all!" roared Mirbeau peremptorily, and he would have been ready to knock down the first man who contradicted him. Jules Renard used to say that Mirbeau got up furious every morning and spent the rest of the day seeking more excuses for anger. When his natural turbulence was disciplined it produced work of rare passion. His *les Affaires sont les affaires* is one of the few plays to analyze the business mentality with conviction. It gave Lucien Guitry one of his most powerful roles as a tycoon who conquers the commercial world and goes on to juggle with newspapers and politics. Business is business for the central character, who in the midst of tragic personal sorrow whips himself on to finish the details of a new contract because nothing can subdue his lust for managing men and affairs.

"Never collaborate!" Mirbeau told Sacha, insisting that his talent was now fully fledged. So Sacha went ahead and wrote another three-act play, a fantasy called *Chez les Zoaques*. This was accepted by André Antoine, whose experimental productions of Ibsen and Strindberg were among the most significant events in the French theater of the time. He had thrown up his menial job with the Paris Gas Company for what in those days seemed the little more promising activity of producing Gerhart Hauptmann and Björnsen in cramped attics. At his Théâtre Antoine he specialized in the naturalistic drama which was beginning to make its presence felt. It may be that he found in Sacha an excuse for lightening the Scandinavian gloom that tended to shroud his programs. Halfway through the 1914–1918 war he left the theater, having in the meantime revolutionized production methods and scenic design, and turned to the cinema. Here again he was ahead of his time, making nearly a dozen films in which he used natural settings and non-professional casts, as opposed to the essentially theatrical method which then prevailed. He never returned to the stage, where presumably he had done all that he wanted to do, and until the 1939–1945 war this independent thinker earned his living by contributing film criticism to a daily newspaper. Sacha did not forget Antoine's generosity to him at this early stage of his career and was to repay it handsomely forty years or so later.

Chez les Zoaques tells of a mythical country where the natives are tolerant, philosophical folk, and where deceived husbands are held in honor. The play's success was even greater than that of *Nono*, which has since been revived more than half a dozen times, and the author now saw himself enthroned in the favor of Paris. It had reached its eighty-fourth performance when the leading man, for reasons of his own, decided to withdraw. Sacha took his place and for the first time acted in one of his own plays. His earlier unfortunate stage début was forgotten, and despite having had no rehearsal he played with an ease and a charm that captivated his audience. The legend was complete. He could not only write plays but could also act them with an air of improvisation as attractive as the spontaneity of the dialogue.

The supporting cast of *Chez les Zoaques* included one of those old actors whose personalities were as diverting as the characters they portrayed. His name was Dieudonné, and he was in the habit of giving benefit performances every year or so, only to turn up again a fortnight later, having thus ensured that he was not forgotten. He had done everything, romantic lead, feature player, noble father, and was already embarking upon a green old age frequently punctuated with benefit performances. His part in *Chez les Zoaques* called upon him to lisp, and having read it over he made a suggestion: "Since the role is extremely short, would you mind if, instead of lisping, I took the liberty of stammering? That would help to lengthen it a bit." Dieudonné was usually a most amiable man, good-humored and pleasant to all his acquaintances except a certain very famous actress. For her he had conceived a vicious hatred. It was the classic case of a man who has been a woman's first lover and who can never thereafter forgive her for it. He collected all the backstage gossip about her, all the scandals, all the unflattering rumors that her friends purveyed, and made himself an inexhaustible authority on her private affairs. This lifelong pursuit had enabled him to draw up a complete list of her lovers, both past and present. As age began to weaken his memory, he used to take his nine-year-old great-granddaughter to rehearsals with him. His friends, knowing the ritual and naming the actress, would ask: "Who was she going with in '83?" "Hold on a bit, I'll be back," Dieudonné would say, ambling over to his great-granddaughter, who gave the answer to his whispered query. Dieudonné would return triumphantly: "With somebody called Mazurier!" Aware that his failing memory might destroy his labor of love, he had made the child get off his precious list by heart.

Having had two outstanding successes, it was only natural that

Sacha should now please the theatrical world with a failure. He was asked for a new play by Réjane, then one of the finest actresses of light comedy, and he obliged with *la Clef*. Jules Renard thought highly of it. "*La Clef* deals with the eternal triangle, if you like, but it's something new. Something new in the theater! I scarcely dare write the word, and yet I'm sure I'm not exaggerating: it's really new! This remarkably gifted young man, who could so easily write the average sort of play, is only interested in being original. He knows the stage like an old actor and forgets it . . . After *Nono, Chez les Zoaques,* and *la Clef,* one need no longer refrain from telling this young fellow of twenty-two that if he works (and why not? the moment one loves literature one loves nothing else), he will be something quite out of the ordinary. He is already; but let's not be maudlin. . . ." Despite two glowing articles by Renard, it was the third act, which he had singled out for praise, that brought hisses from the audience and the ominous rumble of stamping in unison. The scene is on board a yacht where the husband, at the point when he realizes that he is deceived, is overcome with a bout of seasickness. For once Sacha's gift of distinguishing between comedy and vulgarity had deserted him. The doomed act reached its end and he wandered palely off-stage into the arms of Georges Feydeau, who steered him into Réjane's dressing room.* Standing against the wall were a large espalier with peaches entwined in the latticework and a strawberry bush that Sacha had sent to his leading lady. The kindly Feydeau, anxious to take Sacha's mind off his disaster, chatted amusingly of this and that while they both

---

* Feydeau, the author of more successful farces than anyone could remember, is still played today. *Occupe-toi d'Amélie, la Dame de chez Maxim's,* and *Mais n'te promène donc pas toute nue,* to mention only a few of his beautifully precision-made comedies, always come up as fresh as they ever were. "Take the case off a watch," wrote Sacha, "and look closely at its organs: notched wheels, tiny springs and propellers—a charming mystery, a miracle! That's what a Feydeau play is like seen from the wings. Snap on the case again and turn the watch round: that's what a Feydeau play is like seen from the auditorium—the hours pass by, naturally, quickly and exquisitely. . . ."

absent-mindedly picked at the strawberries. It was ten minutes before they realized they had eaten them all. Sacha went off to dine feeling a little less suicidal than at the curtain-fall that had taken his play with it. Antoine was sitting at a nearby table. He had just become director of the Odéon and he called out cheerfully: "Write me a three-acter for the Odéon. I'll take it sight unseen." And Sacha reflected: "I had been cheered and I had been hissed. Henceforward I considered myself a true playwright. . . . After all, provided it doesn't become a habit, a flop now and again doesn't do any harm. The public forgets it and only remembers successes. But the author remembers it and learns some sort of lesson from it."

His friends rallied round. Mirbeau took him out to Giverny and introduced him to Claude Monet who lived his simple life there, rising with the sun, breakfasting off a grilled eel, spending the day out painting, and going to bed at sunset. It was the beginning of a friendship that lasted until Monet's death. He and Mirbeau formed the habit of calling on Sacha whenever they visited Paris, Mirbeau standing in the doorway and bellowing: "Here are your two friends from the provinces!" Monet had no small talk, contented himself with a yes or a no to most questions, and if he disagreed with a remark he just laughed in the speaker's face. "Monet had known poverty, indifference, and contempt," wrote Sacha. "He told me that at the age of forty-seven he had still not sold a painting for more than fifty francs. He wasn't at all bitter about it, but that surely was the source of his pride. When he became well off—and he had only to say the word to get richer still—he allowed himself but one luxury: his flowers. His garden was one of the loveliest in the world. He would decide its color several months in advance, saying, for example: 'This year I want my garden to be mauve.' " In the early years of their acquaintance, Sacha was anxious to have a souvenir of the great painter and asked if he might take one of his brushes.

"Of course," replied Monet as Sacha looked eagerly through the well-worn brushes on his workbench, "but at least take a new one that'll be of some use to you."

As they became more intimate the painter started to reminisce. "What do you do with your old scenery?" he once asked. Sacha explained that sometimes it was kept against a possible revival, or hired out to a provincial theater, or repainted if the canvas was strong enough—a working life of ten or fifteen years, perhaps. Monet then asked if the scenery of a Meilhac and Halévy play of 1877 were likely to be still in existence. No chance at all, explained Sacha. "A pity," said Monet. The last act took place in a mad artist's studio, and the producer had asked four starving young painters to do a dozen pictures—landscapes, portraits, still-lifes—executed in *trompe-l'œil* on the scenery itself to look as if they were framed and hung. The set was a great success and, as intended, the audience roared with laughter at the "modern" paintings. "It would be interesting to have found that old scenery again," went on Monet, "for the simple reason that those 'rib-tickling' pictures had been commissioned from Renoir, Sisley, Pissarro, and myself." He fell into a reverie. "We often roamed the countryside, Renoir, Sisley, Pissarro, and I, looking for subjects. Pissarro was a Jew, the only one among us. As far as I know, his racial characteristic showed itself but once. Coming out of a little wood, the four of us were suddenly confronted with such a pretty landscape that we all raised our arms to heaven, but Pissarro cut us short by exclaiming: 'Oh, no! This one is *mine!*' "

The great artist provided only one of the distractions that helped to take Sacha's mind off the failure of *la Clef.* There was also the consolation which rarely disappointed throughout his life, the pleasure that never faded, the topic which, together with his work and his love of art, gave him a lasting subject for reflections that were sometimes gay, sometimes bitter, but most often cynically benevolent. Sacha fascinated women and was in turn fascinated by them. He did not find their conquest difficult. As the son of

Lucien Guitry, even though estranged from him, he was courted by aspiring actresses who hoped he would use his influence to get them cast in his father's plays. Then, when he was successful in his own right, they had ambitions to appear with the son. Both in the theater and outside it, he had already found that, "Even the most respectable woman has a complete set of clothes in her wardrobe ready for a possible abduction. You never take a woman by surprise when you tell her you love her. You are always a minute or two behind." And, as he pointed out, a man's optimism is seldom misplaced: "Honest women are inconsolable for the mistakes they haven't made."

Sacha was the first to admit that no one could describe him as handsome. When he looked in the mirror and saw the bull-neck, the stevedore's build, and the prominent nose he had inherited from his father, he murmured regretfully: "My physique doesn't suit me." He did nothing to change it and loathed all exercise. By the age of thirty the trim figure he presented on stage owed more to the art of the corset-maker than to Nature. The impression of lightness which he gave came entirely from the irrepressible stream of his wit, the gestures of his mobile, well-kept hands with their long sparkling nails and gold signet rings, and a smile that illuminated his face and eyes with a charm, a grace that only a misanthrope could resist. He did not run after women. "Those who do," he said, "are the unsuccessful ones. And why run, after all, since women walk . . . ?" On-stage and off, his aim was to please and to amuse. Though he loved happiness for himself, he loved quite as much to make others happy. He might well have been the character of one of his plays who draws up a will and glows with philanthropic warmth as he earmarks large sums for his deserving friends and loving relatives, only to exclaim at the end of it: *"Bon Dieu de bon Dieu!* Where am I going to find all that money?" Women liked him because he obviously wanted to please them and did so in such a flattering way. They liked him because he made them laugh, because he made them believe they

were beautiful, witty, and desirable. To hear Sacha's voice was
to be a little in love with him already. It was, like Sarah's voice,
one of the theater's most caressing and unforgettable sounds. He
could have recited a list of irregular verbs and still have cast a
spell. The tone was deep, hypnotic in its compulsiveness, ending
with the rallentando of a soft drawl. It enchanted not only women
but men as well. Once, to the astonishment of its owner, it enthralled an audience of Japanese businessmen without their un-
derstanding a single word of what he said.

Sacha's voice was the first thing about him to attract. Then
came his personality. His powers of seduction were almost entirely in the mind. The woman who responded, and few did not,
lived in an atmosphere of delight. Whether the transformation
lasted for a day or for a year, it remained a lovely strand in her
memory. For Sacha, an adept in the overture, was no less an
artist at ending an affair. No one could devise with finer skill
the steps of an amorous minuet which gave the greatest pleasure
to both dancers. There was endless enjoyment to be had from the
feints and deceptions which either side could employ, although
it was feminine guile that added the essential spice. "Men," said
Sacha, "are much worse at telling lies than women. You can see
their lies as clearly as the seam in a stocking. And as for actresses,
God preserve us!" Yet this did not prevent him from marrying
one.

Charlotte Lysès, a pertly pretty and fair-haired actress of twenty-
six, had called to see Lucien Guitry in 1903 at his theater. The
result of the interview was the promise of a role in his next production. She was not to know that her real part was to be quite
different. Backstage during rehearsals she made the acquaintance
of a vivacious young man who kissed her hand and treated her
with gratifying respect. "His name was the same as my producer's," she said. "His Christian name was that of the son of
my producer, who was soon to bring us together, since he was
Sacha. . . ." Charlotte appeared with him in *Chez les Zoaques,*

la Clef, and in all his early plays. She was older than him and had had more experience of the stage. It is true to say that she helped form him as an actor. The apprenticeship he had begun by studying his father's technique was completed by what he learned from playing opposite her in his own plays. She is dead now, but she has left a touching memory as a person, as the only woman who ever taught Sacha anything, and as the one who was involuntarily responsible for laying the basis of his legend. Like the British novelist Michael Arlen's long-forgotten heroine Lily Christine, who aroused the loving protection of gentlemen because she was short-sighted, Charlotte had the disability, appealing in a woman, of myopia. It made her seem more deserving of gallantry. "She is slim," wrote Sacha, "slim and lissome as the stem of a flower or a swan's neck. Naturally she's blonde and she's blonde naturally. Behind her glasses she gives the impression that she's looking at you through a keyhole."

But here a digression is necessary. At the age of twenty Sacha had become liable for military service. His brother Jean, who was a year older, had contrived an ingenious escape from this depressing situation. "He was in the cavalry at Melun," wrote Sacha, "though he didn't have a horse. I don't ask why. The reason is unknown to me, but such is the fact. And not only did he lack a horse but he had a motor-bike. Don't start thinking he was a dispatch rider. No—he was in the cavalry but he went around on a motor-bike. This hellish machine was a present my father had given him. He did the whole of his military service astride the monster. It was, however, a service of short duration. When he drove into the barrack yard at a cracking speed, he made such a terrifying din that all the horses reared up. There was always an officer to shout: 'Will you clear off, *nom de Dieu!*' And my brother cleared off. I know it's unbelievable. But I know, too, that it's the truth. Like me, my brother had been thrown out of a dozen schools. Now—and my readers are at liberty to disbelieve me—he was *expelled* from the barracks after a few months. I said to him: 'Don't you go to Melun any more?' He replied: 'No. They don't want anything to do with me.' He was so likeable, indeed, that instead of putting him 'inside' they'd put him 'out'!"

On his first appearance at a medical board Sacha found that, lacking a motor-bike, he had a natural ally in his weight. He tipped the scales at a little over 200 pounds and was deferred for reasons of obeseness. At his next birthday in 1906, the army beckoned again, only to be repulsed by a convenient attack of appendicitis. A year later the Republic was no longer to be denied the services of her son, and Sacha, in the midst of rehearsals, made a desperate appeal to Alfred Edwards, a superlative "fixer" of his time and owner of the influential newspaper *Le Matin*. A brief interview with a general at the Ministry of War seemed to have settled the matter. Then an inflexible colonel took up an attacking position and the dandy of the Faubourg St.-Honoré was later to be seen wearing a shapeless uniform several sizes too large and scribbling plays in the regimental library.

It was fortunate that two of Sacha's admirers occupied high government posts at the time. One of them was Georges Mandel who, about the same age as Sacha, was that rare creature, a politician of wit and refinement. He wore his black hair parted down the middle with geometrical exactness, the stiffest of stiff collars, and, after five o'clock in the evening, a glistening top hat which towered at least half an inch above anyone else's. Struck by the contrast between the pallor of his face and the black suit he always wore, by his outward coldness and by the sharpness of his intellect, somebody once called him "the monk of politics." His integrity was such that the Nazis had no other course in 1944 but to murder him. Like Clemenceau, who respected him but nicknamed him "the Saint-Simon of the Ghetto," he enjoyed Sacha's mercurial company. Clemenceau himself, then Minister of War, had once written a play, *le Voile du bonheur,* later improbably turned into an operetta. (It is set in China and propounds the theory that illusion is preferable to reality and that it is man's duty to ignore ugliness. "Don't forget," said a member of the audience defending the play's extreme length, "that he's been talking in Parliament for twenty years.") At that time Clemenceau was working with Mandel and they did what they could to help Sacha. When an attack of rheumatism put the young playwright in military hospital, telephone calls from the Minister of War enquiring after his progress ensured more deferential treatment for the patient than he might otherwise have expected. Never at a loss to improve the occasion, Sacha created an effective system of bribes for the orderlies who came to tell him, in a voice loud enough to be clearly overheard by those in authority, that the Minister of War was on the line.

The army regulation over which neither Mandel nor Clemenceau could be of any help at all was the one permitting married men to complete their service in the town where they normally lived. Sacha found that being deprived of Paris was the greatest discomfort he had to bear. The obvious solution was Charlotte. On August 14, 1907, they were married at Jumièges, the little town near Rouen which now harbored, besides the famous Benedictine abbey, a villa Sacha had bought and christened "Chez les Zoaques" after his successful play. Tristan Bernard was his best man, a role in which he soon became an expert, for he played it at most of Sacha's weddings, and the proceedings that day had the atmosphere of one of his farces. Sacha wrote his own scenario, which began with the local mayor being summoned to marry a dying man. Garbed in an outfit which hesitated between appropriateness for a marriage and suitability for a burial, the mayor arrived to find Sacha expertly made-up and expiring dramatically in bed, with Charlotte in a summer dress standing beside him. While the rest of the spectators dissembled their laughter, the mayor gravely carried out the ceremony and the bridegroom, with a trembling hand, scrawled a shaky signature on the document. Whereupon the *coup de théâtre* took place and Sacha, springing out of bed, declared himself the happiest and healthiest of men.

The mayor, after grumbling about disrespect to the magistracy, joined in the fun, and the first day of Sacha's first marriage ended in gaiety.

The newly wed couple returned to Paris, where Sacha was to spend the rest of his military service in more pleasing surroundings. And there the youthful husband noted, a trifle apprehensively: "A comedy that ends with a marriage is really the beginning of another comedy—or rather, of a drama."

Chapter 7

Chérie, I'm wondering if you don't play too great a role in your life.

SACHA GUITRY

Sacha's marriage brought no reaction from Lucien. He did not care much for Charlotte, and the violet eyes that charmed the son left the father cold. The couple established themselves at number 8, rue d'Anjou. It had an interesting pedigree, for here had lived Lafayette, the Frenchman whose Revolutionary zeal impelled him to fight in the American War of Independence. The new tenants were more preoccupied with finance than with history. Charlotte had an income which had been left to her by a relative of her mother's. This cousin deserves to be remembered for the splendor of his name, which was Daniel Osiris, and for the fact that he saved Napoleon's house at Malmaison from ruin by handsomely endowing it. He also, less imaginatively, financed yet another of the fifty or so literary prizes awarded annually by the Académie Française. His timely death gave Charlotte a useful revenue of about twenty thousand francs, in the spending of which his legatee had the full and sympathetic aid of her husband.

The Osiris bequest, ample for the needs of a thrifty clerk living in the suburbs, was by no means adequate for a rising young man of the theater with a fashionable apartment, a habit of insisting that his wife should be dressed by Paul Poiret, and a firm belief that: "It is torture to have to deny oneself anything at all." The flood of royalties that was later to bring him millions had not yet started to roll in. His author's rights and performing fees were carefully put away by Charlotte, a shrewd manager who, unlike Sacha, did not agree with Balzac that a debt is a work of the imagination which creditors are too inartistic to appreciate. Bank managers who wrote to tell Sacha that his account was overdrawn were liable to receive a letter profuse in thanks for bringing it to his attention, and enclosing a check to make up the difference. The pocket money doled out by his economical wife soon melted in his hands. One day, finding a neglected franc on the mantelpiece, he rushed off with it to buy some desperately needed cigarettes. On his return he found a nervous Charlotte awaiting him. "I've a pretty good idea that our maid is a thief," she hissed. Intimidated by her anger, he agreed. That evening, shedding copious tears and weighed down by heavy suitcases, the maid was sacked. "Wait a bit, my girl," said Charlotte with a sudden inspiration, "let's see what's in your cases!" The maid's bulging luggage clicked open, revealing quantities of lace, ornaments, and nearly all their silverware to the astonished gaze of the owners.

Next door to the Guitrys at number 10 lived the eighteen-year-old Jean Cocteau, who shared a flat with his widowed mother. The pale, tense youth was the founder of a literary magazine and the sponsor of a poetry reading by Édouard de Max which had recently caused a sensation. As if that was not enough, his first collection of verse was soon to appear with a cover designed by Alfred Jarry. The precocious celebrity moved with ease in the world of Proust. He had seen everything and known everyone before the age of twenty. His disarming brilliance had a paradox and inventiveness that caused duller wits to accuse him of shallowness. The jibe is unfounded. The glitter of his public character masked a warm heart and a loyalty that Sacha cherished all his life. "Sacha was my youth," Cocteau told the present writer. "When we were next-door neighbors in the rue d'Anjou you could see, at the top of the little stairway that led to his front door, a life-size portrait of him that I'd painted, telling callers that here was the flat where that tireless idler wrote play after play and drew poster after poster. We were hardly ever apart. Besides his plays, Sacha used to organize mock lectures, either at the Odéon or at the Athénée. 'Burmese Art' was one of them, when Édouard de Max recited poems in an unknown language. Sacha would pick me out in the audience and publicly ask my mother if I could dine with them (Sacha and Lysès) that evening. All this would be impossible at the present time, for the charming and sponta-neous liberties of a Sacha Guitry no longer exist. . . . In the old days in the rue d'Anjou he used to arrange things so that he didn't need to appear until the second act of his plays. This enabled him to laze about in his dressing gown and read through the *Fliegende Blätter*, a German paper where he would look for witticisms that might be of use to him. I repeat, Sacha mixed idleness with work, and when, recently, Aimé Michel said on the radio that I was one of those lazy people who pile up work, I wondered if this resemblance between us wasn't at the root of our affectionate un-derstanding and close friendship."

This friendship, Sacha remembered at the end of his life, ". . . was unclouded and pretty well half a century old. I can see us all again, with little Cocteau in the town where we spent our holidays, hearing that a lady a hundred years old lived nearby. We decided to go and see her and arrived at her house. An ancient female opened the door and showed us into a drawing room where we found, sitting hunched up beside a wood fire, another even more stunted little old lady. We went up to her and I paid the formal compliment: 'What a moving spectacle, Madame, to contemplate in you a whole century . . .' She stopped me with a gesture and warned us, smiling: 'Mummy will be here immediately!' " Sacha's country house at Jumièges was the scene of many hoaxes and mystifications—Sacha and Cocteau dressing up as a well-known doctor and his wife to baffle their guests; Sacha bestowing the nonexistent medal for *Mérite Agricole* upon a flattered mayor (back in Paris, after a word in the appropriate minister's ear, the unique recipient of this fictitious honor was solemnly gazetted a week later); at a wedding Cocteau sporting a purple carnation and Sacha dressed in full military uniform while the organ slowly played a tune from one of his vaudevilles.

Other close friends who were familiar faces at Sacha's flat in the rue d'Anjou were Colette and her first husband, Henri Gauthier-Villars. Under the pen-name of Willy he was notorious as one of the most amusing and amoral figures in boulevard journalism. In those days Colette was a music-hall actress. She adored her profession and cared for it so much that she always arrived at rehearsals long before time. A prey to self-criticism, each night she was already worrying at six o'clock about the performance she was to give at ten. Sacha dubbed her "Collerette," a nickname with which she took to signing her personal letters, and he tried to make her forget her professional insecurity with his jokes. "Sacha and Charlotte are here for quite a good long time," Colette wrote to a friend when the Guitrys stayed with them in the country, "and Sacha is making us ill with laughter. He's giving me new wrinkles. But we can't make him get up in the morning. . . ." They planned to do a play together that Sacha would write, with Colette as his leading lady. Then she became a journalist, ran her own shop for selling beauty products, and finally settled to writing. "She prefers synonyms," remarked Sacha, "and that's what makes her sentences so beautiful." It may also suggest why readers of today find that her luxuriant style recalls one of those airless and over-furnished drawing rooms of the Victorian era.

In Colette's memoirs, which are an accomplished exercise in malice, it is Willy who suffers most from her acidulousness. She had come, so the story goes, to Paris, a simple country girl barely out of her teens, and there she had been taken advantage of by the charming Monsieur Willy who was fifteen years her senior. He belonged to a distinguished family, the Gauthier-Villars, who owned a famous scientific publishing house which still bears their name. At first Willy seemed to be following the family tradition with his treatises on zoology and astronomy, but a book on Mark Twain showed where his real sympathies lay and he gravitated naturally toward the boulevard. Under a variety of bizarre pseudonyms he wrote music criticism, racy novels, and plays. The team of ghost-writers he employed included Marcel Boulestin, the Anglo-Frenchman who later founded one of London's better restaurants, the austere composer Vincent d'Indy (what was he, of all people, doing in this *galère* one wonders?), and many others who under their own names were clever authors. It is a tribute to Willy's charm that he persuaded such people to devil for him. Like Oscar Wilde, he might have said that he put his genius not into his books but into his life. He dwelt in an eternal maze of intrigue. His secretaries often found themselves commissioned to write letters under false names, both male and female, or were sent on mysterious journeys to fulfill what seemed nonsensical errands in remote townships.

One day when money was short Willy told Colette to write a book about her schooldays. He himself could never face the agony of staring at a blank page. His powers were critical, rather than creative, and when he attached his own name to the *Claudine* novels she had written under his tutelage, Colette's self-pride was bitterly hurt. After he was safely dead she took pains to belittle his share in them, although a friend who has studied the manuscript reports that four-fifths of the text is crossed out and rewritten by Willy in the violet ink he always affected. It was the same with his music criticism which, in spite of relying on the technical advice of his ghostly advisers, contains the irreverence, humor, and pungency that Willy alone could furnish. It increased his newspaper's circulation by many thousands. He was one of the very few to recognize the worth of *l'Après-midi d'un faune,* and Debussy used to say: "Willy is the best music critic of them all. He doesn't know what a double quaver is, but I owe him the best of my reputation."

"I know of only God and perhaps Alfred Dreyfus who are as famous as Willy," wrote Sacha at the time. His tall stove-pipe hat and podgy figure were an integral part of the boulevards, and his neatly tended beard was more eye-catching than even Tristan Bernard's. Willy's flair for getting himself talked about attracted publicity as a sponge soaks up water, even on the rare occasions when he did not seek it. One of these occurred at a concert where he was fiercely upbraided by that quaint composer Erik Satie. He replied with a joke that only increased Satie's rage and was obliged to defend himself with a walking-stick until the police arrived and bundled the furious musician off to the station. A more deliberate publicity device was inspired by his acquaintance with Polaire, then his current mistress and a talented music-hall singer. He dressed Polaire and Colette in identical outfits and paraded them among gossiping spectators at the races and at the theater. His liaison with Polaire bears out the truth of Sacha's remark that the burdens of marriage are too heavy to be borne by two people alone. Colette was neither pretty nor attractive, but she had a rank sexuality that was hard to resist. Both men and women experienced this, since she was what boulevard slang termed *une amphibie.* So was Polaire, and at first it is clear why Colette welcomed her into that versatile household. The welcome was regretted the day Colette surprised her in the arms of a gigolo who catered for her own needs when in an orthodox mood. In the meantime poor Willy, who could not help feeling rather out of it all, had grown weary of the daily hair-pulling and face-scratching, not to mention the damage to furniture and crockery. When Colette became the lover of a grotesque *marquise* who smoked a pipe and wore men's clothes, he seized his opportunity. Mur-

muring: "I can't really say I've been cuckolded," he divorced
Colette and slipped gratefully out of her life.

The play Sacha wrote for Colette was put on at the Gaîeté-
Rochechouart as *C'te pucelle d'Adèle*. The title alone will explain
why neither of them was very keen on referring to it in later life.
Sacha was, in fact, going through a period of insuccess. A piece
he wrote for de Max closed after four nights and another had a
run of only thirty performances. Life in the rue d'Anjou became
straitened. He made more out of the advertising slogans he con-
cocted than out of his plays. The best-known of his efforts in this
direction was a phrase he dashed off for the Elesca coffee firm,
who plastered it on hoardings everywhere in France. It was made
up of seven letters: L.S.K.C.S.K.I., which, if given a French pro-
nunciation, tell the customer that Café Elesca is exquisite.

Sacha's run of ill-luck continued with *la Petite Hollande*, the
play Antoine had commissioned from him after the failure of
la Clef. Like most of his work it is scaled for a small theater where
the closeness of actors and audience favors intimate effects. In the
hangar-like Odéon its charm evaporated. An excited letter from
Jules Renard after the first night told him: "However old you
get, you're not afraid of possessing the same talent. Your pretty
and daring *Petite Hollande* often delighted me. I like it no less
than *la Clef*. . . ." This little comedy is about a young spark
who, whenever his sentimental adventures go wrong, withdraws
to his estate in Holland to console himself with a little Dutch girl.
The memory of his tour of the country and its picture galleries
was always close to Sacha, and he often found its tulips and placid
landscapes a grateful retreat from the complications of Paris.

The play ran for only eight nights in spite of good press notices.
One of them was by the writer who signed himself "Maurice
Boissard" in the *Mercure de France*, then enjoying its palmy days
as the most enterprising of literary periodicals. Many people knew
that Boissard was none other than Paul Léautaud, the author of
a book called *le Petit Ami* which had recently caused a great

scandal. He was the illegitimate son of a prompter at the Comédie-Française and of an actress who thought of the child simply as a misfortune likely to hinder her career. So, in Léautaud's words, she dumped him and left him to get on with it. The only affection he ever received was from his mother's sister, who happened to be another of his father's mistresses, and from an illiterate housemaid. His happiest childhood memories were of playing with the family dog under a table when the adults had forgotten about him. His mother went off on tour, leaving the boy to share a bed with his father and his current *amour*. His schoolteachers were the prostitutes, concierges, and stagedoor riffraff to whom his father abandoned him. They were amused by the precociousness of the pale and undernourished little urchin. Then, at the age of nine, he met his mother again and experienced the cruelest emotional shock of his life. Seeing her in négligé, he fell deeply in love. The disreputable woman half-encouraged him. He wrote her heartrending letters and spent hours at railway stations waiting to give her bunches of violets as she passed through between engagements. She rarely turned up. His passion lasted for seventy-five years and he never forgot her.

As soon as possible his father sent him out to work and pocketed most of his wages. After a brief spell with an insurance company he spent a long period as a notary's clerk and got a fund of legal knowledge. This proved handy in later disputes with landladies over the habits of the pet animals who gave him the affection he never received from humans. Then he was offered a job on the *Mercure de France* by Alfred Vallette, one of the outstanding editors of his time. It was Vallette who had built up the magazine for which the great names of the day were flattered to write. He never read his contributors' work or the books that his literary advisers accepted for publication. It is doubtful whether he was fully acquainted with the contents of any given issue before it went to press. Yet his method worked extremely well and the review that was the pride of his life achieved both literary and financial success. His offer to Léautaud was characteristic. The job was little more than that of an office boy, but at least it gave Léautaud a steady income which enabled him to write as he pleased. Very early in his career Léautaud had sworn that he would never rely on writing to earn a living. This was essential for him to preserve the complete independence which he regarded as the writer's duty. Rhetoric and elaboration were anathema to him. He believed you should write spontaneously and use the first words that came to mind. Recourse to a dictionary or a grammar book was an admission of failure. If he disliked a piece of writing his deadliest insult was to call it "literature." When he published *le Petit Ami,* the story of his childhood and the relationship with his mother, its bluntness gave strong offense. Even Renard's *Poil de carotte* seems reticent beside it.

Writers calling at the *Mercure* to deliver their articles acquired the habit of dropping in at his poky little office upstairs for the pleasure of his sardonic conversation. This was apt to be disconcerting, for in the middle of talk he would start making notes of the dialogue for inclusion in his diary. This *Journal littéraire,* as he called it, took most of his leisure time. Written at home by candlelight and with the aid of his famous goose-quill pen, it was the pursuit for which he rejected nearly everything else that makes life bearable. The nineteen printed volumes cover the literary scene in Paris from 1893 to 1956. They contain gossip—much of it dubious—detailed accounts of his love affairs (some discreetly veiled, as his mistresses occasionally got hold of the pages he left about), and, above all, a self-portrait more genuine and unsparing than Rousseau's. Keeping up his *Journal* and caring for the animals he loved were his two main preoccupations. His appetite for women, which persisted until his eighty-fourth year, ran a close third. When these interests clashed it was the women who suffered. One day, coming home with a cat he had picked up in the streets, he found his mistress packing her bags. "*Ma chère amie,* when one animal goes another comes to take its place," he cackled, pointing at his new pet. He chose to live out in a bleak suburb where he could find a ramshackle house to accommodate his forty-five cats, twenty dogs, two goats, two ducks, and a she-monkey. When they died he buried them in the large garden and replaced them with others. In the garden at night he wandered among the hundreds of little graves with tears in his eyes. He always carried a voluminous bag of scraps and tins of condensed milk to feed the strays he came across in the streets of Paris. Even Vallette, who put up with his eccentric employee's whimsical sense of time and surly temperament, was moved to object when he started drying out mildewed bread, intended for his strays, on the radiators at the *Mercure*.

Léautaud's review of *la Petite Hollande* was the twelfth he had contributed since Vallette had promoted him to drama critic. He wrote in his dilapidated study sitting on a broken chair whose sagging bottom was stuffed with old numbers of the magazine. A monkey perched on his shoulder and cats swarmed over his Louis XIV desk. On the peeling walls hung licentious engravings and prints of writers of the eighteenth century—"A delightful, charming period, the most beautiful the world has ever known or ever will know!" he declared. His refusal to be awed by pretentiousness, which he attacked in the mocking spirit of Diderot, caused the astonishment that is always aroused when a man speaks his mind with honesty. If the play he had just seen bored him, he would write instead on the charms of old Paris, or the horrors of vivisection, or the death of a favorite dog. Readers were either delighted or infuriated, and as the demands to cancel subscriptions rolled in Vallette shrugged his shoulders and said: "There'll be others to take their place." Léautaud enjoyed Sacha's dialogue, for he had himself a gift for tart repartee that he could never resist exercising, even when it was not in his own interest to be witty. He had, too, a fear of old age and death, and Sacha's remark about someone who had died at the age of sixty—"It's a bit young for dying, but it's so old for living"—awoke deeper feelings in him than a conventional witticism could do. He found Sacha's colloquial style a refreshing change from the stilted language of other boulevard playwrights. Sacha, who eagerly read everything that the critics wrote about him, and who shared with Léautaud a defiance of bourgeois convention, sought to make his acquaintance. The shy and impoverished writer started away like a scared rabbit. What did he have in common with this smooth sophisticated figure, he wondered? Yet over the years and the many first nights that succeeded, a hesitant, touching relationship grew up between them across the footlights.

The months between 1909 and 1910 were, for Sacha, a fallow time when he wrote only three or four plays. Among them was *Tell père, Tell fils*. As the punning title indicates, it was a variation on the William Tell theme, the difference in Sacha's play being that the son shoots at the apple on his father's head, misses, and scores a bull's eye in his father's face. It was written while Sacha was in agonies from the disability which eventually gave him permanent exemption from the army. This was a form of rheumatic trouble that made his knees swell up alarmingly and gave intense pain. It dogged him for the rest of his life, often striking at other parts of the body, but provided him incidentally with useful material on the ways of doctors and patients which he turned to good advantage. Another distraction during his convalescence was a series of sketches he wrote for a newspaper. These were later issued in book form as the *Correspondance de Paul Roulier-Davenel*, purporting to be the letters of a well-known scholar among whose works is listed "Mes Mémoires" (forty-one volumes). It contains the most complimentary remarks about a brilliant young dramatist called Sacha Guitry and his friends Alphonse Allais, Laurent Tailhade, and Tristan Bernard. In the course of his letters Monsieur Roulier-Davenel offers reflections very like those of Sacha. "Woman is a perfect creature and never ceases to be so," he observes, "except when she becomes hateful, unbearable, jealous, stupid, malicious and impossible the day she's asked to love with something other than her body." On the theater Roulier-Davenel speaks with a professional accent: "A play is written to be acted and not to be read. The moment a play seems better when read, it's a failure. Read the collected works of Eugène Labiche and Émile Augier . . . you will find that the plays you like best are the ones that didn't succeed." The correspondence ends with a hearty broadside against those traditional enemies of the playwright—the critics. "In what other profession would people put up with this sort of free publicity which can well be harmful to the commercial product one is trying to launch? . . . Publicity, moreover, which is always harmful since it is critical. . . . To write dramatic criticism a man needs to be either fantastically proud or else old enough to have proof of his own ability."

When his next play was produced, Sacha certainly had no reason to complain about its reception. "My dear Sacha, don't bother about criticism," said Octave Mirbeau to whom it was dedicated. "Above all, remain what you are. . . . The critics will get used to it. They get used to everything, to Becque whom they riddled with poisoned darts, to Ibsen whom they laughed at as a clown. . . ." *Le Veilleur de nuit* opened early in 1911 to an almost universal welcome and regained for him all the ground he had lost over the past few years. Sacha played the leading role, and the stage direction reads like a self-portrait: "Jean is the very personification of lively youth and good humor. He is energetic and healthy. He is exuberant, voluble, genial—and if he is sure of himself, he is so without the slightest vanity." Jean is an interior decorator who is commissioned to re-design a beautiful house owned by an elderly member of the Institut. Here the old gentleman has installed his young mistress and, being a man of orderly habits, comes to see her at regular intervals. Inevitably Jean and the young woman fall in love. Her protector becomes aware of what is going on; to their surprise he remains unmoved. He is, in fact, delighted with the situation, for he had been secretly worried by the girl's custom of entertaining her friends so lavishly and spoiling her health with many late nights. Now she has an interest, a hobby so to speak, that will keep her out of mischief. This unexpected development astonishes the couple. "He's clever," says Jean, "he knows very well what his position is and he says to himself: 'I have my pleasure with her and she has hers with him.' And the result is that I'm the mug in this set-up." "Why?" exclaims the girl. "Because I love you! Now, this is what it amounts to: he's not jealous of me, but *I'm* jealous of *him!* It's the finishing touch! When he's near you he's happy. When he's far away from you he's content—he knows *I'm* here! It's unbearable!" And then comes a typical exchange. They decide they must leave the house and set up on their own. "Could you do without all your luxury?" asks the penniless Jean. "Yes!" she thrills with shining eyes. "Well, so far as I'm concerned, I've a feeling *I'd* have difficulty in doing without it!" The old man lends an amiable ear to Jean's expostulations. He reasons that if he'd thrown Jean out he'd only have crept back in again, surreptitiously. It would be much more sensible to carry on as they are and everyone will be happy. Jean finally sees the tolerant logic of the argument and agrees to continue as the "night-watchman" of the title.

In Jean and the old man Sacha personified two sides of his character. On the one hand was the careless impetuosity of youth, and on the other the indulgent philosophy that happiness is the supreme end. Adolphe Brisson, one of the day's most prominent critics, observed that Sacha had written ". . . a comedy of character and manners—bad manners, certainly. . . . He possesses the inestimable gift of gaiety, that prism which re-shapes ugliness, makes it amusing, and softens the crudity of colors that are too sharp. Molière plays would be dismal without the salt of laughter to temper the bitterness." Another interesting comment was made by Léon Blum, who, before reaching the top of the slippery pole in politics, wrote a great deal of dramatic and literary criticism.

He drew attention to a notable feature of Sacha's skill: "The transition from a joking to a serious, even grave tone, is brought off without the slightest apparent or hidden effort. The character of the old gentleman, which was the trickiest and is the most original, is achieved with extraordinary ease. This shrewd and egoistic philosopher does not shock us because he doesn't seek to astonish; sometime, even, he is on the point of moving us, and it is surely an advance in Monsieur Sacha Guitry's style that he should have been able to draw such a character so unerringly." Fortified by praise from the critics and by admiration of a future prime minister, Sacha and his company drew full houses every night.

With *Un Beau Mariage* at the end of 1911, Sacha retained his firm hold on the public. "I'm something better than a bachelor . . . I'm a widower!" exclaims the unscrupulous bookmaker who owes his fortune to sympathetic jockeys. Then, into this raffish world of con men and tipsters, comes his daughter. She announces that the female cousin to whom he had entrusted her has died of pleurisy. "Pleurisy?" he says, "why, that's no laughing matter." "But, Daddy, she didn't laugh," comes the grave reply. Not knowing quite how to fit her into his own way of life, he looks about for a solution. His eye falls on the young tenant of his lower apartment. This gentleman already owes three quarters' rent, and whenever the concierge tries to collect it he fobs him off with the profound remark: "No, no, never between meals." The concierge tries again, and is handed a note for the landlord:

> Dear Sir,
>   Your concierge has already called once to ask me for money. 3,750 francs, if I remember rightly, and I can see that I was wise not to pay him then, because he came back today and again asked me for 3,750 francs. This would have made a total of 7,500 . . .

Another creditor arrives, and in a scene which has since been included in school anthologies ("Ah! to write things that children copy into their exercise books—that's what it means to be a classic!" declared Jules Renard) the resourceful tenant so charms him that he accepts an order for more goods. The young man even stalls the girl friend to whom he owes money. "The day I give it back to you," he warns solemnly, "it will be because we no longer love each other. Don't you understand that I borrowed the money to quicken your love?" "How?" "Obviously, you'd soon have tired of me if you didn't have an interest in remaining my mistress!"

The bookmaker-landlord, realizing he has met his match, now takes a hand. After agile sparring he suggests the tenant marry his daughter—a proposal, naturally, which it is impossible for such an honest and high principled young man to accept . . . until, in the course of an act which studies human nature with an amused eye, he eventually accepts. Now it is true, as Sacha's critics often reproached him, that the characters he draws rarely have an unselfish thought or do a good action. Their behavior is dictated by self-interest and they have no idea of what a social conscience is. On the other hand, it is as difficult in life to find a perfect gentleman as it is to meet a complete rascal. The answer is that Sacha depicted men and women as he saw them and put into their mouths the everyday language he heard them speak. He did no differently from Molière, who, instead of waxing indignant over human faults and follies, was content to laugh at them. Laughter is always more effective than anger, and had anyone asked more of Sacha he would doubtless have reacted like Sam Goldwyn. Questioned about the message of his films, Goldwyn replied that if he had a message he always sent it by Western Union. The very title of Un Beau Mariage reveals irony, and the audiences who laughed so freely were more thoughtful when they left the theater than when they had come. Paul Léautaud was of their number and he was so impressed that he devoted the whole of his fortnightly article to the play. He believed that Sacha had now fulfilled his promise both as writer and actor. "I find that he really has more talent than his father, who is always the same in his roles. One must also speak highly of the scenery, especially in the last act. It represents a garden with a real bloom upon it. Monsieur Sacha Guitry in white and Madame Charlotte Lysès in black, against the green background of trees, make a very successful Manet."

The time was now ripe, or so it seemed, for Sacha to conquer towns outside Paris. He and his company were offered a foreign tour by the flamboyant impresario Schuermann, a personage who fulfilled all the requirements of the profession so perfectly that he was almost a caricature of the impresario type. He was a foreigner in every country and was generally taken for a Dutchman—except in Holland. His talk was consistently entertaining and was inspired by a riotous imagination which blossomed in stories of how he had turned up with a circus wagon at Amsterdam railway station to fetch Sarah Bernhardt; or how he had lost Patti in a game of cards on one of his more unlucky tours abroad. Schuermann was the incarnation of politeness, a grand cross or knight commander in most of the world's orders of chivalry, a polyglot who simply breathed honesty and never kept his word in any one of half a dozen languages. Antoine was horrified to hear of Sacha's plan and told him cautionary stories of Schuermann's gambling desperately to secure rent for the theater the company was to play in. Sacha's mind was filled with visions of ambassadorial receptions, command performances, and foreign decorations, and he was not to be put off. His troupe started the journey in mid-winter and promptly lost seven trunks at the Russian border. In Warsaw, they played in a wooden theater that stood in the middle of a leafless park. In St. Petersburg, they had the Conservatoire, a building twice as large as an average theater, where they were inaudible in the front rows and could be heard twice over in the rest, thanks to a clanging echo. In Moscow, Schuermann had hired a private house with such a low ceiling that, once on the stage, the cast was forced to keep their heads permanently inclined, as if in respect for each other. In Odessa,

Schuermann had surpassed himself. Here he had booked the Jewish theater for them. There is no need to enlarge on the originality of such a move in Imperial Russia of the time.

At this stage of the tour Sacha decided to halt at the land of his birth and to postpone visits to Asia Minor for another time. He took advantage of an option in the contract to interrupt the tour at Odessa. Schuermann agreed, pointing out, though, that he was still waiting for money to come through from Paris, so would Sacha pay for their passage home? Sacha did so. A week later, in Paris, he was sued for having broken the contract. The proof was that he had paid for the tickets to bring his company home. He contested the action and lost, with heavy damages. In spite of it all he could not bring himself to dislike the fantastic Schuermann, and a few weeks later he complied with his request for a photograph "with a few nice words, as a souvenir." From then on Schuermann continued to ask for complimentary seats at his first nights, adding always ". . . don't forget that I'm your mascot. . . ." Sacha, who was superstition itself, never failed to send them.

It was good to be back in Paris, where Sacha could enjoy life again as the *enfant gâté* of the boulevards, and where his slightest action caused a ripple of excited curiosity. "To be a Valentinois," he wrote, "is to be a native of Valence, Draguignanais of Draguignan, and Briochain of Saint-Brieuc—but to be a Parisian doesn't mean that you have been born in Paris: it means you have been reborn there. . . . You don't belong to Paris in the same way as you do to Clermont—you belong to Paris as you do to a club. You are elected a Parisian—elected for life. It is a dignity. It is also a responsibility. You must be at her disposal, ready to take her orders when Paris does you the honor of admitting you. To love Paris makes you proud, for she becomes such a necessity to you that you end by thinking you can be of use to her." He might also have added that you cannot honor Paris without money. The

Schuermann affair and the bills that flowed daily into the rue
d'Anjou were reminders of the disagreeable side of life.

Before the year was out luck favored him again with another
box-office success in *la Prise de Berg-op-Zoom*. The historically
minded will know that Bergen-op-Zoom, as written in English, is
a Dutch town which resisted many famous sieges. In 1588 it was
besieged unsuccessfully by the Spanish; they failed again to take
it in 1622. Then, in 1747, a French commander, the comte de
Lowendal, attacked it and carried off the prize which everyone
had thought impregnable. "Wisely, slowly, prudently, he prepared what was to be the crowning-point of an admirable career,"
commented Sacha. "And when the great moment of his life came,
he concentrated his strength, his intelligence, and his determination . . . Bergen-op-Zoom was taken! I don't know whether I've
made myself understood." There is little need to add that the play
is set in modern times and has nothing whatsoever to do with military history. The reason for the title becomes apparent when the
central character has at last persuaded the object of his siege into
calling at his house.

> HÉRIO: You'll get used to being kissed behind the ear like that
> each time you arrive . . . which will allow me . . .
> (*Going to his calendar*), on Tuesday the 22nd . . .
> Revocation of the Edict of Nantes . . . a delightful
> anniversary, don't you think? . . . which, as I say,
> will allow me, on Tuesday the 22nd, to let my kiss
> slip gently down from your neck to your mouth.
>
> PAULETTE: Can you see that happening?
>
> HÉRIO: Can I? I can see it as if I was there!
>
> PAULETTE: And then?
>
> HÉRIO: Then? Ah . . . (*Returning to the calendar*) . . .
> Thursday the 24th . . . H'm, yes, we must include
> that . . . Thursday the 24th . . . The taking of
> Bergen–op-Zoom by the comte de Lowendal . . . Let's
> not miss it! . . .

Written between the acts during performances of *Un Beau Mariage*, the play was put on at the Vaudeville. Although the subject matter is vintage Palais Royal, the treatment is quite different. Adolphe Brisson, usually a severe critic, evoked Molière acting beside his wife Armande Béjart in speaking of Sacha and Charlotte Lysès. He added: "Whatever offensiveness it may contain is saved by the lightness of the performance. There is nothing crude or heavy about it. It is the equal for vivacity and elegance of the gayest pictures by the light-hearted storytellers of the eighteenth century." The cast also included two of those old actors whom Sacha liked to engage. It was a pleasant habit which his experience during the Schuermann tour had not changed. On that occasion he had with him a player called Chelles who had in his time been an excellent comedy actor but who had now almost lost his memory. He made his entry and was asked by a servant what name should be announced. "Announce Monsieur . . . h'm . . . h'm . . . Chelles," came the reply. Next evening the curtain rose and Chelles, turning to Sacha with the look of a drowning man, inquired: "What play are we doing tonight?" In *la Prise de Berg-op-Zoom* Sacha had cast Baron *fils* and Dieudonné, that libelous master of the vendetta whom we have already met. In his old age Baron suffered from deafness and absent-mindedness. The duc d'Orléans came to his dressing room one evening and the duke's secretary murmured quickly to Baron: "His Royal Highness the duc d'Orléans wishes to congratulate you." "Ah," said Baron to the duke, "you're from Orléans? A charming town. I played there in 1867 and have the pleasantest memories of it. . . ." Tristan Bernard met Baron in the street one day and greeted him. Baron raised his hat without a glimmer of recognition and passed on. "Tristan Bernard. . . ." the other reminded him. "I am not he, Monsieur," replied Baron.

Another venerable representative of past glories was the comedy actor Noblet, a jovial egoist who retired after a long career to Monaco. There a seventy-seven-year-old Englishwoman fell in love with him and, as a New Year gift, insisted on paying his rent. This went on for five years and each time Noblet graciously recognized her kindness with a bunch of anemones. On the sixth year she died. Noblet instantly sent a dignified letter to Sacha, who realized what was expected of him and arranged for Noblet's rent to be paid for the rest of his days. By return he received a telegram, not of thanks, and not, as might be expected, of praise for a generous action, but consisting of one word: BRAVO! Noblet wasn't thanking him, he was congratulating him.

It was inevitable that Sacha should put him into his next play, la Pèlerine écossaise, as a raving cuckold, with Baron fils again as an incompetent village mayor. The play has hardly any plot and shows a day in the life of an average married couple. The trivial details and routine incidents are told with such fantasy and wit that they cease to be commonplace. Despite the reply made by the husband when asked his age—"Let me see, I'm thirty years old and I've been married for six years . . . which makes me thirty-six"—the moral emerges, quite painlessly, that in marriage neither partner should take the other for granted.* It is as if the Balzac of the Physiologie du mariage had turned his subject into an evening's entertainment with a similar light hand. The bizarre figure of Paul Léautaud nodded approval. He looked odder than usual that night for he wore two jackets, one on top of the other to keep out the cold January air. His companion stared around him at the rest of the smart audience in evening dress and said: "We're probably the poorest of anyone here tonight." "Very likely," said Léautaud, "but you can't deny I'm wearing two jackets. Find me someone else in the audience who can show as many." His jocular mood faded during the interval at news of a stray cat which had spent a fortnight on a roof and refused to come down. Everything else became unimportant at the thought of an animal

---

* Francis Bacon had a similar opinion. In a letter to Lord Chancellor Ellesmere he observed that a married man ". . . is seven years older in his thoughts the first day."

exposed to such bad weather. Léautaud hurriedly explained the
need for some sort of trap to entice it back to ground-level. Only
when he had given instructions to a reliable friend on how to cope
with the emergency did he feel able to go back to his seat and
enjoy the rest of the play—which he did wholeheartedly. Sacha,
he wrote in a perceptive notice, ". . . sets himself the most
difficult task of all in writing his plays. 'To amuse is my only
aim,' he says. . . . You will see that the aim Monsieur Sacha
Guitry puts forward and which, even better, he nearly always
achieves, is neither so modest nor so negligible. Not to be boring!
The most natural and yet the most difficult thing of all, bearing
in mind that it cannot be achieved by wishing it alone."

By contrast with the lighthearted *Pèlerine écossaise,* another
play Sacha wrote at the same time under the title of *les Deux
couverts* showed that when he wished he could make a point
effectively in one act alone. A widowed father awaits his sixteen-
year-old son who has just failed his exams. He plans a consolation
dinner with a table laid for two. The woman who loves him
arrives unexpectedly and he has to calm her fears by explaining
the reason for the two settings. "I've never spoken to you again
about our marriage—which I long for so much—since you made
me understand we had to give up everything because of your
son," she says. "So for the sake of love I put up with an existence
that isn't very pleasant, believe me. Because I'm proud of you,
I'd like to love you openly . . . but it's forbidden me. Out of
respect for that young man I can only come to see you secretly,
between five and seven o'clock. . . ." Jealous and reluctant she
makes way for the son. The latter conceals his feelings with a
display of nonchalance and shrugs his shoulders at his father's
loving concern. It is the eternal situation of youthful egotism
accepting, and despising, parental self-sacrifice. The father appeals
in vain for him to pull himself together. His mother died fourteen years ago, he reminds him. "I was thirty-six years old then,
and I'm fifty now. I was young . . . but I'm not any longer. I've

grown old for you, I've devoted myself completely to you. Twice I could have married again. The first time you were too little . . . and the second time you were too big. Think of that from time to time." The boy, unmoved, announces that he is off to dine with a school friend and asks what his father plans for the evening. "See for yourself," is the brave reply. "You can read the menu and can see I'm not dining on my own. Look . . . two places. . . ." And the boy goes, leaving him to begin his lonely meal. The play was written in a few hours and read aloud to Octave Mirbeau who happened to be staying with Sacha at the time. At the end the audience of one remained disturbingly silent. Then: "Read it to me again!" cried Mirbeau, who, after the second reading, took it off enthusiastically to the Comédie-Française where it was accepted within forty-eight hours and produced in the March of 1914. It remains in the repertoire and has since had nearly fifty revivals. "For once," wrote Paul Léautaud, "a playwright who has had successes in other theaters makes his début at the Comédie-Française and has not shown himself inferior—quite the contrary, in fact. For this reason Monsieur Sacha Guitry is doubly deserving of praise."

Almost immediately Sacha underwent tribulations in the form of rheumatic trouble. "That unfortunate Sacha is being martyred," Colette wrote to a friend, "and his attack of rheumatism just doesn't seem to let up. A temperature of a hundred and four, and inhuman pains; he's stopped acting but doesn't stop suffering . . . and the poor creature even arouses the pity of strangers . . . Lysès works miracles, as very woman knows how. She acts at matinées and evening performances, and spends her nights and mornings turning Sacha (!) in his bed thirty times in twelve hours. . . . In the end, to save her from pegging out, they've brought in a night-nurse. Your poor Sacha-child hasn't seen his play at the Comédie-Française [Deux couverts]—a good piece of work, well written, well proportioned, compassionate and moving, which cannot help but please everybody. . . ." It was from this illness that Sacha dated his long career as an invalid. The events in his life came to be situated by the phrase: "Some time before my illness. . . ." or else: "A short while after my illness. . . ." He kept an hour-by-hour diary which was later issued in a de luxe edition entitled *la Maladie*. It reproduced his handwriting which varied from a scrawled record of high temperatures to its usual clear and cursive form when he had recovered.

"An invalid is no longer a man," wrote Sacha painfully on the thirteenth day of his month-long sentence. "When you're ill you no longer have a name, age, fortune, or friends—you have a temperature. What am I saying? You don't even have that! It's the others who've got your temperature: the moment you have it they take it away from you and carry it quickly into the room next door!" He found that doctors have much in common with actors in that they always play a part—one of grave impassiveness. "They don't even have the happiness of being able to express their legitimate satisfaction. On the contrary, they have to keep a close watch on themselves and must be careful not to let slip the gesture, the remark, the grimace, which reveal the awful truth. They have to be liars." Which explains why, in a moment of depression, he noted: "I don't like the doctor I saw yesterday. He wasn't a good actor." And before slipping one evening into a drugged stupor he scribbled: "Morphine was invented so that our doctors could enjoy a good night's sleep."

After three weeks in bed Sacha was well enough to look more objectively at the relationship between doctor and patient. "They don't see things from the same point of view: the patient only thinks of health, the doctor is only concerned with illness. I'd already noticed this, and to a friend who asked me how I felt, I replied: 'Oh, my illness is extremely well . . . unfortunately, my health isn't all that good!' " When he had begun to improve he was able to offer advice to other invalids: "If you're ill, don't stay like it too long. Try not to overshoot the regulation three weeks, because—you can't ignore it—the patience of the best of friends is quite short and you'll soon feel you're being deserted. Your relatives themselves won't be slow in showing a certain weariness and sometimes a little annoyance. And after the twenty-second day you'd see one of your nearest and dearest asking the doctor who's come *for you* whether he couldn't prescribe something *for him* as a tonic. There's nothing in the world, it must be confessed, quite so tedious as an illness that drags on. It's rather like very old people who die in fits and starts, who have good moments and bad, who seem to fade away and then keep on rallying, who can't, in a word, make up their minds—it becomes tiresome in the end!" On the twenty-eighth day Sacha got out of bed and drew the curtains of his window overlooking the rue d'Anjou: ". . . I was blinded, or dazzled rather, stifled, almost overcome by the sun that rushed into my room like somebody who's been waiting for an hour and who at last has just been let in . . . the air itself was so light, so clear, so thin, that nothing separated me from the trees, the houses, and the people going by in the street below—and I thought that by stretching out my arms I could have reached them. How lovely it was! Just look at that little roof with the old tiles opposite. Not much to get excited about, is it? Well, at six o'clock, under the sun, it was unrecognizable! And it'll last a long time because it's new every morning! Well, well! I'm no longer talking exclusively about myself—I think this is it, I'm better!"

By the end of April Sacha was convalescing. "They say that rheumatism protects you from tuberculosis. I can see no other advantage in it. During all the years my rheumatism and I have lived together, I've had plenty of time to study its drawbacks and oddities. It is a strange and devilish individual. . . . However much you get used to it, in the long run it always manages to take you by surprise. It amuses itself one day in making you think you've a bad back—which turns out to be lumbago in disguise. Next month you're wondering whether you've dislocated your collar bone—and that sharp, localized pain is found to be rheumatism. That raging toothache you get one day is caused by the same culprit. That sharp twinge of pain you feel on breathing isn't an attack of pleurisy—no, no, it's your old enemy, as always. It changes its face and takes every form—and sometimes it *de*-forms you."

In Deauville, where he went to recover, he found himself in the same hotel as Isadora Duncan. The latter-day priestess of the Greek dance had come there to get over the deaths of her two small children in a swimming accident. Dressed in white veils, her hair cut short, she lay prostrate in a room which, with the aid of a few Algerian scarves, she had turned into a Greek temple. "She did not rebel, she no longer wept, she smiled at all the innumerable little photographs that surrounded her. 'Look . . . there . . . how lovely they are! And there, look, in the garden . . . and there, both asleep . . .'" At the time Sacha knew her she already had an aura of other-worldliness. Sacha remembered seeing her leave the hotel ". . . dressed in a great violet cloak. It was the time when night falls. She went on the beach, took off her sandals, and, for herself alone, she began to dance barefoot on the sand to the rhythm of the waves. . . ." For a moment the perfect egoist had forgotten his own ills as he watched her silently from the window.

Chapter 8

Be careful not to tell your wife about the dirty tricks her predecessors played on you. It's not worth putting ideas into her head.

SACHA GUITRY

One day in 1914, the painter Auguste Renoir happened to be away from home when Sacha and Charlotte came to visit him at Cagnes. Apologizing for his absence he wrote, in the shaky handwriting caused by the paralysis of his last years, that he had been to see his doctor in Nice. "I came back empty-handed a quarter of an hour after you left my house. Believe me, I'm the first to regret it. . . ." Renoir, who was very fond of the young actor-dramatist and his wife, taught Sacha a lot about art. As time went by and Sacha amassed one of the finest of private collections, he was especially proud of his Renoir nudes, flower pictures, child studies, and the famous portrait of Mallarmé, for which he had had to wait sixteen anxious years before it came into his hands.

Their friendship was behind Renoir's appearance in a film Sacha made at the time. A group of German intellectuals had issued a manifesto at the beginning of the war that deeply irritated Sacha. By way of a patriotic reply he decided to make a film which would show some of France's greatest men in the arts. The cinema until then had interested him hardly at all. Though he was later to write, direct, and act in nearly forty films himself, he never rated the medium higher than a magic lantern. Its main value, he contended, was documentary. His admiration for Mary Pickford and Charlie Chaplin did not affect his preference for factual reportage. "So far as the past is concerned," he wrote, "we only have written accounts which are sometimes contradictory and very often vague. The cinema changes everything and will enable us to leave exact information about important events and famous people." So he called on Renoir with a camera. The choice of time was unfortunate. That very day Renoir's wife was to be buried. Sacha went to the old man who sat huddled arthritically in his wheel chair and murmured: "It must be terribly painful, Monsieur Renoir, and you have my deepest sympathy." "Painful?" he replied, shifting his racked limbs, "you bet my foot is painful!" They pushed him in his chair up to a canvas, and, while Sacha leaned watching over his shoulder, Renoir jabbed at the picture with brushes attached to hands which had captured so much beauty but which now were shriveled like birds' claws. The flattering reminder that he was being filmed for posterity had no effect on the man who, on being awarded the cravat of a *Commandeur* of the Légion d'honneur, had said: "How can you expect me to wear a cravat when I never wear a collar?"

Another artist whom Sacha filmed was also unimpressed. "Call it what you will, it's still nothing more than photography," said Rodin. He was pictured in that magnificent studio which has since been turned into a museum by those who failed to recognize his genius during his lifetime. The neglect and the bitter opposition which his sculpture provoked were sweetened by the companionship of his wife. At the age of seventy-five, in 1913, he wrote to her what Sacha always considered to be one of the finest love letters he had ever seen—all the more so as love letters are usually written in the hope of rewards to come, whereas Rodin was writing to someone of whom he was absolutely sure. *"Ma bonne Rose,"* he began. "I send you this letter as a sort of reflection on the greatness of the present God made me in putting you beside me. Put it in your generous heart. I shall be back on Tuesday. *Ton ami,* Auguste Rodin." They filmed him in his garden, the sculptor still believing there was no difference between cinematography and ordinary snapshots: "Tell me to stop when you're ready so that I shan't move," he said. Then he stood before the camera in a black beret and oddly spruce pin-striped suit to chisel at a piece of marble.

From Rodin the camera team went on to Monet who was discovered, a cigarette drooping from his mouth, working myopically at a picture which might have been *les Nymphéas.* The elusive Degas refused to be filmed, so Sacha lurked outside his house on the boulevard de Clichy one morning and caught him emerging, stumpy and white-bearded, a coat and umbrella hanging from his arm as he looked suspiciously around before scurrying down the street. The next celebrity to be bagged was Saint-Saëns. He had written a suite of incidental film music some time before and on this occasion he was not unwilling to appear on the other side of the camera. The octogenarian composer obligingly played one of his showiest piano pieces, all fingers and *fortissimo,* and then, with a jaunty baton, took an orchestra at a brisk trot through the ballet music from his opera *Henry VIII.* Somehow it was the writers who proved the most docile "subjects." Edmond Rostand in a razor-sharp wing collar meekly did as he was told and pretended to write a sonnet; Anatole France, observed in his medievalesque library and at his desk, had great difficulty in keeping a straight face as he contemplated the latest mechanical invention of an absurd age; and even the fiery Octave Mirbeau agreed to stare briefly at the camera, thumbs in waistcoat and arms akimbo.

The theater was represented by Antoine, who was shown directing a scene from a play; by Sarah Bernhardt; by Lucien Guitry; and by Henri Robert. The inclusion among actors of Maître Henri

Robert, who was a noted trial lawyer, and the star of many famous cases, may cause surprise. Reflection will show that the art of the advocate differs little from that of the actor. In fact, the sequence depicting Maître Robert was the most elaborately stagemanaged of the whole film. It was given out that Sacha, with the aid of a very small camera, had slipped into a provincial courtroom and actually filmed Maître Robert as he pleaded the defense of a woman accused of horrible crimes. The audience saw no reason to doubt this as the lawyer's eloquent face and impassioned gestures filled the screen, with a pause now and then to consult an impassive notebook. What really happened was that the scene took place in the courtyard of Maître Robert's Paris home, with a curtain hiding the windows, a kitchen table mounted on empty tins, and the cook's account book doing service as the lawyer's brief. While the camera turned Maître Robert improvised one of his finest speeches and worked in effects which he never surpassed in the most dramatic of his causes. This interlude was for Sacha an appetizing taste of the things one could do with a camera.

Crude though the arrangement may seem to a generation familiar with the optical wizardry of the modern cinema, such enterprise in 1915 was unusual, and Sacha was not entirely wrong in regarding the camera as little more than a superlative box of tricks. Again, in the episode with Sarah Bernhardt, he introduced a novelty when he showed her first at a distance and then in what has become known as a "close-up." She sat on a park bench and recited poetry, the index finger of her left hand pointing heavenward, with Sacha at her side in a straw hat and wing-collar which looked as if it had been borrowed from Rostand.

The film was entitled *Ceux de chez nous* and was first projected on 22 November, 1915, at the Théâtre des Variétés, with a one-act play to make up the bill. The method of presentation entitled Sacha to a possible credit as the inventor of the sound film, or at least of post-synchronization. After he had talked about what the audience were going to see, he joined Charlotte Lysès in an obscure corner beneath the screen. Linking shots portrayed him and his wife calling at the houses of the people involved. With a slight sensation of alarm spectators saw and heard Sacha and Charlotte turn toward the camera and speak aloud. The passages had been carefully rehearsed and the two players fitted their speech to the filmed movement of their lips with uncanny exactitude. The illusion was complete. Yet for many years Sacha did not care to pursue his experiments as an inheritor of Georges Méliès. Only a short while before *Ceux de chez nous* he had declared enigmatically: "I consider that the cinema is already past its best." Later, he observed: "The cinema is a meat-packer's art. I don't like it."

A film studio could never replace the warmth and excitement that Sacha found on the stage, and he returned to the theater in 1916 with a play that is one of his most characteristic and enjoyable. It has been revived countless times, has been made into a successful film, and, years after his death, continues to delight audiences with its freshness. *Faisons un rêve,* which takes its title from a poem by Victor Hugo, was written in three days; and there are three characters only—the husband, the wife, and the lover. The play opens with husband and wife calling by appointment on a young man whom they have met several times at dinner parties over the past year. They are kept waiting, and as the clock hands move slowly toward four o'clock the husband becomes more and more irritable. He is not a very imaginative fellow. He finds it difficult to disguise, for the benefit of his wife, a date with his mistress at four as an appointment with a business acquaintance. In the course of their dialogue the mysterious businessman grows into a South American with the name of Lopez Quita de la Mañana, but of what country of that interesting continent he is a native, the husband is not quite sure. "You never know whether they're Brazilians, Chileans, Argentinians, or anything else," he says, talking a little too fast. "When they've said 'South American' they've said everything. Anyway, they never know themselves. Brazilians usually have their family in Chile, their domicile in Argentina, and their money in Guatemala. How can you expect them to know who they are?" By ten past four the wife, who has a nice nature, is agreeing that life together is only possible on a basis of mutual trust and confidence, and the relieved husband is flying off to his appointment.

After a decent interval their host comes in from next door, where he has been patiently listening to their conversation and waiting for the husband to go. He tells the wife how he has known her for over a year, how he has longed to talk alone with her, how for the last three weeks their eyes have been "speaking" to each other, how he is madly in love with her, how he implores her to come to him this evening at nine o'clock. . . . All of which only gives her time to agree and say: *"Je t'aime!"* before the curtain falls. The whole of the second act is a soliloquy, a *tour de force* for the actor who plays the young man waiting for her to arrive. It contains all the thoughts and all the anxieties of all the lovers who ever found themselves in this situation since history began. He pictures her emerging from her house and calling a taxi. He sees her, nestling nervously in her seat, as the taxi crosses the Champs-Élysées and goes up the rue Washington (that's a two-minute journey, enough time for him to lower the lights in his apartment), before taking the boulevard Haussmann ("Take it, *mon amour*, it's yours, I give it to you . . ."), and arriving in the avenue de Messines where he lives. In his mind he visualizes her coming up the stairs and counts the steps . . . 21, 20, 19, 18, 17, 16. . . . He waits for the bell. It rings at that very moment, only to herald a telegram from a friend. Women, he reflects bitterly, unpunctual and unreliable, women are dreadful bores. How awful to be married to one! What can you do with them apart from making love? "If someone said to me: 'One day you'll strangle a postman on the road to Vésinet,' I'd say: 'Perhaps!' If someone said to me: 'One day you'll be Archbishop of Clermont-Ferrand,' I'd reply: 'It's possible!' But if someone said to me: 'One day you'll be married,' I'd say: 'No, General'—provided, of course, it was a General who'd said it to me." And he fidgets about the room with a scent bottle, spraying the air and a bowl of flowers, and then, as an afterthought, the bed, as the minutes tick away. Suddenly he hears a car outside and rushes to the window. The car-door opens, he glimpses with rising excitement the hem of a skirt . . . but: *"Merde!* it's a curé!" There follows some excellent business when, in desperation, he tries to telephone her, performs acrobatics as he lights his cigarette with a box of matches from the other side of the room, and finds himself making intimate declarations on a crossed line to a housewife ordering cherries from her grocer. While he fumes into the receiver, pleading for a word from the beautiful subscriber, the wife appears in the doorway at his back and tiptoes over to him with a smile.

Next morning she awakes in that mood of remorse that women usually feel it their duty to assume. She thinks with horror of her husband returning home at ten o'clock the previous night and of his surprise at finding her away. Her lover gaily proposes several ingenious but irrelevant solutions to the dilemma. She brushes them aside and in a mood of great seriousness declares that she must get a divorce and marry him. He instantly agrees and quotes the Hugo poem of the title: lovers receding into the distance on their palfreys, birds singing in the woods. . . . He is quite carried away with the romance of it all. At that moment they hear the husband demanding to be let in. Petrified, she rushes into the bathroom while her lover quakingly slips a revolver into his dressing-gown pocket. The husband enters, stony and dramatic. As he speaks the tension relaxes, for he has come seeking help. He has spent the night with his mistress and will his good friend support him with an alibi? The reassured lover regrets that he can't, discreetly indicating as his reason the closed door of the bathroom. ("Actress?" asks the husband with a connoisseur's interest. "No." "Society woman?" "That's it!" "Married?" "Of course." "Her husband on a business trip?" "That's a good idea," mutters the lover to himself. "Oh well, one cuckold the more!" "Quite." "And how many there are already!" "I'm glad to hear you say that. It's comforting . . . ," replies the lover. "Is the husband a close friend of yours?" "Hmm . . ." "Anyway, he's that much closer to you now," chuckles the husband.) The lover sets his brain to work and improvises a plausible story based on the husband's providential disclosure that he has an elderly aunt living in Orléans. The South American, the husband will tell his wife, was a kindly invention to spare her worry. His aunt was very ill and he had had to rush to her bedside. From time to time he will send telegrams reporting his aunt's gradual recovery, and after two days he will return to his wife. The husband faintly protests that two boring days in provincial Orléans is a lot to expect. "Think of your poor little wife weeping at home," he is sternly reminded, "and tell yourself that there must not be the slightest ground for doubt in her mind. Now, she'll never be able to accept that you've inflicted such a sacrifice on yourself—two days in Orléans!—just to keep in her good books. When you tell a lie, believe me, you must cultivate it with the greatest care." "Yes, it's very true. You have to make it believable." "And that way," concludes the lover persuasively, "it becomes a tribute you pay to the person you're deceiving." So the husband, full of thanks for this excellent advice, speeds away to exile. The wife emerges from her hiding place: "He's gone? Then . . . we have the whole of life in front of us?" "You weren't listening! We've something better than that, something better than the whole of life!" she is told. "Better than the whole of life?" "Yes," exclaims her lover in a magnificent curtain line, "we've got two whole days!"

Sacha played the lover—"Thirty years old, not a handsome chap, if you will, but it's all the same thing, happy to be alive, pleased with other people, delighted with himself. . . ." runs the stage direction—and Charlotte appeared as the wife. As the husband, Raimu had one of his finest parts. The sly raising of his eyebrow, the clumsy cunning of his grimace, the nasal Provençal accent, in itself a richly suggestive aid, were never more expressively used. *Faisons un rêve* marks the beginning of his success on the Parisian stage. Born thirty-three years previously as Jean Auguste César Muraire—a pleasing baptismal coincidence which foreshadows his international fame as Marcel Pagnol's film character—he came from Toulon. In that town his father, who with much fortitude answered to the name of Mucius Scaevola Muraire, kept an upholstery business. Raimu was always stage-struck and toured the music halls of Toulon and Marseille with a singing act which he afterwards described as "horribly bad." Then came revues in Paris where he adopted his pseudonym and came to the notice of Lucien Guitry. The latter summoned him to his dressing room. "I'd like to know what you're messing about at in the music hall," Lucien told Raimu who was stiff with shyness. "You ought to go into the theater." Raimu took his advice and was grateful ever afterwards. Whenever Sacha wanted to engage him he always accepted with the feeling of repaying a debt to Lucien.

Like many comic actors, in private life Raimu was melancholy, abrupt, and often very bad-tempered. A hard-driven business deal gave him more pleasure than anything else, apart from the elegant suits which he continued to buy at the same tailor's for over forty years. His miserliness was proverbial and he was so sensitive about it that he never agreed to play *l'Avare* at the Comédie-Française. "It might cause unnecessary comment," he remarked drily. He had a beautiful flat off the Champs-Élysées where he lived with his wife, mother-in-law, and daughter. It was furnished in the most correct eighteenth-century style and hung with English engravings which he collected tenaciously. At mealtimes he always sat on the right of his mother-in-law, a napkin firmly tied round his neck, and made polite conversation with her. Then he would go out for a drink at Fouquet's, at the cross road of the Champs-Élysées, where his example made it a rendezvous for producers, directors, and film people. There he held court daily, surrounded by hangers-on and those other strange fauna who haunt the purlieus of the cinema world. He watched them all with a sardonic eye and spoke to them in gravelly monosyllables. Yet despite his gruff exterior he was extremely sensitive, ready to see offense in the smallest detail, and prone to be deeply wounded by unintentional oversights. This made him a very difficult man to work with, but he would not otherwise have been the artist he was.

At about the same time as he gave Raimu his first opportunity on the Paris stage, Sacha made another "discovery." Only a few weeks after *Faisons un rêve* he presented the first of his "biographical" plays, *Jean de la Fontaine,* a four-act piece dedicated to Anatole France, "who did this play the honor of liking it." La Fontaine was a congenial subject. He had married a fourteen-year-old bride when his father intimated that it was time he settled down. The combination of her ample dowry with the succession to his father's government post seemed calculated to give him the maximum leisure for writing. Poetry was the one thing he really cared about. He proved a tolerant husband, an indifferent father. Love was a pleasant relaxation, a useful stimulus to writing, and anything more permanent filled him with horror. After the inevitable separation from his wife he drifted from one noble household to another, the pet of various fashionable ladies who accepted his neglect of their deeper emotions as the penalty they paid for giving shelter to a genius such as he. It is quite impossible for a schoolboy to appreciate La Fontaine. His fables are written in perfect French with an exquisite choice of words that makes translation out of the question. His philosophy can be savored only by a grown man who knows the world. Those deceptively simple tales of rats and mice and frogs embody a realistic view of men and their affairs which springs from a cold-eyed disenchantment with humankind. In Sacha's play La Fontaine hears a seven-year-old boy reciting one of his fables and he is made to declare: "It's flattering, but perhaps it makes me run a greater risk. From that it's only a short step to becoming an imposition. Isn't it diminishing the value of my fables to use them as a mechanical exercise for children's memories? These children will one day be men and I've no doubt they'll have the worst possible recollection of the lines they were forced to learn and repeated like parrots! Admitted they'll know by heart eight or ten fables of mine—but will they want to know any more?"

Jean de la Fontaine opens with a clever piece of stagecraft. Madame de la Fontaine is discovered embroidering, ostensibly alone. Her lover enters. "Are you on your own?" he enquires. "No," says a sharp voice, and the audience are just as surprised as he at seeing the husband's face peering from behind a large armchair which is placed with its back to them. Without paying too much attention to historical fact, Sacha draws a convincingly rounded picture of the famous *mal marié*, who, it is clear, had much in common with him. "He's a man whose egoism seems to increase every week," says Madame of her husband. "You don't know what it's like to live at close quarters with a man who doesn't want to act like everyone else." Another revealing comment is La Fontaine's line: "Although we're very different from each other we both have a priceless gift, mysterious and irresistible, and that gift is the gift of pleasing." Elsewhere he reflects: "As for the first man ever to marry, well, there's nothing to say to him. But really, the second was unforgiveable!" However, Sacha cannot resist a happy ending, and after La Fontaine has rung many sophistical changes on the theme that he prefers to be unfaithful but not disloyal, he is reunited against all evidence with his wife in illustration of his remark: "Indulgence—that's the great quality! Don't be the enemy of the other's pleasures." It is worth remembering that the dedicatee of the play, Anatole France, had once noted that when an author proposes to talk about another author, what he really means is that he is going to write about him *à propos* of himself.

Sacha wore the ruffs and silver buckles he loved to dress up in and Charlotte played his wife. The other important part was that of La Fontaine's mistress. In the play she is stolen from him by the composer Lully—a cold-blooded historical liberty, since the debauched Florentine's real tastes lay in more unusual directions —and it was necessary for her to have a good voice, as she had a number of songs to sing. One evening Charlotte happened to see a revue in which a thin girl with big eyes and a small but pleasing voice performed a skit on the famous Sacha Guitry, whose mannerisms she imitated with spry irreverence. Charlotte, greatly amused, made her acquaintance, and some time later brought Sacha to see the spectacle. That was how his wife introduced him to Yvonne Printemps, then not yet twenty years old. She had been christened Yvonne Wignolle. Overheard singing in her mother's shop by two revue writers, she had been taken by them to see the late Paul Derval, who was the owner for what seemed a century of the Folies-Bergère. "We'll call you Printemps [Spring], which is normal at your age," they decided, adding ungallantly: "By contrast, your mother will be Madame Hiver [Winter]." Their protégée made her début in a Folies-Bergère revue at the age of thirteen. Each evening she arrived at the theater escorted by her watchful mother, and as soon as the performance was over they scuttled off to catch a train back to their suburban home. On matinée days, while her mother warmed up some food in the stage doorkeeper's office, Yvonne's great joy was to stamp the complimentary tickets. No one had seen in her urchin charm the actress whose grace and femininity were to mature so quickly in a few short years and to entrance the young actor-playwright.

During the run of *Jean de la Fontaine* the stage-hands were often gratified with the touching view of Sacha taking Yvonne Printemps' little dog for a walk accompanied by its owner, her long fair hair drifting close to her leading man's shoulder. Once again his current play, though acted in seventeenth-century costume, followed the pattern by reproducing the events of his private life. Charlotte did not need to be told by gossip what was happening. "I had to go," she said years later, "because, like the ant in the La Fontaine fable, I'm not keen on sharing." Her exit was dignified. She went quietly one day, without recrimination. Friends helped her at this difficult period, which she felt deeply but spoke little of; among them were Raimu, Maurice Chevalier, and Jean Cocteau. "He'll come back to you," Cocteau tried to console her. "Spring has always been a short season." Colette found her a home in Brittany, a picturesque old mill, and dreamed one night that Sacha had returned. But Colette's wishful fancy was not to come true, and Charlotte was left with the hundreds of letters he had written her during the ten lively years of their marriage, and the theater programs that linked their names together. She kept them until her death. Each time she took them out for another look, the paper had grown a little yellower. Once more she began to appear on the stage, in smaller parts and in less fashionable theaters. With a sense of disloyalty to the theater she loved, she played opposite Jan Kiepura in a film. Other films followed, but the stage always called her back in the end. She wrote a play, produced it, and designed the costumes, and then took up again the long series of decently obscure supporting roles which managers knew she could be relied upon to fill with competence. It would not be true to say that she vanished without a trace. Her living memorial was the actor Sacha Guitry.

The divorce was concluded in the last year of the war. Long before then Sacha had been training Yvonne Printemps, as he did with the rest of his wives, and making an actress out of her. Before meeting him she had been classed as a soubrette with a pretty voice. Under his tuition she developed an acting talent and a personality that made her an unforgettable partner in the twenty or so plays he wrote for them together. When he judged the time had come to introduce his new creation to Paris audiences, he opened with a play called *l'Illusionniste*. It is a happy title, for no one had an easier gift than Sacha for creating a stage illusion or for juggling with fantasy. He played a conjurer and performed card tricks with professional deftness, relishing the opportunity to display his long and elegant fingers. He had been a passionate devotee of the yoyo craze when it arrived. He owned dozens of packs of fake cards and "clairvoyant" outfits which he manipulated before baffled spectators to the accompaniment of breathtaking patter. This was illusion at its purest for the man who had written: "To act is to tell lies with the aim of deceiving. Everything around one should tell lies. The good actor should say 'I love you' with greater conviction to an actress he doesn't love than to one whom he does. And he should convince the audience that he is eating on stage when in reality he is not. The refinement of refinements is to *appear* to be in love with an actress whom one does really love —it's like eating a genuine chicken while making believe it's cardboard."

The theater was turned into a music hall and *l'Illusionniste* began with twenty minutes of acrobats, singers, and trick cyclists before Sacha arrived with his nonchalant conjuring act. A woman in the audience catches his attention and after the show he makes advances to her. She finds them offensive. "There's only one thing a woman really finds offensive," he tells her, "and that's not being desired." She hesitates as he invites her to join his romantic wandering life. He weaves a bewitching picture of the tour that awaits her: London, which she loves; the week after, Stockholm and its glittering snows; then Turkey and its veiled women; moonlight in Bokhara; Rome, the city of love; Monte Carlo and the thrill of the tables. . . . (It was Léautaud who said that to be really successful with women you need something of the vulgarity of a commercial traveler.) His tactic succeeds. She trumps up a quarrel with her unknowing lover and spends the night with the illusionist. Next day she is full of excitement at the prospect before them. But he is already bored and eager to be off on his next conquest. Anyhow, it's the foggy season in London now, he tells her, destroying the romance as efficiently as he created it, and it's horribly cold in Stockholm. His agent has canceled the engagement in Turkey, the contract isn't yet certain for Bokhara, and instead of Rome and Monte Carlo he's down for a tour of the

provinces. Why did he go to such trouble and tell her such wonderful things, all for the sake of one night? she asks, hurt and
confused. "Yes, but what a night!" he says. "I don't regret it. The
second night wouldn't have been difficult to get. The second night
is success, but the first is a triumph . . . Last night I brought
off a charming sleight-of-hand. I made you appear and then dis-
appear from my life, and it will be a lasting memory for me." One
of the many memories, she supposes bitterly. "No, Madame, I've
got one for every town in the world. Only Paris was missing, and
now I have it, thanks to you." He goes and, a few moments later,
the lover returns to find her in tears. "Why, *chérie*," he says, as
the curtain falls on the unwitting irony of the remark, "why are
you crying? I've come back." The end is worthy of Becque.

There was, as the audience felt, a profound sadness in this disillusioned play. "The pretty decorations only mitigate the horror
it conceals," wrote one critic. "The flowers hide ruins." Paul
Léautaud found in *l'Illusionniste* a tract for the times. Everything
is illusion, he decided. Illusion creates marriage and love affairs.
Duty is illusion. So are work, happiness, and sorrow. Léautaud
was then embroiled with the most impossible of his mistresses, a
woman whose character he loathed but whose unrivaled love-
making he could not do without. ("If she died under me I
wouldn't feel the slightest sorrow.") The theme of the play gave
him cause to develop his theory that pleasure can be exclusive
of love, and that pleasure itself remains an illusion. "So I come
to M. Sacha Guitry's *l'Illusionniste*. I don't need to tell you that
the author has kept to the sentimental, romantic side, and that as
always we find him in this play charming, witty, mocking, insolent, almost cynical, and so full of attraction that, for my part,
under his spell as I am, he could from time to time show weak-
nesses that I would refuse to see."

The opening night of *l'Illusionniste* was the first occasion when
Yvonne Printemps danced, sang, and acted with the inimitable
poise Sacha had helped her to achieve. That night the French

theater acquired one of its most attractive personalities. It was Sacha who had recognized her potential, groomed her, and placed her in a setting where her talent flourished. Her versatility was as captivating as the uses to which she put it. There are few women who can sing as gracefully as they act, or who can dance as prettily as they speak their words. To all these gifts Yvonne Printemps allied a character which enabled her to handle any sort of situation with tact. At a reception in London she was surrounded by a group of hearty young men who were flattered by the way she appreciated their jokes. Her expression showed the sincerest enjoyment and she laughed at all the right moments. No one could have guessed that she did not understand a single word of English.

In the midst of all the celebrations for *l'Illusionniste*, the champagne, the telegrams, the bouquets, news came that Octave Mirbeau was dying. For some time now it had been clear that he was faltering. Sacha hurried to the bedside of his old mentor and found him propped feebly against heaped-up pillows. At the age of sixty-nine he had given up the fight. The violent arguments and slashing campaigns were now far away. For an hour Mirbeau stared at Sacha from a hooded eye. Sacha leaned forward and embraced him. "Never collaborate!" whispered Mirbeau, repeating the last of the many counsels he had given him throughout life.

To follow up Yvonne Printemps's triumph, Sacha wrote a play that would give her the chance to act *en travesti* as well as sing. For his subject he chose Deburau, the great mime, whose art died with him but whose memory lives in theatrical history. Yvonne was to play both the heroine and Deburau's young son. The Harlequin of Deburau was a mute, sad commentator on life. From his birthplace near Warsaw, Deburau had come in the early nineteenth century to France, where his father hoped to claim an estate. On their way through Europe the family earned their bread by tumbling. They put down their worn carpet in the villages they passed through and performed acrobatics when a large enough crowd had assembled. Although his sisters turned neat somersaults and his brothers glided smoothly along the slack wire, poor blundering Deburau was too clumsy to rival their skill. Night after night he would miss his footing and sprawl on the ground to mocking laughter, often bleeding and in pain. Eventually he was engaged to play Harlequin at the Théâtre des Funambules in Paris. At a starvation wage and with his dressing room in a cellar so damp that mushrooms grew in it, he perfected over the years his version of Watteau's "Gilles," that moon-eyed personage with a death-white face, big buttons, and white floppy robes. Deburau impersonated the old-clothes dealers, the junk men, the scavengers, the charcoal vendors, who worked the streets of Paris. His art, popular in its origins, expressed the poverty and the suffering of the humbler classes, not with anger but with compassionate realism. He never spoke. Everything flowed from gesture, stance, gait, or grimace, and the turn ended with an eccentric dance. The working-class audiences squeezed onto the narrow wooden benches hailed him as one of their own. They disapproved of the fashionable people, the intellectuals such as George Sand and Balzac, who, attracted by Deburau's fame, were often in the small boxes at the side of the stage. "He had made a vocation out of a handicap, an art out of a craft, a joy out of a torment," said an admirer.

Sacha wrote his play in free verse, a medium that lent itself to the romantic world he evoked. It was the world of popular entertainment in the eighteen-forties, the Parisian world of *ombres chinoises,* of puppets, rope dancers, and the *théâtres à quatre sous* or "penny gaffs," to which Deburau belonged. The set reproduced his tiny theater, its narrow facade lit with glimmering lanterns, and the cramped auditorium whose stage was only inches away from the front row. In these surroundings, where Deburau had played five times a day and nine times on Sunday, Sacha brought to life again the blanched face daubed with flour and the tragic round eyes. It does not matter that he stretches coincidence by giving Deburau a hopeless love affair with Marie Duplessis, the original of *la Dame aux camélias,* nor that the mime is far wittier and more eloquent than he really was. In any case, as someone remarked, you began criticizing too late, after the charm had operated and you had left the theater. What does matter is that an atmosphere had been created and the feeling of the man and his setting conveyed. For Paul Léautaud the result was enchantment. He had once known a man, another Pierrot, who had acted with Deburau's son. Léautaud remembered the old Pierrot coming to dinner and pausing at the door, his rubber-like face assuming the expression it had taken thousands of times before on long-forgotten stages. His lips were pursed and his eyes glittered with greed as he exclaimed: "Ah! Sweeties! More sweeties!" How much closer to life, how infinitely truer were the old comedians, said Léautaud, than the boring tragedies of Corneille and the absurd dramas of Victor Hugo. "Doesn't it show the most unfettered, picturesque, sensitive, and inventive mind to have remembered the Pierrot of the Théâtre des Funambules and the actors of that curious little theater, and to have put on the stage their leader, the creator of a *genre,* Deburau in person?"

The success of *Deburau* was increased by the incidental music André Messager later wrote for it. The fate of theatrical composers only too often is to see their work die as soon as the play is taken off. Messager's music is underestimated and does not deserve the snobbish disdain it frequently receives. A musician enjoying the respect of Debussy, who dedicated *Pelléas et Mélisande* to him, and of Fauré, is not to be dismissed so easily. His operettas, in appearance so light and facile, are composed with skill and harmonic subtlety, for he was an expert orchestrator. In addition to being a prolific composer he was for some time manager of the Paris Opéra; conductor of the Conservatoire Orchestra; and musical adviser to Covent Garden. As a practical man of the theater he wrote music for *Deburau* which is perfect of its kind. It is scored for cornet, tuba, big drum, two violins, double bass, and piano. Among the different sections is a pantomime which movingly illustrates Deburau's act as the old-clothes dealer. This is succeeded by a fairground waltz that somehow combines brassiness with pathos. Then comes soft music to accompany Deburau's monologue as he recalls the hardness and the humiliations of his early life. "I was the shame of the troupe," he says, remembering the punishments he suffered for bungling tricks. A tender melody rises from the double-bass to dissolve into a cadence reminiscent of a phrase in Brahms's B♭ minor Intermezzo. There were also a song for Yvonne Printemps and several entr'actes which established the mood quite exquisitely. It is possible that the absence of this lovely music helps to account for the failure of Harley Granville-Barker's London production a few years later.

There is in *Deburau* a touching scene where the mime's young son tells him that he, too, wants to go on the stage. Deburau smiles tolerantly, but his mood changes when the boy says that he will act under his own name. "A name is a sacred thing when one has created it oneself," he declares heatedly. "I've created mine —you mustn't touch it. I don't want you to spoil it." (As Sacha himself once said, referring to his own parentage: "My surname was made, so I made myself a first name.") Later on Deburau becomes reconciled to the idea and instructs his son in the tricks of the trade. "Love your profession—it's the most beautiful in the world," he concludes, after dwelling on the necessity for an actor to feel stage fright if he is to give a good performance. All these passages became intensely significant one afternoon in 1918 when Sacha heard that his father had taken a box for the matinée. Never had the stage fright which always caused him distress been such a torture. Lucien had taken his seat, to watch his son act for the first time, long before the play began. When Sacha made his entry, heart thudding violently, eyes dazzled by the footlights, he had a vision of himself in Russia, a boy of five again, in his father's arms. At the fall of the curtain Lucien vanished. A short time afterwards Tristan Bernard appeared in Sacha's dressing room with a letter. "I expect you for lunch tomorrow . . . ," Lucien had written.

The following day Sacha arrived to find Lucien awaiting him. There was a silence as they embraced. The shadow of their thirteen-year-old estrangement disappeared at Lucien's first words: "While you were acting yesterday, do you know how I was seeing you? As a boy of five, in Russia, in my arms." Ten minutes later they were joined by Yvonne Printemps and the reconciliation was complete. "And now," said Lucien, "write me a play—quickly!" For some time Sacha had been haunted by a subject which he had only been prevented from dramatizing by the difficulty of finding a great actor to play the title part. Within five days of their meeting he had written *Pasteur*.

Chapter 9

To Sacha Guitry who, like myself, does not write in chains, and who, indeed, should have written this play.

BERNARD SHAW

(INSCRIBED ON SACHA'S COPY OF St. Joan)

The news that France's leading boulevard dramatist had written a play about the father-in-law of Dr. Vallery-Radot did not please the Doctor himself. "I should like you to know," he informed Sacha, "that my wife and I will do everything in our power to prevent its performance." With grudging coolness they agreed to hear a reading of the play. By the time Sacha had reached the end of the first act there was no more talk of banning it. When it was finished both Vallery-Radot and his wife were enthusiastic. They wished to change only one remark in the script because, they said, it was something quite out of character for Pasteur to say. Sacha was able to point out that it was a direct quotation from a speech Pasteur had made. One of the features that gives the play its authenticity is the use made of the scientist's own recorded comments. The lengthy quotations, italicized in the text, are handled with great dramatic skill. The early years of Pasteur's unpopularity and his subsequent fame are shown in

116

brief scenes which highlight the important events in his life. There were, of course, objections that minor facts had been overlooked or altered. In a work of imaginative recreation this does not matter provided that the result has emotional truth and avoids distorting the general impression. What Sacha aimed at was the theatrical presentation of a man in all his humility and achievement. His success in doing so gave him a technique, which he employed in later plays, for overcoming the problems of what is always a difficulty in the theater.

Pasteur is in several ways an unusual play for Sacha to have written. It has an all-male cast and it depends on the theme of spontaneous generation to create dramatic interest. It is also one of his few plays which did not contain a part for himself. He was content to place his stagecraft at the service of Lucien, who, in the title role, gave one of his best performances. In the course of a portrayal which included many rare moments, no one could ever forget his first entry. The curtain rose on six of Pasteur's students talking about him with admiration and so preparing his entry in the classic Shakespearian manner. The distant noise of a door being slammed was suddenly heard. During the next twenty or so seconds came the ever-louder steps of a man walking along a corridor. The students turned toward the door, the sound of steps ceased, and there, on the threshold, the embodiment of Pasteur, stood Lucien Guitry. He said nothing, he did nothing, but he was superb. Among the audience that night was Arnold Bennett, who declared: "It seems a lot to say, but at every moment he was perfect." Then came the scene where, faced with a boy who has been savaged by a mad dog, Pasteur has the first opportunity of testing his method. Shall he take the risk? Or will he lack faith in himself and his life's work? He decides to inoculate the boy and to wait until he knows success or failure. "As Lucien Guitry began the long agonizing vigil, upon the result of which all that Pasteur had fought for depended," wrote C. B. Cochran, the famous English manager, "the audience was held with that tenseness which one experiences only once or twice in a lifetime. And then the curtain fell, with the audience gasping, and then breaking into frenzied applause."

"Papa!" cried Pasteur's daughter when she saw Lucien's realistic make-up and performance. "No," Sacha corrected her with a smile, *"Papa!"* At the end of the play and after twenty curtain calls, Lucien stepped forward and replied to shouts for the author. "It would be impossible for me to call him 'Monsieur.' I shall therefore not tell you who the author of this play is. But I shall owe you the greatest happiness of my life if you will be good enough to let me show him to you." And Sacha appeared at his side to confirm their unparalleled relationship. One of the play's keenest spectators was a man who watched from the wings and who, during the scene of the inoculation, even opened the door of the stage-set to see more clearly. Sacha, aghast, told him to step back. The man explained that he was a caretaker at the Institut Pasteur and particularly wanted to see the episode. "Why?" asked Sacha. "Because that's me." "You? Which one?" "The boy," was his reply. "That's me. I was the first person whose life was to be saved by Monsieur Pasteur."

The chorus of praise that greeted *Pasteur* was unanimous except for a lone voice that rang out in harsh disagreement. It belonged to Paul Léautaud. He loved animals with such devotion that he execrated the name of Pasteur. What a pity, he complained in his review, that after writing so many charming plays Sacha should have chosen to erect a monument to human stupidity! It was ridiculous to make such a fuss over the life of a boy when any day you could see brats of his sort maltreating animals in the streets of Paris. No sensible man would wish to consecrate a torturer who had subjected animals to the horrors of vivisection. While the rest of the audience heard with rapt attention Pasteur's remark about the "fine living eyes" of the boy he had just cured, Léautaud squirmed disgustedly in his seat. "What about the animals sacrificed to his so-called science?" he hissed. *"They* had fine living eyes too, eyes that were full of a light children's eyes rarely have." The evening had been ruined for him. From then on Léautaud redoubled the vigils he kept outside the Medical Faculty of the Sorbonne; there he watched for the vans delivering strays for research, and tried to comfort the wretched creatures against the sufferings ahead.

Soon after *Pasteur,* Sacha and Yvonne Printemps took the opportunity of getting themselves married. The cast was ideal for the occasion. The witnesses included Georges Feydeau, who characteristically arrived late. He was in the habit of sleeping during the day and only getting up at night, so his presence was a notable sign of friendship. Once again Tristan Bernard was there as accredited attendant at Sacha's weddings. Yvonne ostensibly played the leading role though she tended to be overshadowed by Sarah Bernhardt. The indomitable *monstre sacré* was borne into the mayor's parlor on a sort of elaborate palanquin. The choice of conveyance was not entirely due to her sense of drama, for at the age of seventy she had had her left leg amputated following an illness. (Her refusal to wear a wooden leg rather spoiled the point of many unkind stories. "What'll she do now?" somebody asked. "She can always rap out the *trois coups,*" replied a wit.) Yvonne's gentle picture-hat of tulle and ostrich plumes lacked the stark majesty of the billowing chinchilla and the silver fox helmet that cascaded down over Sarah's ruined features. Raddled with illness and old age, Sarah had proved that although she had no speaking part she could still dominate any gathering, even one of which Lucien was a member. For the bridegroom's father, who this time warmly approved of his son's bride, was there in person with his own current wife.

A new home was found in the rue Scheffer, an oppressively expensive street where only rich dramatists and the more successful left-wing politicians can afford to live. Round about the same time Sacha got rid of "Chez les Zoaques," the country house in Normandy. Perhaps it reminded him too much of Charlotte

Lysès. In any case he had wearied of its bogus Tudor style and the large garden that surrounded it, and he was ready to let it go for something less than the million francs he was asking. In its place he bought a house on the Riviera at Cap d'Ail and baptized it "Gioia Mia." A jewel it certainly was. It was reached by way of a narrow zig-zag path and stood inside walls ornamented with cupolas and statuettes. Palm trees and mimosas waved around it in the gentle breeze. From the spacious hall looking out over the blue sea Cap Ferrat was clearly to be seen at the right. On the left was Monte Carlo. For Sacha the born gambler, its baize-covered tables presented a more alluring prospect than Cap Ferrat with his forbidding if involuntary neighbor Somerset Maugham.

Eleven days after it had been written, on a train journey from Brussels, Yvonne appeared in a new play with a title which seemed to announce that she had now moved definitely into Sacha's world. It was called, *le Mari, la femme et l'amant*. By a charmingly unexpected piece of casting the husband was played by Jean Périer, the opera singer who had created the role of Pelléas in the first performance of Debussy's *Pelléas et Mélisande*, and who had left the world of opera for the boulevard theater. Burrowing his way out from underneath the piles of furious letters which his *Pasteur* notice had brought him, Paul Léautaud thankfully greeted Sacha's reversion to normal. "It's witty, light, utterly immoral, even rather dissolute, to complete the picture. It's a trifle, but extremely amusing to listen to," said Léautaud, rather in the tone of a father welcoming the return of a prodigal son. "Here we have Monsieur Guitry, after *Pasteur,* back with the sort of play in which he excels, full of happy discoveries, ingenious ideas and fantasy, with a great sense of comedy and often a surprising gift of observation." The hermit of Fontenay went home to his swarm of pets with a feeling of relief that his favorite playwright had recovered from the aberration which led him to glorify an arch-vivisectionist.

During the next five years the names of Sacha, Lucien, and

Yvonne Printemps were rarely absent from theatrical posters. The first play in which the famous triumvirate appeared was *Mon Père avait raison*. It inaugurated their triple reign on the Paris stage by taking more at the box office than had any other play since Rostand's *Chantecler* ten years before. This disillusioned account of three generations—the first act presented Lucien as the grand-father, Sacha as the father, and a child actor as the son—has been described as a "light tragedy." In the second act, twenty years later, Lucien is the father and Sacha the grown-up son. It is at this point that the older generation, fearful that the same mistakes will be made again, tries to influence the turn of events. Fortunately it does not succeed, and the father makes a profound remark: "In trying to stop you from being unhappy, I nearly prevented you from being happy." The audience which laughed at the careless wit and ingenious situations realized much later the inference that an unshakeable egotism, an indifference to other people's misfortunes, and a brute confidence in life were the only sure guarantees of happiness in this world. (One thinks of the centenarian who, according to the Scottish writer Norman Douglas, when asked how he had preserved his astonishing health was wont to shake his head and reply: "By not going a step out of my way to please anyone but myself!") Yet while the play was in progress it was easy to overlook this desolate wisdom and to fix the attention instead on the charms of Yvonne Printemps or the flashing dialogue between Lucien and Sacha. An unexpected admirer of the play was François Mauriac. He wanted, he said, to shout out like the old man on the first night of Molière's *les Précieuses ridicules*: "Bravo, Sacha Guitry, here's a good play!"

A more innocent entertainment was *Béranger*, a dramatized biography of the humble poet whose songs have become a part of folklore. *Le roi d'Yvetot*, relegated these days to the nursery, was a satire on Napoleon, whose legend, by an attractive irony, Béranger was to help keep alive with the songs of his later years. The simple *chansonnier* wrote with a genuineness and an artistry which pleased both the common people, who sang his songs all over France, and such figures as Chateaubriand, Sainte-Beuve, and Robert Louis Stevenson. Béranger's letters, pronounced Stevenson, are ". . . full of wisdom and kindness, with a smack of Montaigne, and now and then a vein of pleasantry that will remind the English reader of Charles Lamb." Sacha himself impersonated this attractive figure, Yvonne was the "Lisette" of so many of Béranger's songs (she was also the Marie, the Madeleine, and the Marguerite of his private life), and Lucien was observed in the guise of Talleyrand. Sacha had long wanted the excuse to do something about Talleyrand, a personality who had caught his imagination, and here, with a chillingly Goya-esque performance by Lucien, he offered a sketch for the full-length portrait he was to draw some twenty years later in his play of the same name. The final scene shows Béranger drinking in a tavern, old and half-forgotten, even though his songs are the rage of the country. Nearby some young men are talking politics and repeating the usual party clap-trap. As one who has lived under half a dozen régimes and who has known imprisonment for his opinions, Béranger tells them: "Beware of politics like the plague! Politics aren't pretty to look at from close quarters, believe me. You mustn't go too near to power if you really want to keep any illusions about democracy." The advice was excellent, but, alas, Sacha was not to follow it himself during the years of the Occupation.

Early in the nineteen-twenties Sacha took the lease of a theater which was to prove an excellent setting for the talents of himself, his wife, and his father. The Théâtre Édouard VII, tucked away between the Madeleine and the Opéra, is one of the smallest and prettiest of its kind. Doubtless this is why it is periodically rumored to be under threat of demolition to make way for office blocks. It was built in 1913 to the plan of an English architect; knew brief indignity as a cinema; became Sacha's fief until 1931, when it was lost to films again; and in 1940 returned to its proper function. The intimate, almost confidential atmosphere was perfectly suited to the key in which Sacha preferred to work, and here he produced well over a dozen of his plays in the next decade. He began with *Je t'aime*, which foreshadows the rigors of Sartre's *Huis-Clos* in the remark: "If someone were to give us the certainty that our love is eternal . . . we'd probably stop loving each other." And when the hero's mistress asks him if he will keep the oath he has sworn to love her always, he replies: "Well, I don't know," adding by way of explanation: "But that's what love is, and that's what makes it so wonderful!"

Lucien came into his own at the new theater with *le Comédien*, specially written for him by Sacha and so full of personal details that it has a biographical interest. It is the story of a great actor who falls in love with a stage-struck girl many years his junior. Against his professional instincts he lets her play opposite him. The experiment proves that she has no talent. Despite her threat to leave him if he does not keep her in the cast, he prefers to lose her rather than compromise with his art. His dresser taps at the door and asks if he is alone. "Yes," he says, "but . . . I've a date . . . tomorrow evening, with twelve hundred people." Whoever serves the theater serves not a job but a passion, declares the author. With a great actor in the part of a great actor the effect of the drama was overwhelming. The girl was played by Renée Falconetti, a young actress whose beautiful performance contributed much to the popularity of the play.* *Le Comédien* did not lack for humorous touches. Sacha's own stage-manager and the director of the Théâtre Édouard VII were cast in their real-life roles, to the amusement of those who were in on the joke. The play was, though Lucien never remarked on it, a filial tribute. Sacha made this clear when he wrote an introduction to the published script and spoke of his feelings on playing opposite his father: "You seemed to be improvising *my* text and giving

---

* Her one venture into the cinema as the leading player in Carl Dreyer's moving silent film about Joan of Arc has tended to overshadow her career on the stage. She died an early death in 1946.

it its true meaning. While you were speaking I stood with my back to the audience and marveled! You were not just satisfied with being an admirable actor. You were not only the perfect interpreter of an already written text. You inspired me with remarks, sentences, thoughts and whole speeches that my play lacked. Ever since that day I have understood how a great actor can reveal to the playwright of his time possibilities they had never before dreamed of."

Only once in the last seven years of his life did Lucien appear in a new play written by anyone other than his son. For the rest, he revived several of his early pieces and put on a Molière season at the Édouard VII which remains a landmark in theatrical history. He had meditated the part of Alceste in *le Misanthrope* for over forty years. Having played it once at the age of seventeen, he had resolved never to attempt it again until he was satisfied that he could convey every shade of meaning within the role. Alceste is one of the great characters in the repertory and as much of a test for a French actor as Hamlet is for the English-speaking actor. The classic problem is whether Alceste should be played as an ill-tempered grumbler, a buffoon whose crabbiness is a source of easy laughs, or whether he should be presented as a figure of tragedy. Lucien chose the second approach. He played Alceste as a lover, not as a clown, presenting him as a man who suffers from his love and whose torments make him turn against society. His production of *le Misanthrope* in 1922, on the occasion of Molière's tricentenary, provoked a lively argument which continues today.

His *Tartuffe* was also controversial and raised the same violent objections from the critics, "those venerable gentlemen," as Octave Mirbeau once said, "who aren't at all keen on people disturbing their habits." Speaking with a harsh Auvergnat accent but otherwise faithfully conforming to Molière's directions, Lucien's Tartuffe, tragic and comic at the same time, inspired a searching reappraisal of an acting tradition nearly three centuries old. As his final tribute to the world's greatest comic author, Lucien rounded off the triptych with a performance of Arnolphe in *l'École des femmes* which again avoided obvious comic effects. It emphasized that delicate blend of tragedy imperceptibly merged with comedy which is so characteristic of Molière and of real life. In 1924 he performed all three plays one after another in a single short season at the Édouard VII. These productions, untrammeled by the ritual that had grown up during the centuries at the Comédie-Française, sprang direct from independent study of the text. They were done at the peak of Lucien's career, and represent, together with the acting style he bequeathed, his lasting revolutionary contribution to the theater in France. However his approach may have seemed to the defenders of orthodox tradition, it was informed with a passionate love for the dramatist. "After Molière's death," said Lucien in a brief speech before *le Misanthrope,* "the Church declared him an actor, refusing to his poor soulless corpse a grave dug in holy ground and a few drops of holy water. Molière was an actor, as he has been throughout the centuries and will remain so for ever. He is our patron saint as actors. Let us keep him, love him, and serve him." To which might be added Sacha's remark: "Molière died with his make-up on. Where is the actor who would not envy him?"

Not long after the Guitry family had settled in at the Édouard VII, they opened, as it were, a foreign branch of the business in London. The agent who managed it was C. B. Cochran, a man possessing all the talents of an impresario in addition to taste and the ability to inspire affection. Without Cochran the London theater during the first half of the century would have been a much duller place. Whether he was presenting Max Reinhardt's *The Miracle* or a rodeo at the vast Wembley Stadium, he did so with equal gusto and showmanship. He brought Hackenschmidt and Madrali the Terrible Turk to London and shared with packed houses his delight in good wrestling; he built up the fantastic Houdini and popularized the two Dolly Sisters;

he staged epic prize-fights with Georges Carpentier and Bombardier Billy Wells; he showed diplomatic gifts of the highest order by "managing" both Eleanora Duse and her rival Sarah Bernhardt. A long succession of revues mounted at the London Pavilion testified to his unrivalled mastery of the genre. At the same time he guided the theatrical destiny of a bewildering multitude of dwarfs, cowboy hypnotists, lion tamers, and roller-skating stars. This lovable man, whose only criterion was that an entertainment should be the best of its kind, met with spectacular bankruptcies and flirted with debts that a Balzac would have admired. He never complained when audiences were misguided enough to stay away from the sumptuous diversions he offered them.

Cochran was a Francophile and eager to add the Guitrys to a list of clients which already included Alice Delysia, Mistinguett, and Gaby Deslys. In 1920 he took the Aldwych Theatre for a "Grande Saison Parisienne," as his advertisements proudly announced. The season was inaugurated with a reception given by Lady Cunard in her home in Carlton House Terrace. There, after paying the customary tribute to his father's contemporary, Gerald du Maurier, Sacha electrified the four hundred guests by stating that his favorite actor was Little Tich, the music-hall performer, whom he described as the quintessence of art. Both Sacha and Lucien had an intense admiration for the comedian, and when they were not on-stage themselves they haunted the music halls where he was appearing. The English impresario Henry Sherek remembered an occasion when Lucien, carried away with enthusiasm, rose from his seat, massive in his black cloak and broad-brimmed hat, and roared at the audience: "Get up, all of you, in homage to the world's greatest genius!" At curtain-fall he rushed back-stage and, kneeling down, kissed the tiny performer on both cheeks. The reaction of Little Tich has not been passed on to us. He was a scholarly man who had taught himself to speak fluent French, so doubtless he was no stranger to the exuberance of the

Latin race. (He also, we are told, suffered from the twin disability of possessing five fingers and a thumb to each hand, and of always falling in love with tall women.) What is certain is that when he retired he gave to Sacha the big boots, long as he was high, with which he used to do his famous dance. These mementoes were ever after treated as sacred relics by the delighted recipient.

The Guitry season filled the Aldwych at every performance and had to be extended for another week. It competed as the triumph of the year with those other West End perennials of the time, *Chu Chin Chow* and *Tilly of Bloomsbury*. The critics compared Sacha to Charles Wyndham at his best. *The Daily Telegraph* invoked another great actor-producer, Hawtrey, and *The Sunday Times* wrote: "Polish of acting is a special prerogative of the French. It is second nature to them, and with these players the smoothness, the shine, the grace, the flexibility of their performances eclipse all the nature and many vulgarities of the story. . . . His [Sacha's] heartless philosophy sparkles like dry champagne on parched lips." *The Times,* as was only proper, had Anglo-Saxon reserves about the suitability of the entertainment for young persons, but having made a quick bow to the conventions the paper found it ". . . impossible not to laugh at the gay, easy, witty cynicism of the thing and to delight in the smooth voluble patter of Sacha Guitry, the knowing innocence of Yvonne Printemps. . . . The art of acting as the French can when they choose to practise it, is an art really fine."

The climax of the season was Lucien's appearance in *Pasteur*. An excited house demanded forty curtain-calls and showed even warmer enthusiasm than the French audience. "I have never known a greater night in a playhouse," said Forbes-Robertson with the grave diction expected of a senior theatrical knight. Yet another English actor-manager, Seymour Hicks, remarked simply to Gerald du Maurier as he left the theater: "I shall be ashamed to act again." Maurice Baring analyzed the reason for the incredible demonstration of applause: "In the last month we have been favoured with a manifestation of French art at its best in the shape of M. Lucien Guitry's acting, and with a delicious expression of French wit in the plays of M. Sacha Guitry . . . M. Lucien Guitry belongs to the great race of French actors. His name will be written in letters of gold with the names of Delaunay, Frédérick Lemaître, Coquelin, and Got. . . . Every detail, every gesture, every intonation, every look is perfect; but so quickly is each nuance indicated that it has happened before you know how it has happened, just as in real life. . . . There is never the millionth part of a shade of anything too much. He knows so surely when not to move his hands and when to keep the expression of his eyes under control. His art is an example of supreme reserve and rigid economy, and it reminds one of the sentence of one of the younger French writers that 'la langue française est un piano sans pédale.' M. Lucien Guitry plays the pianoforte without a pedal, and yet his crescendos are tremendous and his forte overwhelming."

The conquest of London had been complete, and the Guitrys departed leaving Cochran already making plans for their next visit. To be greeted every night by an adoring audience and to be paid forty thousand francs for each performance was enough to make any man fond of the city. Even the acute pangs of seasickness, from which both Sacha and Lucien suffered, were not too high a price to pay for their London visits. The annual appearances of what the English press now called "the incomparable family" became a fixed date in the London season, with full houses even on Derby Day in high season. One of their keenest admirers was Queen Mary, a frequent spectator in the Royal Box where the discreet play of handkerchief and fan veiled her amusement at the more outrageous lines.

The news of Lucien's gratifying experience in England did not surprise Sarah Bernhardt. To the young actors who constantly surrounded her she always gave one piece of advice: take Lucien as a model. She told them to watch his every movement and to study his every intonation. He was, she said, the last of the giants, just as she herself was the last of her race. For even she was beginning to feel the weight of her years. Sacha had been with her a few weeks after the amputation of her leg when she took delivery of the articulated limb she had ordered. She asked Edmond Rostand and other friends to write a few lines on it. The contraption included a thick belt which was designed to prevent the leg from twisting round and which had to be fastened to the waist. But Madame Sarah had never worn a corset in her life and she tried to avoid this clumsy arrangement by substituting a braid of cloth. When she took her first step the foot jiggled like a puppet's. Overcome by the sadness and the horror of the thing, she never attempted to wear it again, and from then on she went about in the palanquin that had conveyed her to Sacha's wedding. Though she had to be carried bodily on and off the stage, she still refused in her seventy-eighth year to give up the theater. She bravely revived her production of *Athalie*, the play in which, as a young actress more than half a century before, she had first won renown. Her face worn and lined by the pain of uremia, she came to the famous and cruelly appropriate lines:

> Dont elle eut soin de peindre et d'orner son visage
> Pour réparer des ans l'irréparable outrage.

It had become a tradition to deliver this couplet almost in a scream. Sarah took it differently and spoke with great deliberation, the golden voice almost hushed. The house burst into unprecedented applause and cheered for minutes until, as if by some hidden signal, each member of the audience got to his feet. Then the miracle happened. Sarah stood up, unassisted, and acknowledged them.

Sacha was to write two plays for Sarah. One of these was put on at a benefit performance and was called *Comment on écrit l'histoire*. The first act was set in the mid-nineteenth century and told how Mariette, an operetta singer played by Yvonne Printemps, became the mistress of Louis Napoléon. The final scenes take place in the twentieth century when Mariette, now played by Sarah, is a hundred years old and the admiration of all for her vivacity and modern outlook. A journalist comes to record her reminiscences for posterity. He marvels at her exact memory and is increasingly excited at the historical revelations she makes in the course of an account which, as the audience well knows, is a wholly inaccurate figment of her imagination. And that, concludes Sacha, is how history gets written.

The other play for Sarah was quite different. With *Un Sujet de roman* Sacha wrote one of his most powerful dramas. The idea was suggested by the famous literary salon presided over for many years after her husband's death by Madame Alphonse Daudet. She was the last witness of a vanished epoch, and over her house, which she preserved like a waxworks museum, there hovered the spirits of Flaubert, Zola, and the Goncourt brothers. The dark rooms were heavily brocaded and filled with the clinging scent of chypre and lavender diffused by invisible perfume burners. The terrifying old lady, swathed in muslin, darted malicious looks from beneath drooping eyelids as she offered her beringed hand to the guests who called every Sunday. Tenacious of her husband's glory, she had turned the place into a shrine of which she was the priestess. The acolytes were her two sons, the dandified Lucien Daudet and his brother Léon, the turbulent political pamphleteer. From time to time they were assisted by her daughter. Mademoiselle Daudet had rashly wedded the millionnaire André Germain, one of the more exotic figures of the *belle époque,* and had realized too late that his painted face and elaborate toilettes did not qualify him to be the ideal husband.

Of course, the Daudet salon only gave Sacha the point of departure for his play. He puts on the stage an elderly author, who, dissatisfied with his latest novel, throws it on the fire. His wife berates him and complains that he has published nothing important for five years. A lifetime of resentment boils up when he tells her that he married her for her beauty—and that she married him for his reputation. She has never understood his work. Her only interest has been to make a "celebrity" out of him and to bask in his reflected glory. It is better for them to part, as domestic scenes at their time of life are undignified. His future son-in-law arrives, himself an ambitious writer. If you want to write something worth-while, the older man advises him, don't marry yet—the daughter may turn out to be like the mother! He then has a stroke and his wife watches in silence as he struggles against it, only to relapse into immobility. After satisfying herself that he is now entirely helpless, she calls the doctor. "What playwright wouldn't be jealous of that first act?" asked Colette. "Its noble structure, its simple and life-like dialogue are worthy of the subject—of the two subjects that go to make up the play, conjugal hatred and the poison of literature." The wife is free at last to carry out all her ambitions. Under the glassy stare of her dumb and motionless husband she arranges to employ a ghost-writer to cobble up a "last" novel from his notes. "I am the guardian of his reputation at present," she declares gleefully, "and I will fulfil my mission!" She organizes a publicity campaign to launch a complete edition of his works and dreams of having a salon like Madame Daudet's. She even drafts a letter requesting the Légion d'honneur and forces her powerless husband to sign it. But in the last act he confounds his doctor and makes a complete recovery. His wife happens to discover letters written to him by humble admirers revealing how his novels had helped them. Their sincerity fills her with remorse when she realizes the duplicity of her schemes. Her husband accepts her plea for forgiveness, and in a speech of autumnal resignation he admits that he, too, has been a little in the wrong. He will forgive her because they have lived forty years together. Their story, he adds, is a good subject for a novel. If he had used it he would have given it this happy but dignified ending.

The idea and its vigorous treatment are far removed from the world of usual boulevard comedy. The dramatic possibilities in the wife's part were seized on by Sarah with tremendous enthusiasm. Lucien was cast as the novelist husband and rehearsals began immediately. Sarah delivered her key speech in a passionate voice sharp with lacerating venom. There followed a long silence in the empty theater. Lucien was unable to take up his cue. He was weeping at the spectacle of the actress who, not far short of her eightieth year, still had the power to move and amaze with her performance. On the night of the dress rehearsal she collapsed on stage, murmuring as she came round: "When shall I appear again?" Only the awareness that she was slowly dying forced her to ask Sacha to replace her. Her part was played by another actress who, many years before, had been one of Lucien's mistresses. The play's lancinating exchanges between him and his partner had a tang of irony which audiences relished as a bonus.

On the first night Sarah demanded to be told the exact time at which the different acts began. "This evening," she said, lying at home in bed, "I shall act the play here," and while Lucien acted out the drama on the stage of the Édouard VII, she recited all her speeches to him in the lonely room. She would not call off the struggle yet. If she could not appear on the stage, Sacha proposed, why not make a film? So he brought along the equipment to her apartment, and there, under the ruthless blaze of spotlights, a gaunt white-faced Sarah trembled through her part. She could not keep it up. In the end she resigned herself to sitting about in a dress of pink Venetian velvet Sacha had given her. While journalists waited in the street below for the inevitable news she gave instructions for her funeral. She who had died dramatically so many times was anxious that on this occasion every detail should be correct. "I want flowers, lots of white flowers," she ordered, "and above all, let the *décor* be bright and happy." Dressed in the costume of *l'Aiglon* she was laid in the rosewood coffin that had accompanied her everywhere. On a clear March day the funeral procession wound its way through sanded streets. After a brief halt outside her own theater, the Théâtre Sarah Bernhardt, the lofty catafalque smothered in flowers arrived at Père Lachaise. The *décor* was everything she had wished.

One result of Sarah's death was to add a notable figure to Sacha's entourage. Her secretary, Paul Dufrény, now joined the household in the same nominal capacity—nominal because he was helpless, incompetent, and wholly destitute of secretarial talent. A schoolboy habit of writing out his English exercises during the history lesson had flowered into the quirk of lighting the fire when he was asked to check on the laundry, or of telling an unwelcome visitor that Sacha was at home when he had been instructed to say that he was out. Nevertheless he was intelligent, chaotically so, with an amazing store of useless information such as the weight of the Eiffel Tower, the length of the rue de Rivoli, or the quantity of water contained in the yolk of an egg. For many years this attractive idiot was cherished for the element of fantasy he brought to his employer's affairs.

One evening, in spite of Dufrény's anarchical rule, the composer Ivan Caryll made his way into Sacha's dressing room. The Belgian-born musician had begun his career with adaptations of Chabrier and Audran before conquering the Edwardian musical-comedy stage with his own operettas, *The Duchess of Dantzig*, *The Earl and the Girl*, *Our Miss Gibbs*, and other pieces designed to exhibit the famous "Gaiety Girls" until such time as, ineluctably, they married into the peerage. He was shrewd enough to keep up with the times, as the inclusion of a fox-trot in one of his latest musical comedies proved, and he had come to ask Sacha for a libretto. The suggestion was taken and Sacha quickly wrote *l'Amour masqué*, the comedy of a beautiful *cocotte* who lives in luxury thanks to her two elderly lovers whom she plays off one against the other. Her adroitness is challenged early in the play when one of them arrives to announce that his wife is deceiving him and that at last he has an excellent excuse to divorce her and marry the *cocotte*. He makes off to surprise the couple at their assignation. She telephones to warn them, so avoiding for herself a dreadful fate. There is, of course, a third man in her life, neither poor nor honest, and during a masked ball she gives the slip to the other two and makes off with the hero who can give her both love and money. Before Ivan Caryll could actually set this libretto, he died on a visit to New York.

The need for a collaborator led Sacha to Messager, with whom he had worked so congenially on *Deburau*. The composer was eager to try his hand at the new genre of musical comedy. He produced a score much better than the usual efforts in this field, the best thing he wrote during his last years. The melodies, ranging from the feathery semi-quaver arabesques of the *cocotte* to the luscious curving sweep of the ensembles, are fresh and spontaneous. The part-writing is neatly laid out, the modulations are delicious in their unexpectedness, and Messager's gift for novel harmonies is at its best. Even in the most obvious conventions of musical comedy he shows his originality. The big waltz tune, for example, sets off in the accepted Viennese tradition and then as it develops becomes something much more poignant. The orchestration, as always with Messager, was perfectly judged. He made a virtue out of necessity, for the dimensions of the Édouard VII were too small to accommodate a large orchestra. Careful study of the ingenious work done by those neglected artists, the musicians who accompanied silent films, helped him, together with his own craftsmanship, to show that a composer can achieve all the effects he wants by the simplest means. In other words, sonority does not depend on the number of instruments available.

Of the many compliments Messager received on his work, the one that gave him most pleasure was a tribute from Gabriel Fauré, now ailing and deaf but still enthusiastic about his friend's triumph. "I know you've had a great big success with *l'Amour masqué,*" Fauré wrote to him, "and I'm deeply happy, as are all my friends. The inside of a theater is still denied to me, alas, so I can't go and applaud you, and neither can I enjoy a play that I'm told is very amusing and admirably acted. However, I've been lent your score. Your wit is the same as ever—it never grows old— and so are your charm and very personal brand of music that always remains exquisite, even amid the broadest clowning. What I miss particularly is the enjoyment of the orchestra, and I can just imagine what you got out of it. I'm happy, my dear André, *et je t'embrasse de tout mon cœur.*"

Yvonne Printemps's voice pleased Messager no less than the full houses *l'Amour masqué* drew at every performance. "On occasion it achieves extraordinary lustre and power," he remarked. He could not say the same of Sacha, who, anticipating Professor Higgins in *My Fair Lady,* chanted and drawled his words rhythmically to the musical accompaniment. During their work together he had been impressed by the richness of Sacha's speaking voice and had reasoned that he might also be able to sing. Asked to produce a note, Sacha obligingly squawked an: "A-a-a-ah!" which froze Messager to the piano stool. "You're not in luck," he said when he got his breath back. "That note just isn't on the keyboard."

It would not be true to assume that Sacha's music-making hastened Messager's end, for he was already subject to the kidney disease from which he died six years later at the age of seventy- five. The composer was to write two more operettas, both of them with libretti by Alfred Willemetz, a lyricist who, by a coincidence, also began working with Sacha at about this time. Willemetz had been Clemenceau's private secretary, and there is little doubt that his chief secretly sympathized when the young man left him for the stage. As manager of the Bouffes-Parisiens for many years, Willemetz was at the center of the French operetta world, and his varied activities have closely linked his name with its development. He wrote over two thousand songs, among them Maurice Chevalier's famous "Valentine" and Mistinguett's equally celebrated "Mon Homme." The numerous revues and musical comedies for which he provided the words have titles unforgettably redolent of that earnest naughtiness which was the hallmark of the 'twenties and 'thirties. They include *Pas sur la bouche, Ta bouche,* and *Trois jeunes filles nues.* (Yet even his industry is surpassed by another popular writer, Vincent Scotto, who helped give the period its flavor with the aid of Joséphine Baker and more than five thousand songs.) The first of the Willemetz-Guitry tandems was *la Revue de Printemps* written around Yvonne, who surprised the audience, and perhaps herself, by appearing in quick succession as the Prince of Wales, as Diane de Poitiers, as half of the Dolly Sisters, as Yvette Guilbert, and as that much-bejeweled *cocotte* La Païva. Sacha, with greater modesty, limited himself to the duc de Morny and Little Tich. Revue gave him the best opportunities he had yet known for his favorite hobby of dressing up.

These pleasantries were checkered by a recurrence of Sacha's rheumatism. He left the stifling heat of Paris to take a cure at Luchon, where the inhabitants of that attractive spa were intrigued by the retinue which accompanied him on tour. Here he received in the manner of a visiting Emperor at luncheons served by a tall butler dressed in a blue uniform with gold froggings. The conversation impressed one of the guests as a series of repartees delivered and exchanged with the brio of crack tennis players, while Sacha and Yvonne gave their celebrated performance as a happily married couple. The amusements of the holiday were overshadowed by news of Lucien. He was currently acting in a play and earning applause for his realistic portrayal of a man stricken with a heart attack. No one knew that he had been suffering lately from coronary trouble and that in the wings he had experienced the symptoms of a real attack. A stubborn man, he ignored the advice of his doctors and, although a diabetic, persisted in eating dozens of oranges stuffed with sugar. When he was thirsty he drank a whole bottle of Évian water. On the eve of his final illness a robust appetite, ever the admiration of friends, enabled him to swallow a hundred snails at one sitting. His physical maladies had been aggravated by the death a few years before of his son Jean. Sacha's brother had followed a successful acting career and had been specially acclaimed for his playing in Tristan Bernard's comedies. Lucien was deeply attached to both of his children. "The father and the sons can't look at each other without smiling," noted Jules Renard. "The smile saves them from embarrassment." After Jean's love of speed and fast motorbikes had involved him in a fatal road accident, Lucien never left off mourning clothes. He thought of him ceaselessly, visited his grave twice a week, and was unable to speak his name until the day of his own death.

The ever-present pain of this bereavement diminished Lucien's will to live when he was eventually confined to his sick bed, though he made light of his illness to Messager, Tristan Bernard, and other anxious visitors. Sacha tried to distract him with news of plans which included a piece about Frans Hals for Lucien and one on Mozart for Yvonne. Then his specialist examined him and sought to conceal what he had discovered. Lucien regarded him with courteous amusement. "You are a very great doctor, a master, and you immediately realized that my heart wasn't very brilliant . . . but to hide it from me, Monsieur, you would have needed to rehearse your lines for a good month!" A few days later he put on evening dress and entertained Sacha and Yvonne at dinner. He took out a red leather wallet and handed over some small items of jewelry: gold cuff links, pendants, a stock-pin given him by the Emperor of Russia, a photograph of Jean . . . They left for the evening performance and looked in at midnight on the way home. He asked about the box-office takings and was satisfied with the answer. "Write *Mozart*," he whispered, dropping off to sleep. Next evening, in the middle of a violent heart attack, he muttered his last words: "And Sacha?"

When Gabriele d'Annunzio sent his condolences and described Lucien as an artist whose understanding ". . . equaled and sometimes surpassed that of his authors with acting so profound that it became a revelation," he went a long way toward defining Lucien's unique gift. At the funeral Antoine was deputed by his colleagues to speak for them. He did so with a single sentence: "In the name of French actors, I salute the greatest of all actors." With his own death coming so soon after Sarah Bernhardt's, Lucien made it possible for historians of the stage to assert with precision that a golden period of the French theater ended on Monday, June 1, 1925.

Chapter 10

"*Consider, Sir, celebrated men, such as you have mentioned, have had their applause at a distance; but Garrick had it dashed in his face, sounded in his ears, and went home every night with the plaudits of a thousand in his cranium . . . If all this had happened to me, I should have had a couple of fellows with long poles walking before me, to knock down every body that stood in the way . . . Sir, a man who has a nation to admire him every night, may well expect to be elated.*"

BOSWELL,
Life of Johnson

*T*here were few complications attached to the dispersal of Lucien Guitry's estate. It chiefly involved the payment of a large quantity of debts and the clearing up of his two houses, one in the country and the other in Paris. The first of these was sold within a few months of his death—much to the disapproval of Colette who lived nearby and who did not realize the need for cash to satisfy an army of creditors. It would have been sacrilege for Sacha to have put the Paris house on the market, so he kept it himself. This extravagant dwelling was very much of his father's creation. Number 18, avenue Élisée-Reclus, stood in the shadow of the Eiffel Tower beside the chestnut trees around the Champ de Mars. The stretch of land it overlooked had been destined by Napoleon as the scene of splendid military tattoos, though now it is an elegant park where children of that wealthy neighborhood play games on soil once trodden by the Grande

Armée. The house was small and its high fences enclosed a tiny
ornamental garden.

The plot of land on which it was built had come up for sale
in 1908. Lucien bought it with the proceeds of a South American
tour as a first step in realizing his long cherished dream of a house
of his own. The following year, despite a voyage that meant three
weeks of painful seasickness, he played the circuit again, from
Rio de Janeiro to Santiago, and his fee was enough to cover
the building costs. The first tour earned him the land and the
second brought him the house, so that when he invited the
Brazilian Ambassador to lunch he was able to say with special
emphasis: "You'll feel at home here!" The architect whom he
commissioned to draw up the plans asked him what ideas he had.
With his actor's eye Lucien envisaged a staircase, a majestic staircase on which he could make an impressive "entrance" as in the
theater . . . and a few rooms. That was all he wanted and he
could not be bothered with details. The dream home began to
take shape as a staircase with rooms grouped around it. One day
he declared to his long-suffering architect: "I want my private
apartment to be on the ground floor and to consist of three rooms
without windows. Since I come back from the theater at midnight
they'd be closed anyway, and when I wake up at dawn they still
wouldn't be open—they'd be utterly useless. Don't make any."
His wish was carried out. Too proud to go back on his word,
he spent most of his time upstairs. The three little rooms on the
ground floor consisted of his bedroom, the dining room, which took
six people with ease but became constricted with eight, and a
tiny study. It was linked to the upstairs by a narrow and awkward
contrivance like the fire escape in a theater.

In the entrance hall everything was magnificence. The staircase
led up to a pair of glass doors opening on a long, high-ceilinged
gallery of marble which was Lucien's version of the Hall of
Mirrors at Versailles. It was lined with Louis XIV chairs and a
gilt wooden table. A portrait of the Grand Monarch stared eter-

nally into the glass over a high chimney piece opposite. This setting of pink marble, a flawless reproduction of the *grand siècle*, was the background to his rehearsals of *le Misanthrope*, which on the stage he played against an elaborate Gobelins tapestry borrowed from his room. He adored his home more than any mistress and was continually buying furniture or pictures or carpets to enhance its beauty. Servants were anathema to him, perhaps because he was jealous of sharing his house with others. He was content with the ministrations of a single attendant, the elderly Élise who guarded him like a watchdog. Her devotion was such that when she entered Sacha's employ she could never bring herself to tell the laundry to change the initials L.G. on the linen.

The son chose a more sociable way of life than the father and when he moved in he somehow found room for a large domestic staff—a liveried butler, a cook, a team of maids, and a chauffeur. If Sacha's ingenuity had been extended in finding a place for them all, it was tested still further by the problem of making space for his own art collections. For over twenty years he had been a collector. It all began in 1900 with an autograph letter of Delacroix given him by his grandfather; a dedicated book presented by Jules Renard; a Forain water-color offered by Lucien. These were the three things of which, apart from women, who were easier to find than a Molière first edition, he was an avid collector all his life. "If I could count up all the hours, days, months, years that I've spent in choosing the items in my collection, in waiting for them, hunting for them, pursuing and finding them, I'd realize I'd given them more time than I needed to write my hundred and twenty-odd plays," he once reflected. "I'm prepared to agree that you have to be a bit crazy to be a collector. Greed soon enters into it—insatiableness appears in its turn—and eventually you get a mania for symmetry. Autographs pile up, and not to have a single letter of Descartes becomes a tragedy, while twelve hundred of Déjazet [the nineteenth-century actress] become an embarrassment. The agonizing choice between two different frames for a picture of the same size is enough to prevent you from sleeping. And to own a nude torso of a Roman ephebe without also owning a female nude of the same epoch makes you wonder if you're worthy of it! . . . When the items you have acquired— each time through love, never through self-interest or vanity— are grouped with discernment and form a harmonious, varied whole, and when the neighbors you have chosen do not clash— for example, the green of your Gauguin shouldn't contradict the blue of its Rouault companion—and they all of them, canvas, marble, drawing, bronze, go happily together and seem in a word to be the reflection of yourself, then you have the right to describe yourself as a collector."

Sacha's method of collecting was simple. Instead of putting aside his money to pay the vast tax demands that time inevitably brought —Louis XIV never asked Molière to pay income tax, he would argue to bemused officials—he spent it all in the Salle Drouot and other auction rooms, where the heady thrill of bidding added excitement to the game. He wanted the Picasso dove ". . . at all costs. And that was what I paid for it!" he told a friend. A dealer wrote to him that he could offer Becque's manuscript of *les Corbeaux* for a few thousand francs. Sacha replied in a seventy-seven word telegram that he would only go up to several hundred. The manuscript went to another collector for thirteen thousand. On his death Sacha bought it for twenty-five thousand, and the dealer sardonically offered him the telegram to bind in with it. . . . There was no such thing as a top price for Sacha. An epic battle in the saleroom left him with a first edition of *l'École des femmes* at many thousands more than its valued price. On arriving home he found that at page fifty-two the word *amour* had been crossed out and replaced with the word *esprit* in Molière's own hand. (Molière autographs are almost as rare as Shakespeare's.) The volume took its place alongside the autographed copy of Racine's *Athalie,* Bossuet's annotated *Oraison funèbre,* a book with a malicious commentary by Voltaire, and others of the same nature, for it was Sacha's rule as a collector of rare editions to buy only those which had been inscribed or written in by their authors.

There were also thousands of autograph letters and manuscripts to be accommodated somewhere. They had come to Sacha in many different ways, and it is impossible to view without envy the advantage he enjoyed in having so many authors as his friends. The complete manuscript of *Poil de carotte* was given to him by Jules Renard, just as *les Affaires sont les affaires* was a gift from Octave Mirbeau. Corrected proofs and manuscripts of Anatole France's novels had been offered by the author to Lucien who in turn bequeathed them to Sacha. The provenance of other treasures was often as interesting as the items themselves. Such was a drawing by Captain Marryat, the creator of schoolboy adventures before the mast, who was aboard the *Bellerophon* and sketched Napoleon from the bridge as the exiled Emperor sailed off to St. Helena. Somehow it had come into the possession of Henry Irving, who gave it to Sarah Bernhardt who passed it on to Sacha. The manuscript of Flaubert's only play, *le Candidat,* mysteriously came to light in the theater where *Deburau* was being played and a stage-manager rescued it from a bundle of old papers intended for the dustbin. As a manuscript it ranked with the same author's *l'Éducation sentimentale,* two thousand six hundred pages of corrections, crossings-out, and revisions in small handwriting containing phrases which, so spontaneous and "right" in print, are seen to be the result of innumerable second thoughts. There are few more exciting experiences than to hold in one's own hands the manuscript of a classic work, and it was this unusual privilege that Sacha could allow himself every day with writings by Stendhal, Zola, Musset, André Gide, Barrès, and Renan. The saleroom battles to obtain them added to the value of these trophies. If a friend had been thoughtless enough not to give him a manuscript Sacha did not hesitate to brave the auctioneer's eye when the opportunity arose. One day he realized that he possessed nothing by Georges Courteline. The manuscript of *Messieurs les ronds de cuir,* that contemptuous satire on bureaucracy, came up at the Salle Drouot and Sacha carried it off. He telephoned Courteline with the news. "How much did it make?" asked the peppery author. "Thirty-five thousand francs." "Thirty-five thousand?" "Yes," replied Sacha. "What silly ——— paid thirty-five thousand for it?" snorted Courteline. "I did," Sacha beamed.

The manuscripts, including many of Sacha's own plays, were housed in fine bindings, some of them from Napoleon's own library with the Imperial arms embossed in gold on the covers. The letters were kept in files according to their subject, which was principally love. It wasn't difficult to classify the letters from Napoleon to Josephine, or the correspondence between George Sand and Musset or Chopin. They figured in the same section as those by Wagner and Mathilde Wesendonck, Henri IV and Marie de Médicis, Potemkin and Catherine II, Victor Hugo and Juliette Drouet, Voltaire and his niece Madame Denis, Rousseau and Madame d'Houdetot, Beaumarchais and Madame de Goddeville, Dumas *fils* and Marie Duplessis, Liszt and Madame d'Agoult. There is no doubt that, had they existed, Sacha would have possessed the letters of Héloïse and Abélard. As it was, he made do with the regrettable absent-mindedness of Verlaine, who would begin a passionate letter with the words "My dear Hortense," and end "Farewell, my dear Adèle . . ."; or in the offer of marriage, a result of curiosity perhaps, made by an old soldier to the famous transvestite Chevalier d'Éon. So they accumulated, the files, the drawers, the frames, stuffed to overflowing with documents and letters in the writing of Goethe, Mozart, Beethoven, Berlioz, Debussy, Proust, Schopenhauer, Saint-Simon, Talleyrand, Cagliostro, Richelieu, Baudelaire, and the kings and queens of France. It is tiring even to list them, these always moving, often pathetic, and frequently comic glimpses into the most secret lives of so many great men and women. "The question for me," Sacha would say, "isn't to know whether or not I own one of the finest autograph collections anywhere. In my eyes it shines with incomparable charm, and the least one can say is that it is unique by the fact alone that *every* autograph is unique."

There comes a time when the passion to acquire these intimate revelations of the past extends to the objects worn or used by the people who wrote them. Inscribed photographs or pictures are the most obvious items, but they cannot rival milk bowls moulded from the breasts of Marie Antoinette, Flaubert's ring and dressing-gown, Hugo's inkwell, and Napoleon's hat, all of which Sacha possessed. They were arranged in illuminated glass cabinets where an astonishing heterogeneous collection of articles were identified on enquiry as Robespierre's waistcoat, Clemenceau's gloves and scarf, Joffre's Order of the Day at the Battle of the Marne, some withered flowers picked by Napoleon and the telescope he owned. These keepsakes were displayed in the gallery which Lucien had once vowed to the colder formality of a Louis XIV décor. They took up most of the floor space, and the visitor trod carefully to avoid upsetting Tanagra statuettes, Greek sculptures, Ming china and ceramics which were scattered about on stands and plinths beneath the ironical stare of Richelieu's death mask.

The only other space left was on the walls, and these were covered so thickly with pictures that only a few square inches of the surface remained. Many of these were gifts by artist friends—portraits of Lucien and Sacha by Oswald Birley and Vuillard, one of Monet's *Nymphéas* studies, and a Toulouse-Lautrec poster commissioned by Lucien. Sacha had several Lautrecs which recalled his meeting with the artist one evening in Lucien's dressing room. The bowler-hatted dwarf squatted in the depths of an armchair, his legs dangling over the edge, drunk and helpless. "Now, Henry, we must go," said his companion. "Yes," muttered Lautrec, "we'll go to the brothel." "No, we'll go to bed." "Yes," agreed the painter, "we'll go to bed in the brothel. . . ." By contrast with Lautrec's miserable existence there were souvenirs of Rodin, whose tender letters to Madame Rodin were prized items among Sacha's autographs. These souvenirs included Rodin's head of Balzac, his bust of Hugo, and his powerful statue of "Iris, Messenger of the Gods," so huge that it was kept out in the garden. Every school of art was represented on the crowded walls, from Rembrandt and Tiepolo to Cézanne and Modigliani, whose haunting *Portrait d'un jeune homme* struck a melancholy note among the bright profusion of flowers and nudes by Gauguin, van Gogh, and Renoir. The macabre visions of his Goyas, the stark lines of his Utrillos, were set off by the placid sheen of his Corots and his van Dycks. The charm of collecting is that it never ends, and Sacha followed an interminable path that led him to heap Degas upon Manet, Braque upon Courbet, Seurat upon Delacroix, Guardi upon Watteau, until there was no longer an available centimeter of wall space to be found and pyramids of canvases grew in the cellar where the overflow inevitably came to rest.

Paintings had the unique quality of autographs for Sacha. "If I re-read *le Misanthrope*," he wrote, "I say to myself that five other people are reading it at the moment, perhaps ten, perhaps a thousand. But if I stand alone for twenty-five minutes in front of Manet's *le Joueur de fifre*, I can tell myself that during those twenty-five minutes I am the only person in the world to have seen Manet's picture." All of Sacha's art collection gave him pleasure, not least a perfect little Matisse drawing of a woman in a hood, which he summed up in unconscious paraphrase of Whistler's riposte when the judge, in the celebrated libel case against Ruskin, expressed surprise at the speed with which he drew: "There are twenty-five pencil strokes, not one more, not one less. I've counted them. Reckon four seconds to each line. Twenty-five multiplied by four gives a hundred seconds, or one minute and forty seconds, which is probably the time Matisse took to do this drawing. However, to be fair, one should add to those hundred seconds the twenty-five years of work Matisse needed to be able one day to draw such a lovely picture in one minute and forty seconds." The curve of a line inspired Sacha to write: "A sketch is neither the beginning of a masterpiece nor its conclusion—it is essential. Look at those trees created by a stroke, those looks imagined by a dot, those hands shaped by a shadow! Have you admired the way in which Rodin, his eye fixed on the theme, cuts out the body of an odalisque? Have you seen how La Tour can sketch a smile? how Daumier can set Rosinante at a trot? how Degas arranges things so that his dancer has brushed the ground a second in advance? how Watteau makes a marquis sit down, very comfortably, even though he has neglected to give him a chair? Strokes of the pencil, strokes of genius. Wonderful moments which have already perpetuated themselves for ever!"

Sacha divided collectors into two—the "cupboard" type and the "display" type. To the former category belonged Calouste Gulbenkian, the secretive oil billionaire, who kept his fabulous art treasures locked up in a vast house in the avenue d'Iéna, where the only people who ever saw them apart from the owner were two footmen and a nightwatchman. It was not in Sacha's nature to be so jealous of his possessions, and there were few things he enjoyed more than showing a sympathetic friend around his well displayed and cleverly lit collection. At this point there comes a further subdivision in the collecting species, for Sacha was one of those who liked to dress the part. There is a long tradition in this which goes back some hundred years to the collector of North Americana who, when showing off his private museum, always put on the trappings and weapons of an Indian savage. In our own time there is talk of the Chilean who equips himself with lorgnette, cane, and ruffles before touring his eighteenth-century collection. Sacha's choice of clothes was eighteenth-century too. He wore a canary-colored dressing-gown, a soft scarf of rare material round his neck, and a turban modeled from a La Tour pastel such as the artist may have worn when he painted Madame de Pompadour. As he paused over an Houdon statuette or traced with his finger the gentle contours of a Sèvres pastille burner, his beautiful hand with its emerald ring equaled in whiteness the smooth texture of the porcelain. Here among his collection he passed some of his busiest hours, devoting poignant thought to the exact placing of a Khmer head or meditating the agonizing decision to consign a Largillière to the cellar and make way for a newly bought van Dongen.

Sacha did not go out much into society. His life crystallized around his home and the stage, and his daily travels were mostly confined to a straight line between the avenue Élisée-Reclus and the theater where he was currently appearing. He made no distinction between domestic and theatrical life, for wherever he happened to be was temporarily metamorphosed into a theater. A room became a stage-set, the people around him became an audience. "He acted all the time, even at breakfast. It was awful," exclaimed one of his exhausted former wives. When you had entered the shadowy cupola'd hall you were confronted with the white steps of the famous staircase which rose in the penumbra to the small landing above. The peaceful silence was broken only by the gentle click of a distant typewriter. As you mounted the stairs there was a feeling in the air rather like the atmosphere in a theater before the rise of the curtain. When you reached the last step on to the landing, the glass doors swung open as on a perfectly timed cue, and there was Sacha, wrapped in one of his flamboyant dressing-gowns, both hands outstretched to welcome you with the gravity of a Renaissance prince, the velvet charm of a Talleyrand. It was good theater. At other times he might be wearing some gorgeous costume chosen at the whim of the moment. Unlike most actors Sacha never hired costumes for his productions. He had them all made to measure at his own expense and kept them afterwards, with his elaborate wigs, in a special wardrobe at home. Thus his staff became used to the unusual spectacle of Richelieu dictating to a secretary at her typewriter, and the sight of Louis XIV at the telephone was as commonplace as Napoléon III re-hanging a picture and La Fontaine admiring a Goya print. One of the novelties of working for Sacha was that people never knew whether he was likely to make his appearance as an eighteenth-century marquis or as an Edwardian dandy. The transposition of life into theater was completed by the habit of using his own furniture and pictures on the stage, so that his friends were often uncertain as to whether they were in the auditorium of the Théâtre Édouard VII or in the drawing room of 18, avenue Élisée-Reclus. To the perturbation of his insurance company he would hang his Renoirs and his Rembrandts on the backcloth of his stage-sets and give a lecture from behind his valuable Louis XIV bureau; his financial backers accepted with silent protest his insistence on real flowers, preferably orchids fresh each night, and real food when the characters in a play gave a dinner party, which usually included chicken or pheasant on the menu.

For Sacha the day began late. He was not an early riser and had, moreover, the excuse of only returning from the theater at midnight. After lunch he would go into his study and write, chain smoking the Virginia cigarettes to which, he claimed, he had devoted the two fingers of his left hand. "I've so got into the habit of feeling your gentle warmth between them," he once apostrophized his *"petite amie"* the cigarette, "that these two fingers seem useless and genuinely *gauche* when you're not there. . . . And then, you must admit you're jealous. I'm convinced you are, because when I take a woman into my arms you do everything possible to burn her, and make her start abruptly away from me. You don't even wait until she's in my arms, because your jealousy shows itself the moment I try to talk to her close up. You instantly take her by the throat and make her cough—and, little hypocrite, you let the draught take the blame!" In a cloud of light blue smoke and to the accompaniment of Ravel's *Boléro* turned up to the highest volume on the radiogram, he speedily filled large yellow sheets with his big shapely handwriting. Often it was quicker to dictate, so impatient was he to cream off some of the ideas that crowded his mind, and the secretary who had been woken up at three in the morning to take down the inspiration for a new play would sometimes discover herself, by the afternoon, scribbling frantically to keep up with a new piece on a different subject. On other occasions Sacha found, like Mozart, that billiards improved his concentration, and it was not unusual for him to dictate a complete play in the course of a few hours' sinking reds and potting drop-shots. "I'm so tired!" gasped one of his retinue at the end of a day like this. "What of?" enquired Sacha with genuine astonishment.

At his wide desk, so capacious that it nearly filled the small study, Sacha worked happily amid a carefully ordered disarray of Daumier prints, books, dictionaries, stacks of manuscript, bottles of Vichy water, packets of Laurens cigarettes, tubes of Stricknal Longuet, and boxes of acid drops. On the furthermost edge lay a heap of proofs which had awaited correction for several years. Sacha gladly paid the rent for standing type demanded by the printer; he would do anything to avoid the drudgery of reading through stuff he had written long ago and in which he had lost interest. Why care about yesterday when plans for tomorrow were so much more exciting? One by one the yellow sheets were covered with speeches, cues, blocks of dialogue, cast lists, ideas for articles, and the last scene of a play for which the preceding acts had yet to be written. "Do people think that writing a sentence is easy?" Courteline used to complain. "When it only has a subject, a verb and a complement, it's hell! I've led the life of a stationmaster. You've seen them, haven't you? They take a carriage here, a truck there, blow their whistle, and off it goes. Whereas I take a word here, an adjective there, an adverb from somewhere else; I link them together, I blow my whistle . . . and the whole lot goes off the rails!" The layman often fails to realize that easy reading means hard writing. For all their spontaneity, the speeches that Sacha's characters delivered, the books

1. Sacha Guitry

2. The young Sacha

3. Lucien Guitry (1924)

4. Sacha with Tristan Bernard (left) and Jules Renard (right) on an outing in the Renault

5. Alphonse Allais, the melancholy humorist

6. Aged 28,
with his first wife,
Charlotte Lysès

7. A famous trio: Lucien, Yvonne Printemps, and Sacha

8. Introducing Sarah Bernhardt in his film *Ceux de chez nous* (1915)

9 and 10. Two of Sacha's friends: Paul Léautaud, the critic

Raimu, the actor

11 and 12. Home at
18, avenue Elisée-Reclus,
showing the stairway leading
to the upstairs corridor

13. Sacha takes the lead in *le Roman d'un tricheur* (1936)

14. With his third wife, Jacqueline Delubac, in a scene
from *Bonne Chance* (1935)

15. With Lana Marconi in a scene from *N'écoutez pas, Mesdames!* (1942)

16. Sacha's sketch of his father (1910)

17. A page from the manuscript of *Quadrille* (1937)

18. As Talleyrand in *le Diable boiteux* (1948)

19. Louis XIV (Sacha) and Mme de Montespan (Claudette Colbert) in *Si Versailles m'était conté* (1953)

20. Sacha on the film set: one of the last photographs

and poems that he wrote, went through many a trial and many an error. His manuscripts, with their convoluted crossings-out, often look as if they were sketches of smoke emerging from the railway engine of Courteline's metaphor. Yet his inspiration was so urgent that he worked at a speed few ordinary people could have kept up.

As the afternoon went by in a flurry of writing or dictation, friends would drop in to hear Sacha read the play he had just finished. "Do you really think," they enquired, "that your penniless hero could afford those Modiglianis of yours that you plan to include in the set?" "Of course not." "So?" "So let's hope the audience will be intelligent enough to think they're copies!" replied Sacha, who always fought for the last word. By now it was the time of *l'heure bleue,* that moment when the air of Paris takes on a misty quality and shrouds the buildings and the plane-trees in a delicate blue haze. The Cadillac was ordered and the Guitrys swept out on a lightning raid of the Faubourg Saint-Honoré to track down a diamond necklace for Yvonne, a Boulle cabinet Sacha had glimpsed in an antique-dealer's window and which he thought would look well in the second act that evening, a new scarf from Hermès. . . . They were back by six o'clock and the household began to assume an expectant theatrical rhythm. Into the car went the innumerable items Sacha never traveled without on his way to the evening's work, the bottles of champagne in their ice bucket, the costumes, the scarves, the sweaters for him to put on when he made his exit from the heat of the footlights, make-up boxes, some new drapes to titivate the scenery, and a piece of furniture borrowed at the last minute from the drawing room. Most precious of all were the metal cases with their loose writing paper and a battery of well-sharpened pencils to note down the reflections that occurred to him. As they drove down the avenue Élisée-Reclus he would chuckle and write something like: "Our greatest mistake is not in believing women love us—but much rather in believing that we love them." While they stopped at the traffic lights before the place de la Concorde, he would muse: "To be married, to have a mistress, and to deceive her with somebody else makes it look as if one is becoming faithful to one's wife again—more or less." And, with a sidelong glance at his own wife beside him in the car: "If one day we should want to be bachelors again, we should take care only to marry the most beautiful women."

Sacha detested traffic jams and sudden brakings, all of which reminded him that he was in a car and not in a theater. Yet his nervousness increased as the prospect of his first entrance drew nearer, and, putting away his writing cases, he rehearsed fervently with his partner. In his dressing room he continued to rehearse, shaving, making-up, and adjusting the fall of his cravat while the atmosphere grew tenser. But once he had appeared on the stage and conquered his audience all over again, as he did each night, everything went well. After the curtain had fallen for the last time the car was loaded anew with its varied cargo, including the empty champagne bottles, and the royal progress started off through darkened streets. Neighbors who stayed up late were rewarded with the spectacle of Monsieur and Madame Guitry arriving home in their limousine. (The interior was illuminated so that the crowds in the streets they passed through were able to see every detail of the occupants, as at the theater.) They stepped out and proceeded to the front door between rows of domestics who lined the garden path under orders from the major-domo. Sacha was ready for his evening meal. He had inherited his father's appetite and had a partiality for ten-egg omelettes. After dinner, at one in the morning, he would vanish into his study. With the applause of the evening's audience in his ears and the glow of the theater still warm upon him, he would start to write yet another play.

The pace was unsparing and continuous. One bleak October day Yvonne succumbed to a bout of influenza. "Sacha's household," wrote Colette, "and the health of the two partners, seems to me to be in shreds." The revival of *Nono* in which they were playing had to be closed down and the leading lady sent to convalesce. For Sacha this was just an excuse to write a new piece, and by the following December he had complied with his father's dying wish and written *Mozart*. Sacha was not a musician, as Messager's tingling eardrums bore witness. He was, though, a man of taste perceptive enough to recognize the quality of the sublimest music the world has ever known. "When you have heard a piece by Mozart," he wrote, "the silence that succeeds it is also by him . . . Saint Bernadette was spoken to by a heavenly voice—Mozart had the power to make us hear it." The composer made three visits to Paris during his short life, the first at the age of seven when his father paraded the little virtuoso through the salons before taking him to England, where they lived in Chelsea for a year or so. There was a second trip to the French capital three years later, and he came back for the last time at the age of twenty-two. On this occasion he wrote the "Paris" symphony (K.297) whose glossy showmanship, rather contemptuously tossed in to flatter the ears of the groundlings, cannot hide the stature of the work. (One pities the generations to come who will have missed Sir Thomas Beecham's lovely playing of this symphony.) Mozart's visits to Paris were not among the happiest episodes of his life. In that city he wrote the ballet *les Petits Riens* for the dancer Noverre, who passed it off as his own work. The duc de Guines, who commissioned the Concerto for flute and harp (K.299), neglected in the manner of a true aristocrat to pay him. "You have no idea what a dreadful time I am having here," sighed Mozart, adrift among the conspiracies and intrigues which only a Gluck, with his masterly organizing talent, knew how to turn to advantage.

Sacha was too much of a patriot to dwell on the misfortunes of his hero in Paris and he chose instead to present Mozart as the *enfant terrible* of the drawing rooms, the mischievous darling of noble ladies and their sly maids. He further juggles with dates so

that one of the characters may flourish Beaumarchais's newly written manuscript of le Mariage de Figaro under Mozart's nose.
This is the Baron de Grimm, correspondent of the Empress
Catherine and a literary man-of-all-work, who, with Madame
d'Épinay, sponsors Mozart in Paris. Grimm and Madame d'Épinay
are lovers in approved eighteenth-century fashion. When she reproaches him for his flirtation with La Guimard, the idolized
beauty of the dance who was nominally under the protection of
the Prince de Soubise, and he replies with a teasing reference to
her affair with Rousseau, she ripostes: "Don't pretend to be jealous
as far as he's concerned. You're prouder of my past than you are
of me. You've got such a passion for history that if you heard I'd
seen Jean-Jacques again, you'd forgive me, I'm sure, on condition
you were the first to know of it!" Madame d'Épinay never said
any such thing according to the archives. On the other hand, as
Sacha pointed out, when attacked for his liberties, no one can
disprove it. The lovers' quarrel is interrupted by the appearance
of Mozart at the head of the staircase. This beautifully managed
moment has been recorded by the critic James Agate. He had
seen and appreciated Henry Irving, Bernhardt, and Duse at their
best, and he knew what good acting was all about. "Every theatre-
goer has experienced moments of emotion, for the justification of
which he must search his intelligence in vain . . ." he wrote.
". . . I have not forgotten, though it is twenty years ago, that
people were seen to cry, and by 'cry' I mean shed tears, when
Music's heavenly child appeared at the top of the gilt staircase
and descended it to kneel at the feet of Madame d'Épinay."

Grimm and Madame d'Épinay take the boy in hand. He is
anxious for a girl friend, and Grimm, divining the educative value
at this stage of what Balzac was later to define as la femme de
trente ans, proposes the remedy: "What he needs is a woman of
thirty, ripe, experienced, and triumphant!" And Madame d'Épinay
sees that he gets her—in the person of La Guimard! The musician

who could write his three last great symphonies in a few weeks
proves to be a quick learner. When he takes his farewell at the end
of the play he sings adieu to his mistress. But which one was it?
No one is quite certain after all, and on that delicate note the
curtain falls. The tracery of the plot, slim though it may be, brings
to life again the atmosphere of an age when Mozart, Rousseau,
Voltaire, Gluck, and Diderot were contemporaries. As James Agate
observed: "At the beginning the piece moves slowly, and we are
grateful, since the eye is thereby given leisure to renew acquaintance with a delicious epoch. Those engravings, each with its
coquetry of blue ribbon, can only be after the little painters of the
grand siècle, the spinet must have tinkled its accompaniment to
Orfeo's 'Che farò,' the very furniture prates of great ladies lancing
discreet œillades and petites marquises making fluttering confes-
sions behind their fans."

When Sacha had completed his play he asked Messager to
write a score for him. The idea of placing his own music beside
Mozart's was too much for the unassuming Messager. Sacha then
sent a telegram to Reynaldo Hahn: "Will you collaborate on a
flop with me?" "Gladly," came the reply. Within a few weeks the
music was ready. Reynaldo Hahn is much despised by the musi-
cally naïve. They have a quaint notion that the worker in physically small mediums is inferior to the maker of frescoes. By this
reasoning Meyerbeer is a greater composer than Chopin. The
slaves of fashion are entitled to swoon at the endless verbosity of a
Mahler, but this should not allow them to scorn the craftsmanship of musicians like Reynaldo. He was a Venezuelan who settled
early in Paris and became Massenet's favorite pupil. Music for the
theater was his specialty, and he left a number of ballets and
operettas notable for their expertise and invention. He was an
excellent conductor of Mozart opera, for which he had the most
sensitive touch, and toward the end of his life he was director of
the Paris Opéra. His several books are valuable guides to all

students of singing, of conducting, and of musical performance in general. He had been Sarah Bernhardt's music adviser and wrote a touching memoir about her, in addition to a published journal which gives interesting accounts of the artistic and social circles he knew well, both in France and in England. His taste in painting and sculpture was wide. In literature he is best known for his friendship with Marcel Proust. Their long acquaintance is a pointer to Reynaldo's personal attraction and his culture.

The overture to *Mozart* is one of those bustling allegros which, heard in the concert hall, re-creates the atmosphere of dimmed lights and expectancy just before curtain rise. In mid-course the orchestra throws in a slower melody, a chain of languishing Massenetic phrases which accompany Mozart's entry in the first act; and then, as if suddenly reminded of its job of heightening anticipation, it breathlessly returns to the allegro animato. Mozart's own music is introduced with aptness. While Grimm talks of his first meeting with the composer we hear a quotation from the G minor Sonata (K.9) written in Paris. His spoken references to *Figaro* and *Don Giovanni* are heard to background snatches from the appropriate operas. The prelude to the second act contains the opening bars of the "Paris" symphony's last movement. No excuse is needed for incorporating a generous allowance of *les Petits riens* into dances performed by La Guimard and the famous ballet-master Vestris, accompanied by Mozart at the harpsichord. The numerous *mélodrames*, or passages to accompany spoken words, are mostly by Hahn, and they are handled so well that the listener overlooks the cunningly wrought seams that join his own work to Mozart's. Effect is the sole aim of theater music, and if this is achieved all other criticism is pointless. Music is here only one of the elements employed to suspend disbelief. As Messager pointed out in his review of the play, Reynaldo had avoided pastiche and had succeeded in a perfect marriage between his personal style and that of his model. There is a clear difference between the tactful *Mozart* and that painful farrago which the nineteen-twenties knew as *Lilac Time,* where Schubert was the unfortunate victim.

Mozart was yet another personal triumph for Yvonne Printemps. She played the leading role *en travesti* and lent to her little songs an artless artistry which gave her portrayal of the shy adolescent a delectable appeal. Sacha himself, the benevolent puppetmaster, took the part of Grimm and emphasized the character's avuncular side to bring out Mozart's *gaminerie.* "The success of *Mozart* has been outstanding," wrote Antoine, "and this brilliant spectacle will have a long run. Of all contemporary writers, Sacha Guitry is certainly the only one who can overcome much a challenge. People have often mentioned Molière in speaking of him, and here indeed is something that reminds one of those royal *divertissements* at Versailles. This Mozart has their grace, lightness, and style."

Antoine was right and *Mozart* ran for many months. One of its admirers was Oskar Straus, the Viennese composer, who came with his wife one evening to the Théâtre Édouard VII. At the end of the first act his wife suggested he ask Sacha to write a libretto for him. While Yvonne Printemps in her fetching boy's clothes evoked memories of *Rosenkavalier,* and Madame d'Épinay wove her second-act intrigues, Frau Straus's proposition began to flower in her husband's mind. The interval found the pair of them wandering in the foyer, Straus's perpetual cigar burning his fingers, his lips pursed in a whistle beneath the massive hooked nose. By the end of the play they were in Sacha's dressing room to congratulate him. Their compliments were accepted with flattering courtesy by Sacha, who, not to be outdone, declared himself an admirer of everything *"le Maître"* had composed. At dinner the next evening Sacha delighted them by saying that he and Straus must write an operetta together. "Say yes," he declared, "and you can have the book tonight!" The plot he suggested was that of

Mariette, "or how history gets written," the piece he had done some years previously for Sarah Bernhardt. This story of the heroine whose myth-making capacity in old age inspires her to add a startling footnote to the private life of Napoléon III, was an ideal subject for operetta. Straus provided a score which, though not in the class of his earlier successes, adds a flavor that only he could have contributed. The inevitable waltz that Mariette sings encompasses the generously spaced sixths required by tradition, and the surging melodies crowd in upon each other in an endearing multitude.

Yvonne Printemps sang Mariette, first as the young girl who captivates Louis Napoléon and then as the mendacious centenarian. Her husband doubled the roles of her royal lover and of the journalist who interviews her during the last act. He gave James Agate yet another of those moments which the critic enjoyed recollecting in tranquility: ". . . though its texture is of the lightest you feel that it is strong enough to bear the weight of pathos and of irony. M. Guitry's writing, though it may be nothing to read, has on the stage all that non-seeming strength which is the proper quality of gossamer . . . I can still see that half-bovine, half-imperial Napoléon III sitting in his box putting his heavily kid-gloved hands portentously together. I can still hear that half-whisper: '*Il faut tâcher de ne pas être ridicule.*' " *Mariette* ran for two years. Even when it was staged abroad without Sacha or Yvonne it was equally well received, although few of the other actors repeated his dual role. There was a variety of reasons for this. Louis Napoléon is absent from the last act, and, like his father in *l'Aiglon,* Sacha did not enjoy being off-stage for long. The part of the journalist enabled him to re-appear and saved him from the necessity of loitering in an empty dressing room. Yet as Straus's percipient biographer has pointed out, the true reason lay in the fact that he was an extremely jealous husband. He detested the idea of leaving Yvonne Printemps alone with other actors. Himself an accomplished performer in the field of seduction, he knew only too well the danger of being hoist with his own petard. And so he won extra applause for versatility by capitalizing on a trait in his nature which, a few years later, helped lead to the break-up of the famous partnership.

Chapter 11

As for the man who runs away with your wife, there's no worse punishment than to let him keep her . . .

SACHA GUITRY

One of Sacha's older plays, which he had first acted with Charlotte Lysès, was called *la Jalousie*. He revived it for himself and Yvonne Printemps, and it had the honor of being taken into the repertory of the Comédie-Française, where Edwige Feuillère distinguished herself in one of the leading roles. *La Jalousie*, though it is written with Sacha's customary light touch, goes rather deeper in its study of human nature than usual and gives a penetrating account of the effects of jealousy. A husband arrives home late one evening from an assignation and finds that his wife is not back yet. His own feelings of guilt are immediately translated into a suspicion that she is deceiving him in the same way as he is deceiving her. Full of righteous anger he waits impatiently for her return and flings accusations at her. She refuses to tell him where she has been, for she had gone out to buy a surprise present for him. This happens to be the truth. They make it up, but from then on the husband's whole existence is

infected by jealousy. He dreams about it, thinks of it during all
his waking moments, and even employs a detective to shadow his
wife. The husband's best friend does nothing to reassure him
either when he explains why he doesn't marry: "Because I'm too
fond of other people's wives! When you marry it means you're
ensuring the happiness of your friends! Later on, perhaps, I may
take the plunge, and when I'm old enough to be deceived I shall
probably make the sacrifice and pay my debt to society." The husband begins to suspect him, and so intense are his feelings that
he ends up by driving his wife into the philanderer's arms, whereas
had he not been obsessed by the notion in the first place she
would never have been unfaithful to him.

The point about *la Jalousie* is that, quite unconsciously, Sacha
had put a lot of himself into the portrayal of the husband. During
the time Yvonne Printemps was his wife he stifled her with attention, would never allow her to leave the house alone, and insisted, even though he was working in his study, that she be in
a room near at hand. He gave her many millions of francs' worth
of jewelry but never paid her a fee for her stage appearances;
he bought her dozens of dresses and luxurious toilettes but never
allowed her to make a purchase without his knowledge. She was
surrounded all the time by his watchful care. Even on holiday,
when they went down to the house at Cap d'Ail and the butler
ran up the flag with their initials entwined upon it to announce
that they were in residence, Sacha kept her under surveillance,
complaining that her tennis skirts were too short, hovering anxiously on the beach while she went for a swim, and making sure
that she was safely occupied if he was called away. "It's a gilded
cage," said Yvonne ruefully, "but a cage all the same."

Only with great reluctance would Sacha allow himself to be
torn from his wife's side. One such occasion arose on the death
of Monet. The old artist had written to him: "I've just been going through a bad time with my work, but it's better now and
I'm hopeful for the future." He was then eighty-one. Soon after-

wards he fell ill, and, cruelly enough, he was attacked through his most precious faculty, his eyesight. A cataract had blinded his better eye, and Sacha found him alone in his studio looking miserably at his palette. *"Mon pauvre Sacha!"* he groaned, "I can't see the yellow any more!" When his sight went completely he no longer wanted to live. His old friend Clemenceau rushed to his deathbed. Then the undertaker came to drape the coffin with black. "No!" protested Clemenceau, tearing down the flowered window curtains and throwing them upon the coffin, "no black for Monet!"

With his taste for hagiology Sacha put both Clemenceau and Monet on the stage in his next play. It had been written to inaugurate the Théâtre Pigalle, an elaborately equipped theater with a vast revolving stage, and the owner was anxious to launch his new venture with an entertainment worthy of it. Sacha provided an ambitious spectacle extending from the ancient Gauls, who even in those days would seem to have had Parisian notions of married life, by way of all the kings and queens of France to Monet's garden at Giverny where the artist and Clemenceau discuss Cézanne in front of a backdrop representing the famous water lilies. The music was written by Henri Büsser, a composer of record longevity—he was a pupil of Gounod, was married in his eighties, and today, in his nineties, remains the alert music critic of the *Revue des Deux Mondes*. Like all Sacha's collaborators, he found the experience a tiring one. After long days of research in the Conservatoire library copying out scores Lully had written for Molière and popular songs of the period, he presented the result to Sacha: "No, it's boring—write me some Lully-Büsser!" was the response. Sacha was right. Scholarly editing is not what the theater wants. A bold pastiche will convey an atmosphere more vividly than the most scrupulous "realization." The same may be said of the play itself, whose punning title, *Histoires de France,* aptly indicates the anecdotal nature of the entertainment. Clemenceau at eighty-six was too infirm to come and see how Sacha had presented him on the stage. He sat in his study wearing the little hat that accompanied him everywhere, even indoors. He listened closely as Sacha told him of the emotional cheers that greeted the actor who impersonated him as he made his entry each night. And the yellow Mongolian features quivered with unusual feeling as the callous destroyer of governments told Sacha of his long friendship with Monet and of the last conversation he ever had with him.

The fame of the Guitrys was now as extensive in the Anglo-Saxon world as it was in Europe. The annual season under Cochran in London was followed in 1929 by a tour of the U.S. and Canada. Their manager was Al Woods, an American impresario cast in the traditional mould. He wore sky-blue shirts and he carried torpedo-sized cigars in his breast pockets, six a side, in the way Cossacks used to carry their cartridges. His expansive instincts approved of the eighty Lanvin dresses Yvonne Printemps embarked with as her riposte to the dazzling wardrobe Cécile Sorel had taken on a recent American tour by the Comédie-Française. Faced with a battalion of reporters as he descended from the *Leviathan*, Sacha was asked his opinion of American women. He replied diplomatically that he had none. Actors go on tour, he explained, not to observe other people but to show themselves off. He did concede that American women used make-up more intelligently, adding, as if to compensate for the heresy: "In Paris, when a man passes a woman in the street and looks at her, he almost commits an infidelity. To look at a Frenchwoman and to be seen by her is to write the first page of a love story." After the large cities and the rolling landscapes of North America, Paris looked lovelier still on his return. He reflected: "You oughtn't to stop traveling merely because you've come home. Indeed, you shouldn't go straight back to your house when you return to Paris. You should spend a few days in a hotel and see Paris—at last! The fact that you've 'done' the Louvre is no reason never to go back. There are men who go to the Louvre only when they change mistresses. I know a man who tried to take the woman he loved to the Louvre twice. The first time she didn't dare protest. The second time she cried: 'What again?' "

The democratic ideals of the New World were not, Sacha remembered, much in favor of domestic service. He chose, perhaps as a reaction, to make the hero of his next play a butler. There is a trace of Mirbeau's *Journal d'une femme de chambre* in *Désiré*, where the views of what used to be known as "below stairs" carry the stamp of realism. The members of the servants' quarters discuss how experience has taught them that it is better to have an affair with the employer's son rather than with the employer, since the latter is always unsympathetic. "Sometimes employers end up by marrying you," says the cook. "So that they won't have to go on paying you," rejoins the maid, "or else when they become infirm!" It soon appears that the new butler Désiré is well named, for the employment agency forgets to mention that in every post he has held the mistress of the house has fallen in love with him. When the inevitable happens a few days after his arrival, Désiré addresses his employer's wife in Figaroesque terms: "You shouldn't believe, Madame, that servants only understand what you want them to understand. And neither should you think, however great the distance between two people, that they are at all different . . . Domestic service, Madame, is wonderful! It's a way of existing without having to make decisions. 'Light the fire! Serve the coffee! Shut the window! Open the door!' Those are all other people's ideas! And then, when it's a woman's voice that orders you about, especially a bit sharply, then the feeling is . . . delightful!" Sacha's own butler went to a matinée on his day off and paid his employer the finest compliment he ever received: *"Ce n'est pas bien, Monsieur,"* he said reproachfully, "Monsieur listens at key-holes."

This was the butler who, without the slightest perturbation, appeared in the drawing room one lunch-time to announce: "Monsieur Guitry, His Royal Highness King Manoel of Portugal!"

Sacha blanched. He was alone with his old friend Prince Ponia-towski, and the two of them looked at each other in horror. The invitation to lunch had been forgotten in the excitement of fitting up a new display cabinet. Within minutes the dining room was prepared and Sacha was receiving with his courtliest grace. There was little fault to be found in the organization of a house which could, at such brief notice, entertain a king. On any day of the week the names of Sacha's visitors would have read like a directory of members of that vague body *le tout-Paris,* so difficult to define but, like love, so easy to recognize. His promotion to the rank of *Chevalier* in the Légion d'honneur was an acknowledgment of his place in that fashionable society. He had once, in *l'Amour masqué,* compiled a list of unlikely things—"A woman of fifty who admits to at least forty . . . a taxpayer who declares his income correctly . . . one might even, if one looked hard enough, discover a Frenchman who doesn't have the Légion d'hon-neur . . ."—but like most people who mock honors they do not possess, he was human enough to accept one when it was offered. It coincided with his entry into hospital for a small operation, and the telegrams varied between such messages as: "Delighted to hear the good news," and: "Very sorry at what I've just heard." "I never knew," commented Sacha, "whether they were talking about my decoration or my operation."

Sacha's receipt of the honor in January 1931 opened a year of literary activity that saw the publication of his *Lucien Guitry raconté par son fils.* It was an impressive filial tribute, issued in a limited edition with many excellent plates. Where Sacha wrote an act in an afternoon, a play in a couple of days, he spent three years on this labor of love, checking each date and assembling the massive documentation with infinite care. The work of piety was completed with the unveiling of a bust of Lucien which was set on a pedestal in the corner of the garden, though the depreda-tions of pigeons tended to obscure the dignity of Lucien's gaze.

By comparison with his book on Lucien, Sacha's *la Maison*

de Loti is a slim pamphlet. It speaks with touching respect of the author of those tales of Japan, Tahiti, Constantinople, and other exotic places where the restless traveler gathered the material for his idealized love stories. Sacha had visited Pierre Loti's house at Rochefort and toured the different rooms furnished in the varying styles of the countries Loti knew. There were the Japanese room in red lacquer encrusted with mother-of-pearl and filled with yellow ivories; the mosque upstairs where gold-fringed cushions and prayer carpets were scattered on the floor around a plaster cast of the tomb of Aziyadé, Loti's great love; and the Turkish room, a small alcove containing a divan and the bare table at which he wrote. Sacha stopped for a last look at the tiny garden where a tortoise nearly a hundred years old slowly moved its wrinkled neck. The old sailor who looked after the house paused on the threshold. "He's waiting for his master—and ours. Can Loti be dead? No—he's only set off again on his travels."

The literary tone of Sacha's existence at this time was sustained by a friendship with the Comtesse Anna de Noailles. Her ancestry, which included a Proustian swarm of Greek, Rumanian, and French noble families—the Mavrogordatos, the Bibescos, the Brancovans, the Chimays—would anyway have assured her position in society. The ownership of a pedigree which even the duc de Guermantes could not have questioned in his most exacting mood failed, however, to satisfy "the little genius," as Anatole France described her. She went on to make a second name for herself with poetry of a dashing and emphatic brilliance. Her conversation was as untiring as the verse that flowed from her pen. The personality she revealed to her public recalled those formidable hostesses and their salons of the eighteenth century. "Wasn't it enough that you had your eyes and your smile without having a throatful of birds?" she enquired of Yvonne Printemps. She ordered Sacha to invite her to lunch with the politician Édouard Herriot whom she wanted to meet. The result is best described in Sacha's words: "Lunch was at a quarter past one.

Herriot arrived on the dot. At one-thirty Madame de Noailles was not there. At two o'clock she came in; that is, she could be heard talking before she rang. She was not bringing anybody—she was quite alone; but that did not prevent her talking. She talked to the butler—at some length, though the butler could never tell you what she had said to him. She talked as she shook hands all round. She talked during luncheon, even while eating. It was marvelous. It never stopped being marvelous. Herriot couldn't get a word in. She was talking as we rose from table, and she went on talking as she was accompanied to the door. In the doorway she turned, looked fixedly at Herriot, and said: 'Oh!' Then added: 'And what is more, he has eyes like a bee.' Upon which she vanished down the stairs—still talking."

Another literary acquaintance of Sacha's was Henri Bergson. He was rare among philosophers in that he wrote of his subject in an elegant and persuasive prose. He was a member of the Académie Française, and when a colleague suggested that Sacha be put up for membership, he immediately sent three of his books to Sacha bearing his signature and the words: "An admirer." The immensely flattering implications of the gesture will be appreciated when it is realized that, besides making a round of calls upon the "Immortels," a candidate is required to submit three published works in support of his application. In the latter years of his life acute rheumatism confined Bergson to a wheelchair. When Sacha called to thank him for his courtesy he was sitting, as usual, his knees wrapped in a Scottish plaid, surrounded by towering piles of books and papers which overflowed from his desk on to occasional tables dotted about the room. His deep blue eyes shone strangely out of the pale bony face with its thin nose and slim lips. The features were spiritualized by meditation and physical suffering. He held out a hand whose smooth fingers were twisted by rheumatism. This encounter between the man who wrote the masterly study of the psychology of laughter, le Rire, and the man who had created so much of that emotion, could only have

happened in France, where the republic of letters is not a mere
hackneyed phrase. To imagine such a thing in England it is necessary to visualize Noël Coward, say, or Terence Rattigan being
sponsored for the Royal Society of Literature by Bertrand Russell
or A. N. Whitehead.

The Académie Française owes its existence to Cardinal Richelieu, a statesman so keen of literary reputation that he paid hacks
to turn out the plays which he presented under his own name and
which he himself lacked the ability to write. He even, so it is
said, attempted to buy *le Cid* from Corneille for the same pur-
pose. In 1634 a group of writers who used to meet together in-
formally were somewhat annoyed at receiving the attention of
the Cardinal. To their secret alarm he granted them letters patent
which organized them into an Académie. At one stroke he had
found yet another outlet for his frustrated literary ambition and
had created a useful means of buttressing his power in the world
of letters. The politician distrusts artists and writers. They are unreliable creatures who cannot be depended on to keep to the party
line. Like Napoleon and Stalin, the wily Cardinal was adept at
arranging the arts for political ends and at dangling patronage before the noses of unruly writers. Within a few years the Académie
had reached the mystic number of forty, and all of its members
were assured of immortality by government decree if not by popular assent. When they began to die off elections were necessary
to keep up the original number. So was instituted one of the
customs which over the centuries has provided rich entertainment
for all students of French literature. Thus, for example, official
immortality was refused Descartes, whose unorthodoxy was disliked by Richelieu, and to Corneille, whom the Cardinal detested.
In the nineteenth century a wit invented "the forty-first chair"
for those whom the Académie excluded. Among its occupants
were Verlaine, Rimbaud, Flaubert, Maupassant, and Baudelaire.

This digression is necessary to explain why Sacha, usually so
independent, was tempted by thoughts of the Académie. It is de-

rided as much as it is admired. Every Frenchman will admit the absurdity of pigeon-holing writers by the standards of a government department. Very few can resist the lure of belonging. The Académie is extremely rich. Every year it awards dozens of prizes for various achievements which range from writing books to bringing up a large family on Christian principles. Among the recipients are domestic servants who have spent more than twenty years with the same employer; the daughters of army officers who have been unable to obtain a license for selling tobacco; and deserving young women of illegitimate birth who receive an award that is delicately named the *Prix Anonyme*. It is easy to laugh at the Académie. It is impossible to deny its importance in French life and the prestige which membership confers. The ceremonial reception of a new member, when the Immortals assemble wearing their peculiar costume of knee-breeches, sword and cocked hat, is a social event of great splendor and capable of inspiring deeper feelings, one is almost led to believe, than any World Series.

There was, however, one big obstacle to Sacha's acceptability. "He has a terrible precedent against him," remarked a member. "Molière never belonged to the Académie Française." While boulevard playwrights like Marcel Pagnol and Marcel Achard, and even a living paradox such as Jean Cocteau, may be judged deserving of immortality, a dramatist who stoops so low as to put make-up on his face and to act in his own plays was thought unworthy of dignity as Richelieu conceived it. Although Sacha could count on eleven favorable votes, he decided, in spite of Bergson's encouragement, to give up the idea and not to exchange his theatrical costume for the academician's.

All this time a procession of sober graybeards had been passing through Sacha's home. Eminent persons were entertained to formal meals and there were somber meetings to weigh up, for the twentieth time, Sacha's chances of election. The atmosphere became one of academic reverence. Yvonne Printemps could bear it no longer. She had already evaded her husband's jealous guard to seek diversion elsewhere with an actor whom Sacha had lately engaged. The young man was called Pierre Laudenbach, a name he changed to Fresnay. He had joined Sacha's company straight from the Comédie-Française, where his playing of the classic roles had been well received. Among the plays in which he appeared was *Frans Hals,* an affectionate "biography" of one of Sacha's favorite painters. Sacha did not agree with Horace's *nihil admirari.* He believed that wholehearted admiration was the least one could offer to a creator whose work had pleased. "When a man has given you incomparable happiness through his writing, his painting, or his music, it is impossible to estimate what you owe him," he wrote. "If I suddenly feel that I adore life, if everything charms and delights me, if I love the air I breathe when I wake up, it's all because last night I read a sonnet by Shakespeare." The play was dictated in a couple of evenings and proposes an ingenious reconstruction of what might have passed to bring about Hals's famous picture of the drinking party in Harlem. "I shall play Frans Hals," declared Sacha as he drew up his cast, "Pierre Fresnay will be Adrien van Ostade, my master in painting, and you, Yvonne, will be the charming Annette, my wife . . . and you will become, with my agreement, Pierre Fresnay's mistress, or van Ostade's, that is, because I admire him, because he is my god, because he can only do good in whatever he puts his hand to. . . ." With the same unconscious irony, he wrote these lines for himself to speak: "When you're in love at the age of twenty and for the first time, your beloved is the only woman in the world; by the time you've reached your fourth love you realize that the world's number of women is limitless."

The play coincided with the celebration of Sacha's thirty years on the stage. On the 25 April, 1932, he gave a banquet to mark the event with a menu of appropriate dishes. *Consommé Jacqueline* and *Bombe Illusionniste* recalled some of his successful titles. *Salade de Printemps* was a punning compliment to Yvonne. *Madeleine du théâtre* provided a reminder of the scene of his latest triumphs at the Théâtre de la Madeleine. He and his wife were too accomplished as performers not to give the impression of a blissfully married couple. But their smiles were a little strained as they sat through a post-prandial entertainment which included an impersonator who gave his impressions of Yvonne singing *J'ai deux amants* from *l'Amour masqué*. . . .

For Yvonne life was now a series of encounters on the wing, of fleeting assignations with the man who had taken Sacha's place. One day Sacha received a letter from the actress Berthe Bovy, at the time Madame Fresnay. "If you want to know where they go every day, I'll take you there," she wrote. So the outraged wife and the jealous husband went to the meeting place and saw their suspicions confirmed. The steps of the quadrille were danced with the clumsiness of real life and not with the grace of a play by Sacha. His father in the same situation had said not a word when he learned of his wife's infidelity. Instead, Lucien had preserved complete silence, living with her, eating with her, sleeping with her, but never, despite her pleas, uttering a single remark. After fourteen months of this treatment the desperate woman had vanished to the provinces. Sacha likewise withdrew into dumbness. For a few days he and Yvonne Printemps were seen together in public at the races and at social events. Then she moved out and took a suite at the Hôtel Georges V. The planned revival of *Mozart* went ahead, though with another actor playing Sacha's part. Naturally the box-office takings broke all records. Much hilarity was caused by the choice of incidental music, to which a tactless producer had added the overtures from *The Marriage of Figaro* and *Il Seraglio*. The joke was lost on Sacha. Neither did he relish the exuberant comments of the newspapers for whom the *incident Guitry*, featuring not one, but two, leading men, and no less than two leading ladies, was a boon to circulation. The celebrated partnership trickled away into the arid sands of divorce proceedings, alimony settlements, claims, and counterclaims.

"She's gone. At last I shall be living on my own," reflected Sacha in his lonely house, "and already I'm wondering: with whom?" The answer was close at hand. A few months earlier he had been introduced to a young actress from Lyon. Her name was Jacqueline Delubac and her talent was equal to her ambition, as Sacha had found when he tried her out in a program of one-act plays. She had dark hair, a snub nose, large eyes, and a teasing manner which gave an edge to the small parts she had hitherto played in revues and Palais-Royal farces. Sacha took her out for drives in the Cadillac. They went to Brittany and on to Monte Carlo. They toured Italy where Sacha had an interview with Mussolini and, as one actor to another, was struck by the dictator's magnificent talent for stage-managing the audiences he granted. They came back to Paris and stayed at the Hôtel Élysées-Palace, down the road from Sacha's house where the telephone rang constantly and journalists lay in siege. Hotel life soon palled. Sacha had a bourgeois longing for home, and soon he was back among his collections, reviewing his pictures, cataloguing his autographs, and banishing the Vuillard portrait of Yvonne Printemps from the drawing room to the cellar. Jacqueline took over the household and, with her Lyonnais good sense, made it run as smoothly as ever. "If women knew how much we missed them," mused Sacha as he watched her compiling a menu with exquisite detail, adding an asparagus tip here and white sauce there, "they'd leave us all the more quickly."

Sacha agreed with Oscar Wilde that the only thing worse than being talked about was not being talked about, though even he was taken aback by the commotion his affairs aroused at this point. He was especially wounded by a play which took him as the leading character and titillated Parisian audiences with a caricature of himself and his entourage. *La Voie lactée* was by Alfred Savoir, the author of many light comedies, and it gave a picture of professional egoism which was cruelly true to life. For days Sacha raged about the house vituperating Savoir and his leading actor, Harry Baur, who twenty years before had had one of his finest opportunities in Sacha's own *le Veilleur de nuit*. (By an odd coincidence Marcel Pagnol's recently divorced wife had just written a play about a man who, like her ex-husband, was a schoolmaster from the Midi and came to Paris to achieve success.)

What was worse, *la Voie lactée* was eagerly praised by the critic Pierre Brisson, who in *Figaro* carried on a regular vendetta against Sacha and was an old enemy of many years' standing. Sacha had no use for critics. Their attacks sometimes reduced him to tears. "Why read it?" his friends used to ask. "Why write it?" he would reply. Sacha looked on Pierre Brisson as the incarnation of the pestilential race. He liked to quote a favorite definition of the critic by the eighteenth-century poet Alexis Piron: "He is the eunuch in the seraglio, he never creates anything and harms those who do." Sacha retired to lick his wounds on the Côte d'Azur and opened a new file marked "Savoir" in which to preserve evidence against him. He was cheated of his revenge by Savoir's death two years later. Pierre Brisson outlived them both and continued to place his poisoned darts with unerring accuracy.

By the April of 1933 Sacha had been absent from the stage for at least six months. He remedied this unusual situation with *Châteaux en Espagne,* a new play which gave Jacqueline Delubac her first important part. Stricken with an acute attack of nerves at the thought of her illustrious predecessors and of the Guitry first-night audience, she yet contrived to give a performance both witty and modest. Svengali-Sacha had succeeded again. The acquisition of a new stage partner seemed to give him fresh inspiration, for within a few days he had dictated five plays, including a musical comedy and a historical extravaganza. The latter piece was for Cécile Sorel, that flamboyant star of the Comédie-Française who had descended from the heights of Molière to take the Casino de Paris by storm. It was called *Maîtresses de Rois,* an apt title for a spectacle planned to display the talents of one who saw herself as the Madame Dubarry of the Third Republic. She slept, indeed, in the bed that had belonged to the unfortunate courtesan. Her receptions, for which she prepared herself beforehand by memorizing lines from Pascal or Bergson to be dropped into the conversation, brought together kings and prime ministers, with, on occasional off-nights, a bemused Secretary of State or three.

The musical comedy which belongs to this period was *O mon bel inconnu.* Bored with the company of his wife and daughter, whose feminine chatter he finds unbearably tedious, a middle-aged shopkeeper seeks release. Should he take a mistress? Perhaps not. There are too many complications. "When you separate from a mistress it's because you've chosen her successor. The result is that at that very moment you've three women on your hands— your wife, the mistress you're leaving, and the one you're taking on. Three is too much, anyway, and there's always the fear that the first will learn from the second about the existence of the third. . . ." He decides to put a box-number advertisement in the newspapers announcing that a rich bachelor is looking for a sister-soul. Among the dozens of replies are two from his wife and from his daughter. For several weeks he carries on an anonymous correspondence with them and is astonished to learn more about them during that brief time than during the whole of their existence together. As for the wife and daughter, they are transformed. The plot develops with vertiginous speed and ends with the daughter happily married off and her father and mother reconciled. The verse in which it is written contains many neat lines. Among them are the following, which, unfortunately, are untranslatable because of the play on words and letters:

> *Monsieur, je suis très O.Q.P.,*
> *Et maintenant, j'en E.A.S.*
> *Vous m'ennuyez, vous m'E.N.R.V.*
> *Vous m'assommez, vous m'em . . . B.T.*

Reynaldo Hahn composed a light-footed musical score that underlined the wit of the libretto. There were perky chromatic passages for the song where the maid complains how hard it is to please everyone; some clever Mozartian dissonances for the entr'actes; and for the theme song "O mon bel inconnu" there was one of those simple little waltz-tunes which revolve contentedly in the mind as one leaves the theater.

The part of the wife was played by Arletty with her raucous accent and mischievous eye, apt for expressing infinities of comic roguery. She had been a model for Paul Poiret, the dressmaker, and when she left fashion for the stage she decided that her real name, Léonie Bathiat, was that of a tragic actress rather than of the light comedian she aspired to be. So she became Arlette, shortening the name on second thoughts into Arletty, which she believed, for some quaint reason, to be "chic anglais, up to date, English fashion" (sic). The titles of her films read like a roll-call of vintage cinema—Hôtel du Nord, le Jour se lève, Fric-Frac, les Visiteurs du soir, les Enfants du Paradis, and others equally distinguished. Arletty was an old friend of Jacqueline Delubac. They had acted together before and shared many girlish secrets, rather to Sacha's annoyance. He also engaged for O mon bel inconnu an actor who had known both Arletty and Jacqueline for quite a long time. The part was tedious and unrewarding. It was that of a mute who had to remain on stage for nearly the whole evening. Only the actor and his employer knew why the part was so ungrateful: it represented Sacha's vengeance for the fact that several years previously the actor had been an intimate friend of Jacqueline's.

In between performances of O mon bel inconnu Sacha had written a Molière-style comedy, le Nouveau testament, in which a doctor makes his will, pretends to die, and then has the experience of discovering what his friends' true natures are when they learn of his death. Colette praised its "exceptional mastery" and the piece was well received, but Sacha was bored by long runs. He always had a thousand ideas in his head, and when he had brought one of them to fruition his mercurial brain had already lost interest in it and was ripening the next one. That winter he deserted the stage of the Madeleine and took Jacqueline and Arletty to Switzerland with him. The occupants of the quiet hotel at Gstaad were treated to the sight of Arletty rolling in the snow and playing outrageous jokes, eagerly abetted by Sacha who had reason for his good humor. His divorce from Yvonne Printemps had at last been concluded and he was planning his next production: the announcement of his marriage to Jacqueline. Back in Paris the friends who had been invited to a luncheon-party at the Ritz on February 21, 1935, thought they were celebrating his fiftieth birthday. At the end of the meal, watched by Albert Willemetz and Tristan Bernard, for whom this was Sacha's third marriage as best man, the bridegroom spoke: "As you know, I'm fifty today. Jacqueline is twenty-five. So it was natural that today she should become my better half . . . Before meeting you here we made a little detour, via the town hall, and now it's done. You're the first to know of it."

Chapter 12

Well, cher Monsieur, I create a film in the same way as I create a play, the same way as I do everything in life—for my own pleasure above all and without forethought, without any plan or reservation, with the secret hope of succeeding in what I undertake.

SACHA GUITRY

With a third Madame Guitry at his side, Sacha now launched on a busy period in the cinema, a sphere which he had once disdained. He still agreed with Orson Welles's description of the medium as "a box of toys," though he came more and more to enjoy playing with them. His first sound film, in 1931, had been a version of his play *le Blanc et le noir*. This gave Raimu his earliest role in the cinema as well as introducing Fernand Contandin, otherwise the flashy-toothed Fernandel, in the first of a hundred or so films he was to make. As his director Sacha chose Marc Allégret, who was also responsible for Gide's *Voyage au Congo* (1927) and Marcel Pagnol's *Fanny* (1932).* Four years

---

* Allégret it was who made the pre-war "discovery" of Simone Simon. Ever afterwards he dreamed of repeating his success. Many years later he saw the unknown Mademoiselle Brigitte Bardot on the cover of *Elle*, and excitedly ordered a screen test under the watchful eye of her formidable mother. The result was a disappointment. Bardot spoke her lines, said Allégret with pettish disgust, as if she were wearing her old mother's false teeth. He passed her on to his cutting assistant, Vadim Plemianikoff, alias Roger Vadim, who knew better.

later Sacha filmed *Pasteur* and two other plays, and in 1936 he transferred no less than five to the screen.

In Sacha's approach to the cinema there was something of the attitude of early scholars to the first printed books, which were initially welcomed as a means of avoiding copyists' errors. Once you have filmed your actors at work, explained Sacha, you have preserved their performance and can forget about it, whereas in the theater you never know what your cast will be getting up to. A film is something that has already happened, an event over and done with. It is like the illustrations in a book. "The actor on the screen isn't acting: he *has* acted. He's acted for you, thinking of you—but in your absence. And since you weren't there when he acted, he didn't have stage-fright. Since he didn't have stage-fright, since he didn't run the risk of being booed, he felt more at his ease. But, because he didn't have stage-fright, or didn't have the opportunity of being applauded by you, or perhaps because his heart didn't beat that little bit faster, for that very reason he probably did not act as well as usual. To sum up, let us say that the actor who does not act well is better on the screen, while on the other hand the actor who does act well is not so good when you, the audience, are not there." To those who reproached him for inconsistency when he made five films in one year, he replied: "I haven't changed my opinion. Admittedly I'm filming at the moment. I don't go to the cinema myself, but I go to the studio because I like work. The theater and the cinema are two different arts. One doesn't compare painting with engraving. One is entitled to be fond of engravings." Sacha had not failed to realize either that while his longest-running play would be seen by at most a hundred thousand people, his film of it could reach ten times that number; besides this, films could be made much more quickly than could plays, with their elaborate preparation and boring repeats. At first his sophisticated art might have seemed an unlikely contender in the mass market of the cinema, but by 1939 a survey of French-speaking countries revealed that

Sacha came seventh in a popularity list after Jean Gabin, Fernandel, Louis Jouvet, Raimu, Pierre Fresnay (this must have been annoying), and Charles Boyer—most of them essentially products of the cinema. Of the women film actresses, it is amusing to note, Yvonne Printemps came third.

Sacha quickly grasped the essentials of film-making and directed most of his productions himself, as well as writing the script and acting a leading part. His approach was straightforward. The shooting script was worked out with all the cutting details planned in advance. If René Clair spent hours deliberating where to place the camera, Sacha knew immediately the position he wanted, though for battle scenes or for involved "dolly" shots he wisely engaged the best technicians available. His handling of actors recalled Noël Coward's advice to the young Stanislavsky-trained product who asked him anxiously about the inner significance of the role he was playing. "Just remember your lines and be careful not to trip over the furniture," said Coward benignly. After rehearsing his cast Sacha would sit back with eyes closed and concentrate on their delivery of the speeches. What he most enjoyed about filming was the editing, and in his hands the movieola became a supreme device for juggling with all the wealth of tricks the medium offered. None was more adept than Sacha at cutting a scene at the exact moment, at adjusting a "fade" to produce the right effect, or at getting the fullest impact from a sequence.

The second act of *Faisons un rêve,* consisting entirely of the lover's monologue, was shot straight off in twenty-one minutes, thus anticipating Hitchcock's method in *Rope.* In addition to Raimu playing his original part and Jacqueline Delubac in the role created by Charlotte Lysès, there was a brief prologue featuring a group of famous players whom only Sacha could have brought together. This unique hors d'œuvre offered glimpses of Arletty, Victor Boucher, Claude Dauphin, Michel Simon, and the *diseuse* Yvette Guilbert, now a plump figure and no longer

the scarecrow pictured by Toulouse-Lautrec. Films of *Désiré,
Mon Père avait raison,* and *le Nouveau testament* followed in
a few months, and they proved as successful with cinema audiences
as they had with the more limited public of the Parisian theaters.

At the same time as he was filming Sacha was also writing, directing, and appearing in plays. There were five of them in this
busy year of 1936, which was also to produce the same number of
films. The one that best showed Sacha's gift for airily skirting the
distasteful was *le Mot de Cambronne,* which he described for obvious reasons as a "curtain-lowerer in verse." It was, incidentally,
his hundredth play, and he dedicated it to Edmond Rostand who as
long ago as 1912 had given him the idea on which it is based.
Cambronne, who led one of the last detachments of the French
guards at Waterloo, on being ordered to surrender is said to have
replied: "The Old Guard dies but doesn't surrender." Other versions insist that his reply was much briefer and consisted of the
notorious five-letter French swear word that every schoolboy knows.
"Were you aware," said Rostand, "of the historical fact that Cambronne married an English girl? There's a subject for a play in
it, and it's up to you to imagine the scene between Cambronne
and his wife!" One July morning twenty-four years later Sacha
began to write the play and finished it by lunch-time. It takes place
in the eighteen-twenties when Cambronne is living in retirement
with his wife. She catches him flirting with the maid and snaps:
"We engaged her as a maid-of-all-work. Perhaps you think you're
obliged to take the expression literally." Cambronne makes light of
the situation: "What's wrong, God help me, in saying a word
to her from time to time?" "A word? What word?" says his wife,
instantly on the alert. Does he mean "his" word? It is a word
she has never known, a word that seems to have haunted her since
their marriage and has caused her endless uneasiness on account
of the sly grins and innuendoes of her husband's friends. She
presses him to tell her what this famous word is, but he, irritated
and embarrassed, refuses to enlighten her. Throughout the rest

of the play she tries to worm it out of him, and the dialogue, which is in verse, is a succession of lightly amusing pirouettes around the subject. There is only one rhyme in the French language for Cambronne's word—the third person singular of the present subjunctive of the verb *perdre*—and when it occurs at the end of one of Madame Cambronne's lines the audience waits expectantly. "No!" shouts Cambronne triumphantly, "I shan't fall into the trap you've set!" "What trap?" she asks, bewildered. And just as Cambronne is losing his temper again the maid accidentally drops a loaded tea tray and lets slip the missing rhyme. His wife learns what has been perplexing her over the years and the curtain is lowered very quickly.

Le Mot de Cambronne is Sacha at his most skillful, taking the slimmest of situations and developing it into a string of comic, surprising, and always diverting incidents. He filmed the play in the same year, performing it in the film studios during the day and on the stage at the Madeleine at night. For the part of Cambronne's wife he cast Marguerite Moreno, who imitated an English accent to perfection. Later generations who only know her on the screen as the impersonator of macabre chatelaines, eccentric bureaucrats, and dotty old beldames, find it hard to believe that at the turn of the century she was one of the most beautiful *ingénues* of the Comédie-Française. She was of Spanish descent and took her mother's maiden name on entering the theater. The name, said her lifelong friend Colette, suited the blanched pallor of her complexion and her dark "hidalgo look." The desiccated Léautaud heard her reciting Baudelaire and said: "No other actress has ever caused me so much emotion." She drew tributes from many unexpected sources including Jules Renard, who praised her "Egyptian profile," and from poets who worshipped her "long Gothic fingers." She was loved to distraction by Marcel Schwob, that ultra-refined man of letters whom she eventually married. She went boating on the Seine with Mallarmé who addressed poems to her and explained the meaning of one of his obscurest pieces, *Un coup de dés jamais n'abolira le hasard*. She rushed home to tell her husband . . . only to find, on arriving, that she had forgotten it again. In the nineteen-thirties, her beauty vanished and only the Gothic strangeness remaining, she was dismissed as too old for the stage and Colette persuaded her to take up films. Yet she achieved the greatest triumph of her career at the age of seventy-five as Giraudoux's madwoman of Chaillot. (Sacha, who adored Moreno, remarked of *la Folle de Chaillot*: "I have a feeling that Giraudoux left before the end.") Her rusty voice, dried to a brittle crisp by years of chain-smoking, crackled its bizarre notes on the sound-tracks of close on seventy films. Magnificent ruin though she was, her vitality enabled her to take up piloting aircraft in advanced years. Her godson fell violently in love with her when she was seventy-two. "Can you imagine it?" sighed Moreno. "And me looking like an old priest!" *

That same year Moreno appeared in what is often spoken of as Sacha's best film. It was called *le Roman d'un tricheur* and was taken from a novel he published under the title of *Mémoires d'un tricheur*. The book itself is as delightful as the film. Written in short pungent sentences without a superfluous word, these memoirs of an adventurer present an unassailable case for rascality as a way of life. Even the irony of the ending cannot fault the argument. The narrator is one of a family of twelve whose parents keep a village shop. One day he rifles the till, and as a punishment his father forbids him to join the family in eating some delicious mushrooms that have been prepared for supper. When the meal is over the twelve-year-old boy is the only survivior. The mushrooms were poisonous. The sight of the eleven corpses of his family teaches him a basic truth of life: "I was still alive because I was a thief. It was an easy step to draw the conclusion that the

* At the age of 75 the indomitable Moreno married a young soldier of the Foreign Legion.

others had died because they were honest. And, that night, falling asleep alone in an empty house, my reflections on justice and theft were perhaps a little paradoxical, but forty years' experience have not modified them."

The orphan is taken into the home of relatives, a money-grubbing bourgeois couple who trick him out of his inheritance. A few brief paragraphs give an unforgettable picture of the mean, grasping household which consists of the lawyer, whose grim exterior conceals an even grimmer heart, and his wife, whose ugly features, complete with mustache and pince-nez, are as ugly as her character. The detailed observation has a real-ism worthy of Jules Renard. The boy runs away and as a page in a hotel sees rich people for the first time. He compares them with his penny-pinching relatives who carefully put by every sou: "Money only has value when it leaves your pocket. It has none when you receive it. What use is money when you carry it about with you? . . . When a rich man learns that a deal he's just brought off will earn him two hundred thousand francs, he's not worthy of it in my opinion unless the sum immediately takes the shape for him, according to his tastes, of a jewel for the woman he loves, of a picture he wants, or of a new car. . . . If I were the government, as my concierge says, it would be on the outward signs of false poverty that I'd pitilessly tax people who don't spend their income."

The hero comes to Paris and works in a luxury hotel. There he learns more about human nature than a lifetime's study of books would have taught him, for the art of encouraging tips calls for a knowledge of people and skill in handling them equal to that of a successful diplomatist. He learns, too, how to be a Parisian. After listing the requirements to be fulfilled by those who aspire to such an honor, Sacha concludes: "In conversation you should be optimistic, indulgent, paradoxical, and cruel. If you have wit, use it fiercely and without pity. An epigram is sacred. You can make an epigram against your sister or your wife, if necessary, provided it's amusing. No one has the right to keep a good epigram to himself."

From Paris, where he double-crosses some fellow criminals, the hero goes to Monaco—"you couldn't make an operetta out of it, it's one already"—which is his spiritual home. Everywhere he sees Englishmen, Russians, Frenchmen, Cubans . . . but no Monégasques. Where are they, the natives of this village which is a town which is a country? "They're in the Casino. Croupiers. You don't just become a croupier, you're *born* to it in Monaco. It's an inheritance. At birth every Monégasque finds in his cradle the croupier's traditional black rake." He serves an apprenticeship as gigolo to an insatiable middle-aged countess. "She wore an opaque gauze veil round her neck. She was right. She took it off in front of me. She was wrong." Called up for war service, he is wounded one minute after the offensive begins and is bravely rescued by a man called Charbonnier, whom he only glimpses. After the war he sets up as a professional gambler in Monaco, aided by a mistress who has evolved an infallible system which they operate together with brilliant success. On occasions when she is away, however, he finds that he can't work the system on his own. So they get married, only to discover that, having legalized their partnership, they can no longer work the system. Divorce releases him to continue his career as a lone wolf cheat and a master of disguises, since his own face is too well-known to the Casino proprietors who have suffered from his activities. At this point Sacha, who always gave roulette as his hobby in reference books, is able to expound with loving care his own favorite systems and a selection of cheating ploys which will be familiar to lovers of the game, among them the *poussette aux chances simples* and the charmingly named *récolte des orphelins.*

A magician at baccarat, chemin-de-fer, and roulette, thanks to his fleet conjurer's fingers and the cards up his sleeve, the cheat amasses a huge fortune. He always wins because he is a professional. Gambling for him is not a matter of excitement but a careful maneuver executed with coolness and precision. Only the amateur allows his emotion to get the better of him. Then, one fateful evening at Aix-les-Bains, the cheat encounters a man whose face is vaguely familiar to him. It is the worthy Charbonnier who saved his life at the Front. Charbonnier, simple soul, gambles for pleasure. The cheat partners him with mixed feelings. He cannot help being affected by Charbonnier's innocent exuberance. For the first time in his life he begins to feel excitement at the game. It is the only diversion in the dull and monotonous life of his honest friend. Together they start a winning series and for three weeks their luck holds. Inevitably fortune deserts them. The cheat goes wildly on, alone, until within a few months his honest playing has frittered away the wealth earned over years of crookery. "I'd got the bug—for ever . . . I'd understood what gambling was and I'd begun to love it. I'd mistaken and despised it, cursed it and lived off it—and now it appeared to me in a different light. I realized its charm, I felt its pleasure, I experienced its emotion . . . When you're a gambler, a genuine gambler, you can't cheat, you can't substitute for chance." Now he lives in near-poverty as a clerk in a playing-card factory, piously setting aside a quarter of his wage and devoting it to his weekly gamble "sensibly, religiously."

The film of this cynical little story has become a classic of the cinema. Sacha's originality extends even to the credit titles, where instead of being shown a deadening list of names the audience is introduced to each of the people responsible for making the film. This sets the tone of amused intimacy which is kept up throughout, and after Sacha has presented us to the composer of the incidental music, obligingly running off a few cadenzas, and to the technicians grouped around their cameras, he goes on to tell us the story as if he were recounting an anecdote that happened to have caught his fancy. Except for a few scenes where the actors speak dialogue to each other, the film consists of Sacha's commentary on what is happening on the screen. The idea was not entirely new. Eisenstein had once thought of using this device for his film of Dreiser's *An American Tragedy,* though nothing came of it in the end. An early version of Eugene O'Neill's play *Strange Interlude* had used interior monologue to express the thoughts of the characters, but Sacha was the first director to link episodes together in this way with complete success. From time to time, when in character, he winks knowingly at the audience and takes them into his confidence. Seated at the café table where he is writing his memoirs, he breaks off to initiate sequences prefaced by shots of the lines he has just written, a device which Pabst used also in an early silent film, presented in the form of a diary. There is further novelty in the moving shots and trick wipes that underline the verbal points Sacha makes, and in the reverse motion he invokes when the Palace Guard at Monaco appear to dance a sort of comic ballet. At every juncture there is a cunning twist to carry the story forward. The cast who performed to Sacha's witty counterpoint was impeccable. Jacqueline Delubac was his wife, sly and disabused, and Marguerite Moreno played a raddled countess whose cheeks were as withered as her lasciviousness was evergreen. The part of the bourgeoise aunt who swindles the hero when a boy was taken by Pauline Carton. She was a favorite of Sacha and appeared in dozens of his plays and films. Her specialty was, and still is, impertinent cooks and zany chambermaids who, under the guise of her moonlike features and button nose, take on an existence of their own. "She says of herself that she looks like a duck, and she has in fact the round eye of a certain fowl," wrote Sacha. "She has had parts in plays of mine which could be written out in full on a visiting card— and people never speak of those plays to me without mentioning her name."

Not long afterwards Sacha was promoted to the rank of *Commandeur* in the Légion d'honneur. "I feel as if my country is falling on my neck," he murmured as he tied the ceremonial cravat. This reminder of the world of chivalry and honors found an echo in his next film, *les Perles de la couronne*. It was the first he ever wrote directly for the screen. The story traced the adventures of a royal necklace and how it passed through the hands of Henry VIII, François I, and other historical personages before being stolen by thieves and broken up into its individual pearls. Each pearl is an excuse for a contemporary goose-chase to find its whereabouts in modern times. Sacha could think of a fate for all except the final pearl. His secretary came to the rescue by suggesting it be accidentally dropped from aboard a liner, and that is how the amusing odyssey came to an end. Using the same method as in *le Roman d'un tricheur,* Sacha was seen telling the story to a wide-eyed Jacqueline Delubac, politely leaving the floor on occasion to the Popes and Princes, the Kings and Queens who had their part to play. Arletty was cast as the "black pearl," otherwise the Queen of Ethiopia, and spent days in the studio flirting with a python entwined, rather dangerously Sacha thought, around her neck. She spoke her lines in what sounded like fluent Ethiopian, a linguistic illusion Sacha created by running the soundtrack backwards. Marguerite Moreno was in it and so was Raimu. The latter's role was small and instead of payment he asked Sacha to give his wife a present. Madame Raimu was gratified with a handsome jewel and everyone was pleased. The film company's accountant, not knowing the arrangement, debited the cost of the present as Raimu's salary. Months afterwards Raimu was fined for not declaring it on his tax returns. His hyper-sensitiveness in financial matters was rudely bruised and the misunderstanding caused an abrupt end to a long friendship.

A film on similar lines was *Remontons les Champs-Élysées,* where Sacha told the story of the famous thoroughfare from its beginnings in 1617 as a road cut by Marie de Médicis through marshes and woods. The Champs-Élysées had seen in their day

La Fontaine leaning against an oak watching a reed-fringed pool and meditating *le Chêne et le roseau*. There Jean-Jacques Rousseau had planned to set up a café. There, too, Wagner had been dismissed from his humble post as conductor of a restaurant orchestra when he tried to play some extracts from *Tannhäuser*. "It's the story of four generations who could have lived in the Champs-Élysées," said Sacha. "The ancestor is Louis XV. By his mistress he has a son who later becomes the husband of Marat's daughter. In turn they have a son who marries the natural daughter of Napoleon. This couple's son marries the natural daughter of a Republican, and they produce another son who is now ten years old and who has in his veins the blood of Louis XV, of Marat, of the Emperor, and of a Republican. So the boy is never quite sure whether he should put his hand on his heart like Louis XVI on the scaffold, or in his waistcoat like the Emperor at Austerlitz, or whether he should wave a clenched fist like his Republican ancestor. In a way this boy is the prototype of the average Frenchman who can only agree with all the conflicting opinions inside himself to the extent of uttering the three words: *Vive la France!*" No one was surprised in the course of this pleasant frolic to note the unusual resemblance of Louis XV and Napoléon III to Sacha, nor to realize that the fearsome old woman who knitted while the guillotine did its work looked like Pauline Carton. The simple means that Sacha had at his disposal are primitive compared with the resources of today, yet when revived thirty years later *Remontons les Champs-Élysées* does not fail to entertain. It proves the superiority of one man's wit and intelligence over the machine.

A less distinguished film of this period was *Quadrille*, a version of Sacha's latest play which was a Gallic cousin to Noël Coward's *Private Lives*. By the final curtain the leader of the quartet is edged into marriage with his mistress. "So it's written that I shall never remain as much as twenty-four hours without a wife of my own. How awful!" His future wife asks how it's so awful.

"Because," he answers ruefully, "I shall never be able to have other people's wives." The late Gaby Morlay helped with her sympathetic presence to whip this lighthearted confection into a dazzling froth. Born in Algeria as Blanche Fumoleau, she had won recognition on the Paris stage for her *gamine* roles and played many parts which had been specially written for her by Henry Bernstein. She moved from the dramatic to the pathetic with ease, though her comic gifts, until Sacha came into her life, were apt to be overlooked. Comedy then gave way to character parts and she was seen as the elderly Queen Victoria. It is unlikely that the respectable monarch would have approved Gaby's last notable film appearance as the young heroine's mentor in *Gigi*. With Sacha she repeated her stage performance in the film of *Quadrille*, which was shot with the aid of extras recruited from among Sacha's off-stage friends. At its showing in Monte Carlo during 1938 Sacha stopped the projector after the second act, for he could not bear to be physically absent when more than two or three were gathered together. He played the third act on-stage with his company and then, having satisfied his craving for an audience, gave orders for the projection to continue.

In between all these films and plays Sacha found time to anticipate commercial television. The occasion was *Crions-le sur les toits*, a revue he devised for charity. Each number advertised, with a finesse that modern "commercials" sadly lack, a given product, and the manufacturer paid for the publicity he received. Most of Sacha's friends agreed to lend a hand, among them Tristan Bernard; Arthur Honegger who conducted his new ballet score and Serge Lifar who danced it; Arletty; and Victor Boucher. The only one who insisted on her usual fee was Mistinguett. The elderly charmer continued to display herself in the music hall when she was well over seventy, and she leads one to believe that the French really do prefer their women to be like wine, mature and well-aged. Or perhaps it is because women are less likely to re-sist as they grow older and weaker. "Who does Sacha think he is?"

she growled in her hideous suburban accent to the emissary who approached her. "He's nuts, your boss!" And because she could still command high figures she got what she wanted, for she had not yet reached the age when the ruthless critic D. B. Wyndham-Lewis was to describe her as "a rose-red cutie half as old as Time."

The epoch of Sacha's pre-war films ended gloriously with *Ils étaient neuf célibataires*. "And how delightful it is to move once again in a world of well-bred wit!" exclaimed James Agate on reviewing the film. Jean, a boulevardier of dubious habits, laments that he has so few opportunities of being honest. Twenty times a day a man gets the chance of being dishonest. "The proof is that dishonesty can become a profession. You know that people always talk of 'professional' thieves. It's illegal, of course, but you can live by it. While being honest just isn't a profession. A profession implies technique. Now, there's no technique about honesty. To prove you're honest you must have a profession already. A man who was honest alone and who could be nothing else would die of hunger. Being honest is a negative quality: it means doing nothing dishonest." Jean is able to put his philosophy into practice when he hears of a new law banishing all foreigners from Paris. Foreign women will be allowed to remain if they marry French husbands and acquire French nationality. Here is Jean's opportunity, and he sets up a Home for Old Bachelors. "I'm a middleman," he explains, "which means that I come between the seller and the buyer. I insinuate myself between the man who's on the point of paying a sum of money and the man who's to receive it. I transmit the money, so to speak, and levy a tax on it. You can't deny that in this world half of humanity is seeking the other half. For me, men and women are like apples cut in half: each half is in pursuit of the other. Anyway, don't men often call their wives their better half? Unfortunately, they often pick the wrong half. . . ." He has soon recruited a team of nine old bachelors from among the tramps of Paris, each of them a character in his own right and all nine of them variously blessed with the delectable names of Adolphe, Athanase, Adhémar, Anatole, Aristide, Antonin, Alexandre, Agénor, and Amédée.

Having assembled his masculine moieties Jean advertises for the other halves, which are not long in presenting themselves at his home in the varied shape of a Brazilian shopkeeper, a Chinese dancer, a Dutch millionairess, an American singer, a Russian countess, and two Frenchwomen. One of these French ladies is very rich and anxious for a husband so that she may benefit from the tax relief on married couples. The other is the proprietress of what she euphemistically describes as an underwear shop. She has just learned from the Vice Squad that by law the *directrices* of establishments like hers must be married women. (Such pleasing refinements were ended in the late nineteen-forties by the purity campaigns of the Paris councilor Madame Marthe Richard.) This leaves Jean with two complaining down-and-outs in hand. After all, he reminds them, this is a home for bachelors and some of them must remain here. The fortunes of their colleagues are shown with humor and not a little tenderness. Athanase discovers, to his horror, that by marriage he has acquired two policemen as sons-in-law. While a comfortable bed and good food are not to be lightly given up, he feels the price of freedom is too high and escapes back into the streets. Adhémar, married to the proprietress of the underwear shop, is introduced to what he imagines to be his dozen or so stepdaughters. Among them is a Negress. "That one of my predecessors was," he says, politely concealing his surprise, "a colonial, I presume?" Madame looks bland. "One of our French possessions, I hope?" he adds. Jean himself marries the Russian countess. By a dreadful coincidence Agénor, who had been her choice, turns out to have been the husband of her maid whom he had deserted many years ago. In any case, the countess's marriage ceremony had been rigged so that she was actually, but unknowingly, married to the farseeing Jean. "I love you!" he declares. "I hate you!" she snaps. "Which doesn't mean you don't love me," he assures her. Having chosen for

himself the best of the bunch, he settles down in marital felicity
to help her spend her vast fortune, to which may now be added
the middleman's fees he has garnered from his latest enterprise.

The French cinema has always been rich in players with the
ability to make out of small character parts exquisite cameo
portraits. *Ils étaient neuf célibataires* is like an anthology of them.
Adhémar was played by Saturnin Fabre, whose puffing delivery,
abrupt upward glances, and swooping squints gave a crazed dignity
to his speech. In one of his last films, *Clochemerle,* he played
the minister who inaugurates the useful but controversial edifice
that splits village opinion into two camps. He did so with the
fluttering bravura and devoted inconsequence of which he was
a master. As Sacha's Adhémar he added pathos to his acting.
Athanase was Max Dearly, whose flat features always looked as
if an iron had been passed over them and whose voice suggested
the creaking of a hinge that had never known oil. He was old
enough to have begun his career at the Moulin Rouge in a
novelty dance number with Mistinguett. Now, alas, he is dead, as
are all the others who played the nine bachelors. So, too, is
Marguerite Moreno, appearing with Sacha for the last time as
the much-befurred Brazilian with the reptile eye. Among the few
survivors is Elvire Popesco, the owner of a Rumanian accent and
a sense of fun that have enchanted generations of Parisians. Her
performances, which seem like inspired improvisation, are the
result of meticulous planning. She once took elaborate care in
choosing the exact color of a suit because, she explained, the
tears she had to weep in her part showed up much better on
pearl gray. As the manager of her own theater she has been
embroiled in many lawsuits, but even the plaintiffs have never
denied her their admiration. She is perhaps the last *monstre sacré*
of the French theater, carefully preserving the exotic voice which
thickens with the years as if conscious of its trademark value.
The part of the countess was tailor-made for her by Sacha, and
her haughty flamboyance filled it to perfection.

While Sacha was preparing to film *Ils étaient neuf célibataires*, King George VI and Queen Elizabeth made a State Visit to Paris. The celebrations included a *soirée* at the Palais de l'Élysée, the President's official home, and Sacha was invited to help with the entertainment. He wrote for the occasion a one-act play, *Dieu sauve le Roy*, which imagines the seventeenth-century British Ambassador, Lord Churchill, being received by Louis XIV. The idea was an opportunity for the actors to make graceful compliments to the royal couple in the audience, and at the end the whole company turned toward them and sang Lully's new cantata, *Dieu sauve le Roy*. The soprano Ninon Vallin then gave a brief recital accompanied by Reynaldo Hahn, and they were followed by the Comédie-Française in a Musset play. Sacha's little *à-propos* was played in sumptuous costumes, specially made for the evening, against a Gobelin tapestry. The part of the British Ambassador was taken by Austin Trevor, who, educated abroad, has fluent French and German and had already appeared in French performances of Sacha's plays. *"Tiens, chérie,"* said Sacha to his wife, "he speaks French as well as we do!" It was therefore a little disconcerting for him to be asked to speak with an English inflection, and the royal compliment after the performance had a double-edged ring in his ears: "I lost my program," said George VI, "but I recognized you immediately because of your accent."

Austin Trevor's engagement was handled, as was all Sacha's other business at this time, by an unusual character whose name was Bert Howell. C. B. Cochran had introduced Howell to Sacha in the 'thirties and he had been his impresario ever since. The contrast between Sacha's volatility and the British phlegm of his agent was entrancing. Bert Howell was a pure Cockney who settled in Paris and became a very successful artists' representative. He was lost sight of in the confusion of war and does not seem to have reappeared. In addition to his talent for negotiating contracts he had an astonishing gift for languages. One Christmas Day Cochran and his wife, together with Howell, were the only passengers on a train bound for Budapest. When they drew into the station there Howell said: "Now we start equal. They speak a language here which I know nothing about." By the next morning he had learned enough to ask his way. Within ten hours he was able to conduct small conversations. Before they left a few days later there was very little he did not understand or could not communicate in Hungarian. Howell didn't learn languages, said Cochran, he absorbed them.

It was a pity that Bert Howell could not pass on some of his linguistic accomplishments to Sacha, for a knowledge of English, which he spoke with a deal more fantasy than correctness, would have helped him in his next venture. In 1939 President Lebrun went to London to repay the State Visit of the previous year. There was a Command Performance with Edith Evans, John Gielgud, and Peggy Ashcroft, and Sacha was asked by the President to supply the French element. The courtyard of the India Office, lit by chandeliers beneath a yellow canopy, was filled with gilt chairs on red carpets for an entertainment designed by Sir Edward Lutyens and the grandson of Henry Irving. John Masefield, in his role as Poet Laureate, provided occasional verse of a suitably epic nature, and there was much play with skirling pipers, trumpeters in scarlet and gold, and *tableaux-vivants* of Britannia and Marianne. Sacha brought with him an incongruous playlet he had written under the title of *You're telling me,* in which he appeared with Seymour Hicks. The latter had been very successful with his own translation of *Faisons un rêve,* Englished as *Sleeping Partners,* and had acted Sacha's original part as well. Both actors had a great deal in common, including a determination not to be up-staged. To this end they improvised frenziedly, producing unexpected props and impromptu "business" in the effort to catch the other unawares. Hicks, of course, had the advantage in that Sacha knew little English. But he overplayed his hand. When Sacha realized that his partner was speaking too fast as a deliberate ploy, he withdrew into glacial silence. Discom-

fited, Hicks resumed his normal delivery and the sketch continued as they had first planned.

You're telling me made such an impression that the two actors
were offered billing at the London Coliseum. Three times a day
for a fortnight Sacha appeared with Hicks heading the variety
program, traveling back and forth between the Coliseum and the
Savoy, where his apartment had become a temporary office for
the writing and dictation of more plays, more films, and more
projects. Soon he had had enough. He wanted Paris again, his
house, and his theater. Before he left, however, he had charmed
one of his admirers with a diplomatic witticism. George VI came
to see him in his dressing room at the Coliseum. By the end of the
interval he had still not departed. "Sire," said Sacha, "I must
withdraw. I have an appointment with eight hundred people."
The King went off laughing. He returned at the next interval.
The same thing happened, and as the stage-manager was making
frantic signs, Sacha laid down his stick of make-up and observed:
"I apologize for the hurry, but I've been told that His Majesty the
King is to be among the audience. . . ."

Before leaving Paris Sacha had taken some of the current de-
velopments in his private life and used them for his new play,
Un monde fou. Elvire Popesco, as a headstrong capering wife,
heard him each night give her the benefit of his thoughts on
divorce: "It's a conclusion, a consequence, the logical completion
of a marriage. It's like the last scene in a drama—for isn't it
dramatic when two people live together without loving each
other?" It was Jacqueline Delubac's last play with Sacha. As the
cast took their bow he ostentatiously kissed her hand. "Why
make such an exhibition?" she protested. "Because we're part of
the show," he replied easily. "It's not my wife's hand I'm kissing
but the hand of an excellent actress." He no longer followed her
movements with a jealous eye and was indifferent to her going
on alone. He was only too pleased when she crossed the road to
visit her mother who lived in a block of flats opposite the house

in the avenue Élisée-Reclus. *"Va chez ta mère . . . comme d'habitude,"* he would murmur absently, and switch his attention to other things. Chosen by American newspapers as one of the five best-dressed women in the world, she would go on long solitary tours of the *couturiers* and return with her latest purchase to show him. And then, raising his arms heavenwards, he would say, just like any other husband and not at all in the manner of the great lover: "Tasteless! The green is awful. I hate green. It doesn't go with your eyes at all. Take off that dress and put on your blue one . . ." The next thing the household knew was that he had disappeared on his own to Switzerland. Everyone was surprised except Jacqueline.

Chapter 13

ೂ೨ *Why have I bothered to go through the marriage ceremony
with each of my wives? I have done so, Madame, for the
sake of my English public.*

SACHA GUITRY

*T*he resorts of Lausanne and Montreux are not notorious
for their vivacity. The thought of all those solid Swiss earnestly
making money by catering for wealthy invalids and hearty sports-
men inspires edification rather than excitement. Yet, in a land
whose only concession to frivolity has been the invention of the
cuckoo-clock, Sacha was now enjoying one of his gayest holidays. In
the restaurant of a private clinic a roomful of hypochondriacs quite
forgot their "nerves" as he made a superb entrance, negligently
dropping his fur coat on the almoner who happened to be near
the door, and improvising a comic scene in which the ruffled
proprietor fed him involuntarily with excellent cues. On a shopping trip in Lausanne's most expensive store he took over from a
saleswoman who was battling with an awkward customer and,
after a few moments of voluble flattery, persuaded the dazed
customer to buy a lavish crocodile-skin suitcase. His permanent audience included a young lady whose presence acted as a

stimulant. Her name was Geneviève de Séréville and she was
playing the part Jacqueline Delubac had filled when Sacha had
gone to Switzerland before his divorce from Yvonne Printemps.

Mademoiselle de Séréville came of an old and respected Parisian family. She had spent three years at a finishing school in
England and was preserved from temptation by a battery of chaperones. Her leisure moments were genteelly occupied with lessons
in deportment, singing, dancing, and acting. Or so her family
believed. One night at the theater, when the play happened by a
quaint chance to be *Quadrille,* she was introduced to Sacha by
Baron Max Fould-Springer, a friend who had lent him his country house for location shots of *les Perles de la couronne.* Mademoiselle de Séréville had already flirted, in vague well-bred fashion,
with the entertainment world, for she had been elected "Miss
Cinémonde" by a film magazine. Sacha fully approved the choice
of *Cinémonde* readers. With the energy he reserved for the important things of life, he devoted himself to the pursuit of
Mademoiselle de Séréville. She came to tea at the avenue Élisée-
Reclus, where, having consumed English tea-cakes from *chez*
Smith and Son, she was conducted around the pictures and the
autographs and the art objects under the lackluster eye of Jacqueline Delubac. No chaperone, however watchful, could insulate
her charge against the attraction of the large bouquets which piled
up in the hall, the irresistible notes that accompanied them, or
the telegrams which arrived every hour. Meanwhile, the separation from the third Madame Guitry became a divorce. Jacqueline
Delubac still appears on the stage today. Her tip-tilted nose and
her sparkling eye are as appealing as ever, and the streaks of gray
which now tint her hair make her look even more attractive.

"He'll be after Shirley Temple next," remarked, so it is said,
Yvonne Printemps, speaking this time from the sidelines. Sacha's
prospective father-in-law was less amused. "I can only despise a
man who behaves so lightly and impudently with a young girl,"
he raged. His daughter's suitor was, to be exact, more than thirty

years older than her. The fact was emphasized by an incident which occurred on their return from Switzerland. They were accosted in the street by an elderly woman wearing a veil. "Sacha . . ." she murmured with a trembling voice. "Don't you recognize me?" She raised her veil to uncover the weary features of Charlotte Lysès, his first wife. She wept, and then, swallowing her tears: "Sacha, you don't know what happiness it is for me to see you again. I'd wanted it so much. Be happy, *mon petit*." An embarrassed Sacha replied: "Is there anything I can do for you?" "No, it's over now, there's nothing you can do for me. I can die happy now, I've seen you again. I've known the happiness of talking to you again." She tugged off her glove and stroked his hand with wrinkled faltering fingers. "I have a very sweet memory to take away with me. A sunny one, because I see that *printemps* is at your side. It suits you well. It's always been the season that suits you best." She dropped the veil over her sobs and abruptly walked back down the street. He had married and divorced her twenty years ago before Geneviève's birth. They went on their way haunted by a ghost from the past.

To escape the strained atmosphere at home and the protests of the de Séréville family, they went to Holland and looked at the pictures that always gave Sacha a feeling of peace. From Amsterdam they traveled to Vevey again and on to Salzburg, where the tedium of *Die Meistersinger,* so out of place in the town that belonged to the man whom Sacha termed "the height of art, the heavenly Mozart," drove them out into the foyer. Here they were greeted by a terrifying bellow of "Sâââ . . . châââ" from Chaliapin, whose delight at meeting his friend expressed itself in mighty roars. Over supper and long into the night the two men joked and talked in a cascade of admiring chatter until Geneviève, exhausted with fatigue, crept off to bed leaving Sacha asleep in his chair and Chaliapin extended on a sofa, his great length supported at one end by a heap of cushions. Then came Monte Carlo, La Bourboule, and Geneviève's complaint: "I've got nothing to wear!" At half past nine a small pageboy with a small packet knocked at her door. Inside the packet were handkerchiefs of Alençon lace and the opening sentence of a letter: "Once upon a time. . . ." At ten o'clock a slightly taller pageboy handed her a box containing three Hermès scarves and a further instalment of the letter: "Once upon a time there was. . . ." At a quarter past ten came a medium-sized pageboy with a medium-sized box of underwear and the letter: "Once upon a time there was a gentleman very much in love with. . . ." Quarter of an hour later came a large pageboy with a large box of sweaters and coats: "Once upon a time there was a gentleman very much in love with a girl who. . . ." At half past ten the first pageboy returned with a Lanvin parcel, much too big for him, containing a suit, dress, and coat: "Once upon a time there was a gentleman very much in love with a girl who, having nothing. . . ." Fifteen minutes afterwards the second pageboy came back with an elegantly wrapped fur coat: "Once upon a time there was a gentleman very much in love with a girl who, having nothing to wear, was obliged to agree. . . ." And at half past eleven all the pageboys who had taken part in the little comedy entered carrying cases of clothes and the full letter: "Once upon a time there was a gentleman very much in love with a girl who, having nothing to wear, was obliged to agree to being dressed entirely by him. But morality won't suffer, because the gentleman is her future husband." Whereupon Sacha himself appeared on the threshold his arms full of jewelry: "I forgot all the trinkets that go with it. . . ." he apologized.

Geneviève made one small gesture toward her estranged family by insisting that they be married in a church. An interview with the Archbishop of Paris found Sacha at his most pontifical, and the two men gravely compared notes on prelatical costume. One would have thought the Archbishop was speaking with a colleague in plain dress until Sacha acted several scenes from his plays on the spot. "How do you manage to act churchmen so well without having very much to do with them?" asked His Eminence a shade ironically. Sacha was not unprepared. "It's hereditary," he explained to his startled companion. "Though we were all actors on my father's side, my maternal great-uncle was Bishop of Le Mans." With such impeccable antecedents to back his claim, the hierarchy which had denied a Christian burial to Molière was loath to forbid his descendant from entering its establishments. The marriage took place in the church of Fontenay-le-Fleury, the little village between Versailles and Rambouillet which had become Sacha's parish upon his recent acquisition there of a country house. For the first time he stood with his back to an audience, and for the first time also he played a part with the briefest of speeches and was overshadowed by the officiating Archbishop in his purple robes. After fighting their way through the crowds of sightseers, journalists, and policemen, the newly married couple drove back to the Château de Ternay. It was an excellent spot for a honeymoon. Originally a hunting box owned by Louis XIII, Ternay sat discreetly among well-tailored lawns and vistas of grottoes, ornamental pools, and flower beds that might have been drawn by Poussin. Resplendent guinea-fowl chattered along the gravel in front of the house, and through the miniature farmyard there marched ducks three by three. In a spacious park at the rear Sacha had assembled a collection of rare animals which included Numidian cranes, pink ibis, and deer. He took after Lucien and played the gentleman-farmer, dressing for the part in a Russian shirt buttoned at the shoulder, linen trousers, old knee-boots his father had worn in one of his plays, and a vast straw hat embellished with a feather. His eyes took on the dreamy look of a man used to staring into the distance, his gestures became slow and precise, like a peasant's, and he spoke with a countryman's burr. "We'll turn the place into a farm," he cried, and went on a tour of nearby farmers purchasing animals by the dozen. Vans arrived with drivers asking where to deliver their livestock. "Let them all out and shut the main gate behind you!" he ordered. A multitude of hens, pigeons, ducks, sheep, peacocks, rabbits, cows, and pigs blundered noisily across the lawn, ignoring the instructions he shouted through a megaphone. Then he forgot all about it and left the sheepdogs to snap at the turkeys while he went off and dictated another play.

Next month (it was the August of 1939) they went down to Sacha's house at Cap d'Ail. Sacha needed a rest, for the past few weeks had brought him not only a new wife but also membership of the Académie Goncourt. It is difficult for the Anglo-Saxon to appreciate the importance of this body, which for literary prestige is second only to the Académie Française. Its membership is restricted to ten writers only. Election to its ranks excites as much passion as does election to the "forty" of the Académie. Each year it awards a prize to a current novel, and although the value of the sum has been eroded by years of inflation, the *prix Goncourt* is eagerly solicited for the thousands of extra copies it can add to sales. It is for this, together with their notorious *Journal*, rather than for their unsuccessful plays and depressing novels, that the Goncourt brothers are remembered. They were a snobbish and feline pair, much attached to each other, who wrote all their works together and kept a journal of their association with famous authors of the time. No scandal was too small, no rumor too insubstantial for them to record, and whoever wishes to document the sex life of Daudet or of Flaubert, to mention two of their friends, need only turn to the *Journal*. The Goncourts took a cynical and uncharitable view of their colleagues. For this reason there is hardly an unreadable page in their fascinating *Journal*.

Edmond de Goncourt was the elder and also the last to die. In his will he charged Alphonse Daudet, his executor, with the task of forming a society of men of letters to award an annual prize for a literary work. By the time all the legal complications had been sorted out in 1903, Daudet himself was dead, as were most of those whom Goncourt had hoped would belong, including Flaubert and Zola. The most famous members of the Académie Goncourt as originally constituted became Huysmans, the deca-

dent-turned-Catholic novelist, Octave Mirbeau, and Léon Daudet, the son of Alphonse. Léon was still a member when Sacha's
election was proposed. A ferocious anti-semite and co-editor with
Charles Maurras of the royalist *Action Française,* where his
invective was so extreme that it went beyond even the tolerant
French laws of libel, Daudet was inevitably the center of a storm.
During his forty or so years of violent campaigns there were few
politicians who escaped his excremental abuse. He offered no
objection to Sacha. "Guitry?" he said. "He's a man of the world.
And after all, at least he's never said he likes the Republic." His
friend, the poet Léo Larguier, agreed with him. The novelist
Roland Dorgelès also emerged as a supporter. Francis Carco, an
author of somewhat faded and artificial novels about Montmartre
life, was undecided. Sacha's warmest ally was René Benjamin.
He was a fertile writer whose productions included a popular life
of Balzac, a best-selling novel about trench-warfare, and several
quite shrewdly observed accounts of legal life. Bitter opposition
came, however, from Lucien Descaves. This abrasive personage
had written a grimy little novel entitled *Sous-off's* as far back as
1889. It purported to be a sensational exposure of army life and
owed something to his early friendship with Zola. Since then he
had produced other novels and plays, but his main preoccupation
was the Académie Goncourt. For no good reason, he saw himself
as the guardian of its founder's intention. He rushed around
barking out objurgations and conducting himself like the fiery
sergeant-majors he had satirized in his one successful novel. When
he wrote: "It seems incongruous to me that an actor should sit
at a table once frequented by purely literary men like Huysmans,"
the stage was set for one of those dramas which lend to French
intellectual life so much of its vivaciousness.

Sacha himself was not averse to joining the Goncourt. He had
a personal reason in that Mirbeau, Renard, and Courteline, three
of the writers he most admired, had once belonged to it. Descaves's
fury increased. He was convinced of the virtues of poverty and

wretchedness. It seemed monstrous to him that a rich dramatist and actor should be allowed to rub shoulders with humbler slaves of the pen. The gibes at "our Narcissus, Pacha Guitry," were multiplied, and he even threatened to resign if Sacha were elected. The affair was taken up by the newspapers and opinion was divided between those who, like Descaves, were unable to forgive success, and others who did not happen to suffer from this form of inverted snobbery. At the election meeting, which took place, as did all the transactions of the Académie Goncourt, at the Restaurant Drouot in the place Gaillon, Sacha was voted a member. That evening the new academician replied in a broadcast to the attacks that had been made on him: "For twenty years Descaves has been criticizing my plays. He is more to be pitied than I am if he doesn't like them, because he is obliged to go and see them, whereas I never read his articles. He has spoken of his intention to leave if I entered the Académie Goncourt. That is one of the reasons that encouraged me to let my candidature go forward, since I have never approved of the election of Monsieur Descaves and neither have I understood how he managed it. So I am not dissatisfied at having been the means of getting him out." It was all rather cruel, but the egregious Descaves did nothing to improve his case when he meekly crept back and spoke no more of resigning.

The Goncourt affair would probably have bloomed into further diverting incidents had it not been for the menace of war. Sacha was bored with his friends' talk of strategy and politics. Anxious discussion about Daladier and Gamelin left him cold. He did not understand. The stage was all he knew about and he cared for little else. On the declaration of war in September the theaters were closed. Sacha roamed the house unhappily, rummaging through his wardrobe and make-up box, appearing on the stairs as Louis XIV or limping along the passage as Talleyrand. Then the theaters were re-opened and in October he was able to mount a

program of one-act plays at the Madeleine. With him were Victor
Boucher, Gaby Morlay, and Geneviève, for whom this was her
Parisian début. She was not, as her predecessors had been, a professional actress, but Sacha was able to "produce" her in a way
that skillfully concealed her lack of experience.

A few weeks later he revived *Florence,* a pre-war success he
had put on with Elvire Popesco, and he rounded off the evening
by bringing out again the film *Ceux de chez nous.* Events had
given those brief views of great Frenchmen a fresh poignancy.
Actors, writers, artists, musicians, and sculptors passed across the
screen as a reminder of a heritage threatened anew by sinister
forces. In the bleak opening months of 1940 Sacha was on a tour
of the south. At Nice he gave a lecture which had already formed
the basis of some earlier radio talks called *Lettres d'amour,* and
he delved into his incomparable autograph collection for the
material. From them he drew the conclusions which embodied
his experience of a lifetime. "If I take the liberty of saying that I
don't like women," he warned, "it is, of course, because I adore
them." The effect of these remarks on Geneviève, who heard
them with all the simplicity of her twenty years, was confusing.
She thought that her husband was talking of some other species
of human being. "Beware of the women you marry," Sacha told
his audience, "because the ones who don't deceive you will re-
proach you for it all their lives—as if it were your fault, while
often enough it isn't even theirs!" He spoke of the wives whose
infidelity is the only link that still binds them to their husbands;
and of the women who sometimes imagine they have fallen in love
with a man when all along it's only because they've taken a dislike to his wife. He mentioned with approval a wise friend of his
who had ". . . married his old mistress so as not to be tempted one
day or another into marrying for love." And he ended with a
definition of true love: "It's no very serious matter to love a woman
for her qualities . . . but when you love her for her defects, then

it's the real thing!" Yet after all, with a shrug of the shoulders, he was to admit: "I have always longed to fall into the arms of beautiful women. All I have done is to fall into their hands."

In May they were in the southwest at Dax taking the waters. With a group of friends including Elvire Popesco, Albert Willemetz, and the novelist Pierre Benoit, they gathered in front of the radio to hear Marshal Pétain announce that France was suing for an Armistice. Next month German troops entered the town and the hotel was requisitioned. After inspecting the register their general invited Sacha, the most distinguished of the guests, to have coffee with him. Pale and furious, he went with Geneviève under orders and never referred to the incident afterward except to say: "The coffee was undrinkable." There were now many other exiles from the Paris theaters in Dax, and on hearing of Sacha's interview they rushed to see him. "Who better than you, Sacha," they claimed, "to represent us? Who better than you could defend our interests and those of French actors?" He was flattered by their arguments and touched by their confidence in him. But he was no politician, and he failed to notice that those who were the most persuasive were also the least anxious to support him openly in his negotiations with the occupant. He had made the first in a series of unfortunate misjudgments that were to cost him dear several years later.

Henry Bergson was staying in the hotel next door and Sacha went to seek his advice. He was very ill and racked with pain, though his mind remained lucid. Sacha asked whether he should go to his house at Cap d'Ail or to Paris. "Why, to Paris, of course," replied Bergson, "since you owe everything to Paris! I want to go back there myself, and without delay. I shall try to go through Tours and see if my house is still standing. The next day I shall set off again for Paris." He asked Sacha to get him the safe-conduct pass that was necessary. After visits to the town hall and the Kommandatur, Sacha returned with two safe-conduct passes. The Germans there had spoken of Bergson as "the great philosopher"

—but not as a Jew. Thus he was able to go to Paris and six months later to die as he had wished in his own home.* Sacha and Geneviève made the journey along roads crammed with refugees pushing loaded prams and carts containing their possessions. On either side the verges were littered with abandoned lorries and dead horses.

When they reached the outskirts of Paris they found the country house at Ternay occupied by German troops. Anxious about the fate of his home in the avenue Élisée-Reclus, Sacha pressed on to the city and was relieved to discover it intact. Surrounded once again by his beloved possessions he began to take new heart. His immediate circle again urged him to put himself forward as a kind of ambassador for the French theater. "You're such a clever diplomatist, Sacha!" they murmured. He believed them. Faced with a stiff and heavily departmentalized bureaucracy, he indulged in rash and harebrained schemes to achieve his ends. His excessive confidence in himself, a quality which he had never lacked, his belief that he knew how to handle men and that he possessed the diplomatic gifts of his hero Talleyrand, all combined with his naïvety to lead him deeper into folly. While he imagined that he was cleverly charming concessions out of the Nazi authorities on behalf of less influential people, he was in fact committing imprudence after imprudence. Those who received favors as a result of his intervention were quick to disclaim any knowledge of them, though they were happy enough to benefit from his misguided kindness. A few close friends, among them Albert Willemetz, warned him of the dangerous situation he was creating for himself. They were grandly disregarded.

The theaters, which had closed their doors at the Armistice,

* Bergson deliberately exposed himself to the degrading obligations which the Nazis forced on French Jews. Although he could easily have had exemption, he resigned his chair at the Collège de France; a few weeks before his death he left his bed in slippers and dressing-gown and, leaning on his servant's arm, walked to the local office and registered himself as a Jew. In fact he had been coming round to Catholicism in his later years, but the rise of anti-semitism inspired him to stay in the ranks of the persecuted.

now re-opened again, and Sacha could feel that some good at least had come from the hours spent cooling his heels in the waiting rooms of the Nazi administration. The first attraction to be announced on the posters of the Théâtre des Ambassadeurs indicated a return to normality with the characteristic title *Nous ne sommes pas mariés*. More realistically, the Opéra offered *la Damnation de Faust*. Sacha himself revived *Pasteur*. One evening during its run he took advantage of a visit by a high-ranking German official to ask him for the release of ten French prisoners whose names had been given him by friends. The official agreed. The news soon spread, and for the rest of the war years Sacha was to be inundated with similar appeals from desperate relatives. At the time he was simple enough to feel honored. Only much later did he realize that people can rarely forgive you the good turns you do them.

In August Sacha put on *Ceux de chez nous* again. Night after night Sarah Bernhardt was seen once more, even though the Nazi censorship had decreed that because of her Jewish blood her name was not to be mentioned and her theater was henceforward to be known as the Théâtre de la Cité. "She it is whom I regard as my second mother," Sacha remarked in his spoken commentary on the film. This incautious *boutade* was perhaps responsible for his being denounced as a Jew shortly afterwards, and several collaborationist newspapers seized on the charge. Sacha was forced to go through the imbecile process of collecting his family's birth certificates as far back as his great-grandmother in order to prove his Aryan descent. To make quite sure, he gathered corroborative evidence from the Chief Rabbi of Paris. "Am I Jewish?" he asked. "No, alas!" was the charming reply. These were the days when the rue Henri-Heine was renamed the rue Jean Sébastien-Bach, and when thirty thousand Jewish men, women, and children were herded into the Vélodrome d'Hiver, a famous sports stadium, and sent off to concentration camps. Wearing the yellow star which the Nazis ordered members of their race to display, Tristan

Bernard and his wife were arrested at Cannes. Someone had asked him what he wanted as a New Year's present. *"Un cache-nez* [muffler]," he answered with a mournful pun, gesturing at the unmistakable shape of his nose. He had prefaced a recent lecture with the comment: "I belong, ladies and gentlemen, to what is known as the chosen race . . . or rather, I should say, a race that is up for a second vote." As soon as he heard the news Sacha flew to his aid. A visit to the German Embassy with Arletty and the pianist Alfred Cortot quickly procured the release of the seventy-seven-year-old humorist and his wife, and they were transferred to a hospital. "To Sacha," wrote Tristan in one of his books, "who snatched me, and I shall never forget it, out of the Germans' claws."

There were many others who had cause for gratitude toward Sacha. Paul Valéry wrote asking for help. Sacha put his car at his disposal and managed to obtain coffee and cigarettes for him, "the coal I need to keep my little old factory working," as the chain-smoking Valéry remarked. Colette's Jewish husband was rescued from exile and certain death through Sacha's aid. Among the humble and the famous who sheltered gratefully under Sacha's benevolent wing were Madame Courteline, the widow of Marshal Joffre, the producer Antoine who had fallen on hard days, the poet Max Jacob, the Clemenceau family, Madame Matisse, and innumerable people who came to him begging for help in a variety of matters which ranged from tracing sons vanished in German concentration camps to providing extra milk for aged grandparents. To all of them he gave a sympathetic hearing.

France now was divided into two zones, the Occupied and the "Free" Zone. The pleasant little spa of Vichy was startled to find its name becoming a political term, for it was here that Marshal Pétain set up his government. The quiet tree-shaded walks and trim gardens, recently the scene of nothing more dramatic than the recreation of liverish *bons vivants,* emerged unexpectedly as a background to the myriad plots of an administration which depended for its brittle existence on the favor of a Nazi master. This sad episode in the history of France is marked above all by two figures who stood out in the twilit atmosphere of un-reality, the one a distinguished soldier with a glorious past, the other a subtle and experienced politician. Marshal Pétain was eighty-four when he became Prime Minister, and he already had behind him a career full enough to satisfy any man. An obscure army officer in 1914, he had been abruptly summoned one night from the bed of his mistress to take command at Verdun. His defense of the town made him a national hero, and in 1918 he received the highest honor the French army can bestow. Be-tween the two wars, except for a brief embassy to Spain, he ob-served events from the wings and sharpened his sardonic wit on the politicians and civilians for whom he had a soldier's traditional contempt. An unusually long life encouraged his innate prudence and far-sighted caution (he did not marry until he was sixty-four) and when he opened an official statement with the words: "We, Philippe Pétain, Marshal of France . . ." it was as if the father of the nation was speaking. At the moment of taking office he could draw on an immense fund of goodwill. People generally regarded him as the savior of Verdun, a man above politics and a leader unstained by connections with pre-war governments.

His partner in the grotesque tandem that ran the fragile Vichy regime was Pierre Laval. From his father, a tough Auvergnat tavern-keeper, Laval had inherited his shrewd peasant gift for horse-trading. He was in his element at hostile political meetings, where he nearly always triumphed over unruly audiences. (He defended himself brilliantly at the post-war treason trials. Had the court been guided by logic rather than by a wild desire for vengeance, it is possible that he would not have been executed.) In business, too, he had a golden touch that ensured the prosperity of his big legal practice, his newspaper, and his bottling company which had the monopoly of supplying mineral waters to the French railways. Laval never escaped his earthy origins. He kept his banknotes in a chest and was always counting them in spare moments. His personal foible, the notorious white tie, was for him the height of elegance, yet although he indulged in constant baths he rarely succeeded in making his sallow complexion look quite clean. He took an understandable pride in the expertise that kept him almost a permanent member of the swift kaleidoscope of governments before the war. "If only Ma could see me now!" the former country lad exulted one day as he emerged from the Vatican after an audience with the Pope.

While Pétain at Vichy issued the unexciting exhortation *Travail! Famille! Patrie!* to replace the more inflammatory slogan of *Liberté! Egalité! Fraternité!*, Occupied Paris returned to a life that was more or less normal. If, that is, the adjective may be applied to an existence outwardly policed by a strict bureaucracy, though characterized not far from the surface by unrest, murder and Gestapo savagery in the back rooms of small hotels. The Resistance movement was already in action and went its way undeterred by the brutal executions of innocent Frenchmen. Yet for many people there was little that could be done. Those who are lucky enough never to have seen their country occupied by an enemy power find it difficult to envisage the true situation. They tend to imagine that every man, woman, and child should be perpetually harrying the Occupant, and that those who do not should be branded as traitors and collaborators. Unfortunately, however nasty the circumstances, life has to go on, unless a country wishes to commit suicide. Children must be educated, a living must be earned, food must still be distributed, and trains must be run.

Sacha was only one of the men who carried on with their normal work. In October 1940 he produced *le Bien Aimé* at the Madeleine. He still had the costumes which were made for his film *Remontons les Champs-Élysées,* and it seemed a waste not to use them. The leading characters were Louis XIV and Pompadour, and the play was a light but pointed reference to the achievements of the national genius. While Fragonard draws a picture of Pompadour, Voltaire recites Molière. "Voltaire and Fragonard—France!" says the King on entering. It is not feats of arms that make a country, he reflects: "I think of the victories that are carried off by a La Tour pastel, or by ten lines of your poetry." "By that reckoning, then," says Voltaire, "Molière would have been a Marshal of France." The King agrees: "He *is*, Monsieur— just as Descartes and Pascal are our best ambassadors."

Another play was *Vive l'Empereur!* which had been written in 1938. Its first title, *le Soir d'Austerlitz,* was, with reason, censored by the Nazi authorities who did not wish to be reminded of Napoleon's victory over the Austrians in 1805. The play gave harmless amusement to a lot of people and ran for just under a year. It was succeeded by *N'écoutez pas, Mesdames!* which had six hundred consecutive performances over a period of two years. Sacha played an antique-dealer who, in the first act, comes guardedly on to the stage and addresses the men in the audience: "Don't get married!" he tells them. "And don't listen, ladies, because of course it's the men I'm talking to. Do we realize that when we marry a woman we alter the situation she was in the day we first met, the day we took a fancy to her? Now, didn't we like her precisely because she was in that situation? I'll explain. She was married, I expect. We fell madly in love with her. We got divorced. We married. And we realized, too late, that it was because she was married that we fell in love with her. We fell for a free, independent woman—which is normal. But the moment we married her she ceased to be free, and, as a result, she began to interest us much less."

Among the characters who wander through this unusual antique shop for no other reason than to divert the audience is an ancient lady who is supposed to have worked as a model for Toulouse-Lautrec. She was played, with a ginger wig and a rusty "parigote" accent, by Jeanne Fusier-Gir, another of those accomplished character actresses for whom Sacha always found a place. *N'écoutez pas, Mesdames!* was for many Parisians a bright spot in an atmosphere of increasing gloom. It contained many discreet references to daily life. "Are you really an antique-dealer?" asks one of the characters. "No, I'm standing in for somebody who's run into bad luck," is the reply, which evokes the plight of all those little businesses whose Jewish owners had vanished after a knock on the door at dead of night.

Sacha's other theatrical activities during the Occupation took the form of many charity shows for refugees, prisoners, and war wounded. The gala at the Comédie-Française on behalf of Antoine was an ambitious affair. By raising nearly half a million francs to help the great director, Sacha at once paid tribute to an honored name and discharged something of the personal debt he owed Antoine for encouragement in his early days. The films he made during this period were a strange assortment. The first, a historical confection based on the life of Désirée Clary, was hastily put together in 1941 so that Sacha might have the excuse of pleading other engagements when Nazi film companies asked him to work for them. Two years later, *Donne-moi tes yeux* was remarkable for scenes that featured in person the artists Maurice Vlaminck, Dunoyer de Segonzac, Utrillo, Raoul Dufy, and André Derain. The third film was *la Malibran,* in which a novel piece of casting offered the beautiful Géori Boué as the nineteenth-century contralto, and Jean Cocteau, conscripted in the name of friendship, as a most poetic Alfred de Musset. Another four years were to pass until Sacha's next appearance on the screen, and in any case the production of films under a regime which viewed the medium simply as a vehicle for propaganda aroused difficulties enough.

A more interesting project arose out of a lecture Sacha gave one evening at the Théâtre de la Madeleine. His subject had been five hundred years of French history and two enterprising publishers saw in it an idea for a book. They gave him the freedom of choosing writers and artists to help in compiling a symposium about France and its story, the work to be issued as an *édition de luxe* with the proceeds going to charity. There followed several enjoyable weeks of sharing out subjects among his friends—Paul Valéry chose Descartes, Balzac fell to Colette, Pierre Benoit took Victor Hugo, and Jean Giraudoux and Cocteau, in company with many other noted writers, contributed essays on the Frenchmen of their choice. The editor saw no reason to aryanize his country's history. In a spirit of mischief he went out of his way to give honorable mention to French people of Jewish extraction. He even got away with a reproduction of Zola's historic letter in which he defended Dreyfus against his anti-semitic tormentors.

At last the book was ready. The paper was thick and luxurious. Upon the magnificent binding was stamped in gold letters the title: *1429–1942, de Jeanne d'Arc à Philippe Pétain*. Sacha took the first copy to show to an important person. The latter slowly turned over the pages, stopping sometimes to read aloud a sentence that had caught his attention, or to chuckle at an epigram. Then he closed the book and said: "Monsieur Guitry, it's a very beautiful piece of work. But I don't like the title."

"Why?" asked Sacha.

"You must change it."

"Forgive me, but that's impossible, if only from a practical point of view. And anyway, I like the title."

"You must change it, Monsieur Guitry."

"No. I shall disobey you."

"Very well. You'll be sent to prison."

"All right, I shall go to prison without knowing why."

"Monsieur Guitry, don't you understand that I am telling you this *for your own sake?*" replied Marshal Pétain in a soft voice, his blue eyes full of warning.

Chapter 14

The four years of the Occupation and then the Liberation clearly showed what the spur of political and racial hatred, combined with self-interest and covetousness, could inspire in the way of unworthy acts and words by men who believe themselves to be the most honest people in the world.

FRANÇOIS MAURIAC
Mémoires Intérieures (1959)

One day in the early years of the war a very famous French actress landed on the shores of England after a circuitous flight from Paris. The arrival of this distinguished lady was marked by a press conference at which she was liberal of her views for the benefit of the assembled journalists. "Of all the actors who remained and collaborated, the worst is Sacha Guitry," she declared with more conviction than she was accustomed to show in her dramatic roles. "He is rich. He did not need to sacrifice his honor. Yet he has gone out of his way to cultivate the enemy and entertain General von Stulpnagel." The force of this spirited condemnation was marred by the tiresome fact that Sacha had never set eyes upon General von Stulpnagel. When she had in this manner fulfilled her patriotic duty, the actress then continued her career in films made on British soil until such time as liberated Paris was fortunate enough once more to bask in the radiance of her gracious talent.

In 1942 the good work was furthered by *Life* magazine. Sacha's name was included in their "black list" of Frenchmen sentenced by the underground movement to be shot when France was liberated. He was in good company. Those destined for the tumbril included the novelist Céline, General Weygand, Maurice Chevalier, the artist André Derain, Marcel Pagnol, Mistinguett, and the boxer Georges Carpentier. When Sacha received the press-cutting he thought it a joke in bad taste. "And anyway," he said, "to call oneself *Life* and to ask for death is a rather odd thing to do."

At the same time his marriage was falling apart. Geneviève was bored. If, as Sacha frequently proclaimed, love and the theater were his two great passions in life, then the second was often the more dominant. He sat in his study dreaming up *coups de théâtre,* his thoughts pleasurably engrossed in curtain lines and denouements, while Geneviève drifted fretfully from room to room or fidgeted with a piece of embroidery. She went out on long shopping trips, alone, and Sacha's face remained expressionless when he heard her go. Capricious and voluble, she would explode into a torrent of rebukes at the smallest incident. Sacha's reserve was unshakeable. He listened patiently to her outbursts and turned away to dictate a remark that had just occurred to him: "There are certain people who talk and talk and talk— until they've at last found something to say."

The situation began to resolve itself in time-honored fashion. There were hints of divorce, until Sacha remembered his pledge to Geneviève's father that he would never abandon her. He proposed a solution which would have made an effective second-act curtain. He had, indeed, already used it in one of his plays. The idea was to divorce her and then adopt her as his daughter. Horrified lawyers pointed out that although the court room had much in common with the stage, the legal code had not been drafted by a playwright's hand, and Sacha, regretfully, gave up the plan. In the April of 1944 the fourth Madame Guitry packed her bags and followed the by now well-worn path of her predecessors. Sacha immediately embarked on his favorite pastime of rearranging the pictures, changing the furniture around, and revising the décor so that all memory of Geneviève was neatly tidied away. Down from the attic came the Utrillos he had recently acquired but till now had been unable to find room for; up from the cellar came the Degas sketches, bought years ago, to take the place of the Modiglianis and the van Goghs that reminded him all too sharply of the past few stormy weeks.

A new face appeared in the house, that of a gay and humorous film actress who shall be known as "Mariette." First she came to tea, her dazzling smile contrasting with the petulance that had formerly clouded the atmosphere. Then she began to stay for dinner. When the air raids and a strict curfew made night travel in Paris difficult, she installed herself, at Sacha's suggestion, in a block of flats opposite his house. (It may have amused him that she thus found herself a close neighbor of Jacqueline Delubac who also lived there.) The month of August was excessively hot, and for "Mariette," sunbathing on the terrace, Sacha rehearsed his latest play. She lay there in silent admiration, nodding her head delightedly at his improvised "business" and chuckling as cue succeeded cue. Sacha had never had such a receptive audience. "Come and see," he enthused to his secretary. "She's wonderful. She catches on to everything I say and do. She's full of intelligence. . . ."

Early that month the Germans began to evacuate Paris. Laval was hurriedly escorted from the city and the Resistance movement came out of the shadows. Allied forces landed on the French coast and General Leclerc's tanks began to rumble along dusty roads under the hot white sunshine. They reached the suburbs and thundered into the heart of Paris on the 25 August. As General de Gaulle attended a thanksgiving service in Notre Dame, a fusillade of machine-gun fire sprayed the steps outside. Infuriated crowds bore down upon German prisoners and gouged out their

eyes. Women suspected of collaborating had their heads shaved
and were marched through the streets. "My — is international but
by heart is French!" declared one notorious courtesan with a
Rabelaisian sense of humor that prevailed over the situation in
which she found herself.

The liberation of Paris heralded a period which for bloodshed
and horror far surpassed the days of Terror during the Revolutionary epoch. Committees of purification were set up to punish
traitors and collaborators. It was an excellent opportunity for paying off old scores. Among the culprits who so fully deserved the
penalty they paid there were also many innocent victims. The
denunciations that poured in were often the result of personal
vendettas. A sacked employee, a neighbor with a grudge, a spurned
mistress, all now discovered a potent means of revenge. In the
blaze of anger that swept the country after four years of cruel re-
pression no one was in a mood for careful investigation of each
case. The village squares of obscure hamlets far from the center
of government saw many a killing that owed its origin to private
spite. Although the records of local prefectures are strangely de-
fective, it is estimated that something like forty thousand summary
executions took place. These were the work not of the Gestapo
or of its sinister henchmen in the *Milice,* but of Frenchmen
against Frenchmen.

The "purification" of the literary world benefited from those
resources of rancor and envy that men of letters can always draw
upon so amply. One writer was condemned to death by a jury
which included his former typist. Another was hounded down
because, twenty years before, he had presided over some obscure
Franco-German cultural committee. Others were exposed to public shame for reasons equally notional. One of the most prominent
of the would-be executioners was Albert Camus, that synthetic
tribune of the people, who in daily tirades against authors who
had continued to write during the Occupation, unaccountably
forgot to mention that he had not restrained his own activities

at the time. The Communists were, as always, vociferous denouncers, and while many of them had suffered courageously as members of the Resistance, others were less remarkable for their war deeds than for their noisiness. One writer stood out in particular for the zeal with which he invoked the death sentence. This doughty warrior had undergone his baptism of fire during the Spanish Civil War, which he had spent traveling about in a truck reciting poetry through a loudspeaker to the troops, while his more practically minded comrades were being killed. The Occupation years he put to good use in keeping up a steady production of books that maintained his reputation for being unreadable. The Germans had once arrested him, mistakenly believing him to be someone else, and although his imprisonment lasted for only a few hours, he thenceforward believed himself to be a Resistance hero.

At first Sacha thought that the antics of the purifiers were merely comic. "The novelist So-and-So, who compromised himself during the Occupation, has sworn to 'get' Béraud, Maurras, Paul Chack, and his colleague Thingummyjig," he wrote in his diary, "because he doesn't know that Thingummyjig, who also compromised himself during the Occupation, has sworn to 'get' Béraud, Maurras, Paul Chack—and his colleague So-and-So!" As the days passed there was less cause for amusement. Buying a scarf at Hermès one day, Sacha noticed a famous surgeon of his acquaintance who was trying not to see him and was talking with unnecessary liveliness to an assistant. In the street people looked away when Sacha appeared. His telephone, which in normal times rarely stopped ringing, now fell silent. Friends became uneasy when he spoke to them. They made hurried excuses to be gone and looked anxiously over their shoulders. A telegram arrived one day which read: "Twelve bullets . . . and a stake!"

At eleven o'clock on the morning of August 23 Sacha was writing in his workroom. A group of young men carrying guns entered the house.

"Monsieur Guitry," said one of them, "we have come to arrest you."

"For what reason?" asked Sacha, the smoke from his cigarette rising in a straight unwavering line.

"For intelligence with the enemy. We are the representatives of the Committee of Liberation."

Sacha raised an eyebrow. "You come to deprive me of my liberty in the name of the Committee of Liberation?"

The scene was played with excellent timing. He took a few packets of cigarettes from the desk and walked slowly down the winding staircase. His performance in this impromptu charade was cool and dignified. Outside in the street the bizarre party headed for the local Mairie. Passers-by stopped to gape in astonishment at the young men and their incongruous prisoner. He wore a capacious Panama hat, a vividly colored floral shirt, lemon trousers, and jade-green slippers of crocodile-skin. No one could say that Sacha was not being arrested in the style to which he was accustomed.

At the Mairie they were ushered into the room usually reserved for marriage ceremonies. "Are they going to marry me by force?" wondered Sacha. Here he was photographed and everyone jostled to get into the picture. From the Mairie he was taken to a prison. After the door of his cell had shut behind him, he was entertained by the repartee of his captors who passed the time agreeably in shouting through the judas: "You won't listen to him any more, ladies!" varied with the more robust sallies of: "Any news of Hitler, Monsieur Sacha Guitry?" and such direct statements of fact as: "Not so comfortable here as it is at home, eh, you bastard?" They could none of them recover from the flattering surprise of having a celebrity in their midst. From time to time a sheepish gaoler would sneak in to ask him for his autograph.

A few days later he was bundled off into another cell with Jérôme Carcopino, the classical historian and Minister of Education under Pétain. The welcome Sacha received from the biographer of Julius Caesar was understandably reserved, for with him already in that crowded cell were the Haitian Ambassador and the former Secretary to the Police Chief of the Paris region. The prison can never before have known such distinguished guests. Magistrates and scholars were crammed by the dozen into its narrow confines; surgeons and barristers took exercise in the prisonyard; professors and journalists marched up and down the corridors; while under the brooding eye of an armed guard the man who yesterday had been the Director-General of French Prisons scrupulously emptied his slops in the manner as laid down in regulations.

A convoy of Black Marias arrived at the gates and the prisoners were marched up the steps and driven away. They were taken to the Vélodrome d'Hiver and made to run the gauntlet of an angry crowd. Sacha was helped on his way by a blow on the neck and a hearty kick that should have ruptured his spleen. At the same time a thoughtful policeman struck Carcopino with a truncheon and sent him staggering into Sacha's arms, his face streaming blood. After a night spent in the chilly expanse of the stadium the prisoners were herded out and again made to force their way through a violent mob to the waiting Black Marias. "Who's that one?" asked somebody in the crowd, pointing at Sacha. "Raimu!" replied another.

The next stop was Drancy prison. Here Sacha's company was equally interesting. His neighbor was the octogenarian Abel Hermant, the author of many entertaining novels and plays. He and his fellow collaborator, Abel Bonnard, were known as "the two Abels" and had earned the unenviable nickname of "Gestapettes." His boulevardier elegance was unruffled. He put his head round the door and enquired: "What time do they serve dinner in this establishment?" Another cell-mate was Alfred Fabre-Luce, a polemical writer whose independence of mind has gained for him what must be a unique title to fame. He has at one time or another been imprisoned by the Nazis, incarcerated by the Liberation forces, and arraigned by President de Gaulle under the Fifth Republic.

It was now the middle of September and nearly a month since Sacha's arrest. At last he was called before a commission of enquiry.

"What are the charges brought against me?" he asked.

"To our knowledge, none," said the chairman. "But we have to bear in mind public rumor. If it were somebody other than you we would immediately free him."

"Why not me?"

"Because we fear an insurrection. Under the circumstances it would be better if you stayed here quietly for a few more days."

As the prisoner was taken back to his cell and heard the roars of "Death! death!" coming from the crowds massing round the prison, he understood the chairman's remark. Somebody tried to cheer him up by telling him that his first wife, Charlotte Lysès, had just arrived at Drancy on charges connected with broadcasts during the Occupation. The news had an effect opposite to what the well-wisher had hoped. Sacha threw up his hands dramatically. "Anything I can endure," he groaned, "but that!"

There was another encounter with the Commission of Enquiry, and the proceedings began to look like a Courteline farce. "We are going to charge you, Monsieur Guitry," announced the president—"What with?"—"That's just what we're wondering ourselves."

"Might we say: 'Dealings with the enemy'?" asked one of the Commission rather timidly.

"What dealings could I have had with the enemy?" retorted Sacha icily.

"None whatever, we agree," said the other hastily.

After long and anxious discussion it was agreed to settle for "intelligence with the enemy." On the 18 October Sacha was transferred to Fresnes prison to await interviews with the examining magistrate who, in French law, decides whether there is a case to answer. In the meantime Sacha defeated boredom by writing poetry in his cell (*"Ça fait très André Chénier"*) and conferring with his lawyers. Two days later he was seen by the Juge d'Instruction, who, from the slim file that lay before him, produced five trifling accusations which had been lodged by members of the public. Each one of them was unfounded, and after brief questioning of the witnesses all the accusations were withdrawn. The verdict was delivered: "It clearly emerges from the evidence assembled that none of the charges which originally inspired the opening of judicial proceedings can be held against the accused. At least, thanks to his anonymous accusers, he will have had the time to check the truth of his own remark: 'Do not belong to the ranks of those who hate. Try, rather, to be among those who are hated: you will find yourself in better company.' "

Sacha was free. He went home to find his house in the avenue Élisée-Reclus as he had left it, largely due to the efforts of his secretary, Madame Choisel. "I'll never forgive them, never, do you hear? After all I've done for the theater and those who live by it, after the risks I've taken, they had the bad faith to call me a collaborator!" He was thin and pallid. The bones of the Roman nose stood out in craggy relief and the cheeks were sunken. He relived over and again every humiliation, every degrading insult of the past three months. Ten times a day he abruptly called for Madame Choisel: "Note this down. I was arrested on August the twenty-third. . . ." The faces of those whom he suspected of starting the "public rumor" haunted his mind. Sometimes humor would break through and the old Sacha would emerge. Almost immediately the obsession returned and his features darkened with bitterness.

His doctors kept advising him to relax and he went into a clinic for rest. In pre-war days his room would have been full of visitors. Now, scarcely anyone troubled to call except for a very small number of true friends, among them Jean Cocteau, René Fauchois, and Albert Willemetz, whose loyalty was greater than their self-interest. One curious visitor was Paul Léautaud. During the Occupation he had been summarily thrown out on the street by his employer, a Collaborator who had succeeded to the editorship of the *Mercure de France*. He had accepted the injustice with typical stoicism, just as he had accepted the privations it entailed. It was characteristic of him that at a time when Sacha's fair-weather friends had deserted him, he should go out of his way to see him. One Sunday in December Léautaud climbed the stairs to Sacha's room and was shocked to note the change in him. He had last seen him in one of his plays in 1922 and wouldn't have recognized him on the street.

"His face is colorless, heavily marked," wrote Léautaud in his *Journal*. "The impression was heightened by the fact that he hadn't shaved, that he had much less hair and that what he had was gray. His features are lofty, the forehead high, a handsome face, full of expression and with a delightful smile. He's quite tall, in fact taller than I'd remembered. He wore a dressing-gown that looked to me like black silk, a foulard round his neck, slippers on his feet. From time to time he put on huge tortoiseshell glasses. He spoke most of the time standing up." Sacha told him of his sorry experiences, and the one-time favorite of the Paris public condoled with the modest old pensioner over the bad luck that had stricken them both.

For a time Sacha played with the idea of emigrating and taking American citizenship. Cocteau thought of it also, as did quite a number of other writers disgusted by the excesses of the Libera-tion. By February he had changed his mind and was back in the avenue Élisée-Reclus. The immediate prospect was uninviting. A tax demand for ten million francs waited on his desk. At the same time, as if to increase the interest of the situation, his films, plays, and books were suppressed, his publishing contracts were cancelled, and all his bank accounts were frozen. Despite the official confirmation of his innocence, he was not allowed to receive either fees or royalties. One by one some of his best pictures found their way to the pawnbroker. Yellow rectangles on the walls betrayed the absence of Toulouse-Lautrecs and Renoirs and Cézannes, and the device of replacing them with full-size photographs in their frames was at best a pathetic gesture.

His sixtieth birthday on the 21 February was celebrated with a kind little event organized by friends. A dozen or so of them put on some excerpts from his plays before a private audience that included Jean Cocteau and René Fauchois. "We *must* get him back on the stage as soon as possible!" said Elvire Popesco, her Slavonic tones thicker than ever. "He's bored with not acting. We must pull him out of it and make him forget his miseries." It was not to be—at least for another two years. So far as Sacha's other paramount interest was concerned, "Mariette" had been succeeded by "Henriette," a twenty-year-old blonde who could not conceal her triumph. "I can scarcely believe it, Madame Choisel," she cried, looking around her at the treasures of the house. "When I think I shall be the fifth . . . !" But her fate lay elsewhere. She disappeared within a few weeks, and Sacha went on dictating. "Write this down, Madame Choisel. I was arrested on August the twenty-third. . . ."

He could not live alone, however, and he began to see more of Arletty. He admired her beauty, her independent spirit, and the firmness with which she had openly supported him over the past few months. (At the Liberation a rumor began that Resistants had cut her breasts off. When life returned to normal her neighbor at a dinner party, squinting closely down her corsage, exclaimed: "Ah, *chère amie,* so what they said wasn't true after all!") Suddenly, in his drawing room, Sacha asked her to marry him. She refused. She had known what was coming and had thought deeply. "I'm incapable of being tied. I can't settle down in a house with a man." And she returned to the sparse little hotel room she preferred, with its austere bed and the crucifix above it.

It was through Arletty that Sacha met his fifth and last wife. She spoke to him one evening, and not without forethought, of a very attractive young woman she had recently met. "I tell you, she's the most beautiful girl in Paris at the moment!" exclaimed Arletty. Sacha listened attentively. Even in his present state, beauty was something that did not leave him indifferent. Over the next few days telephone calls went out urgently all over Paris. Eventually they found the mysterious beauty at a Red Cross headquarters engaged in charitable work. Her name was Lana Marconi and she was twenty-eight years old. She had long chestnut hair and a distant manner which froze on occasion into glacial haughtiness. As she entered for the first time the house in the avenue Élisée-Reclus and walked through the long gallery, even Mademoiselle Marconi was impressed by the majesty of her reception. A beam of watery sunlight filtered through the hermetically sealed window, and she could hear the distant cries of children playing on the Champ de Mars. Then Sacha appeared, enveloped in a swirling black cape. "You have the loveliest hands in the world!" he declared, seizing her long slim fingers. He led her into the dining room, and there, on the exquisitely laid tea table, three roses were lying beside her plate.

After she had gone Sacha found a handkerchief she happened to have dropped. It was embroidered with the arms of the royal house of Rumania. Enchanted, he had it framed and prominently displayed. He showed it to all his visitors and invented a fertile variety of romantic explanations none of which was hampered unduly by truthfulness. Within a few weeks her influence was felt all over the house. Caviar sandwiches on silver plates now accompanied the apéritifs; the domestic staff began to take their orders for the day from her; and most of the photographs on the walls were taken down and replaced with photographs of . . . Lana Marconi. There was between the lady who was to become the fifth Madame Guitry and Sacha a friendly rivalry in matters of extravagance. Her taste was traditional so far as the haphazard acquisition of fur coats and jewelry was dictated by passing fancies. Where she ran him close was at the point when she changed her stockings many times a day and had them individually cleaned by a special process. As though to compensate for this, her notion of thrift was to invest heavily in the National Lottery. Each Thursday a servant was dispatched to buy large quantities of tickets. The numbers were selected, perhaps by some superstition attached to her numerical order in the hierarchy of Sacha's wives, according to an obscure system based upon the figure five.

At last Sacha's divorce from Geneviève was concluded. This was the signal for the surprised Exarch of the Metropolitan Church of Central and Western Europe to receive from Sacha a communication which began: "Born and baptized at St. Petersburg in 1885, I wish respectfully to inform you that I belong to the Orthodox Church . . ." The marriage took place in the little Orthodox church in the rue Bizet. "There!" he whispered to Lana as they came out from the ceremony into the cold November air. "I've made a Frenchwoman out of you and you'll make an Orthodox man out of me."

They went home and he rhapsodized over the elegance of her hands, the long supple hands he had had moulded in bronze. "The others were only my wives, but you, *chérie*, you will be my widow," he promised.

Chapter 15

How do the other men manage to live without you?

SACHA GUITRY

"Take this down, Madame Choisel. I was arrested on the 23 August, 1944 . . . ." The refrain persisted, echoing in Sacha's mind as the empty days dragged on. The impudent entertainer was replaced by an aged and embittered man who would never recover from the shock of his disgrace and the injustice of his treatment. For more than two years he went on assembling the documents and papers with which he intended to clear himself. Very few of the people he had helped during the Occupation wished to acknowledge Sacha. Paul Valéry now preferred not to know him. Colette was forgetful of the debt she owed him, both for saving her husband and for introducing her to the Académie Goncourt. Tristan Bernard's son deliberately refused to testify that Sacha had rescued his father. Famous and unknown alike, they thought it more prudent at this time not to admit that he had helped them.

One man came to Sacha's defense, and his testimony was

unanswerable. This was Colonel Rémy, the famous Secret Service Agent who had organized and maintained a Resistance network throughout France. He had been associated with Sacha in the production of *les Perles de la couronne* before the war, and he protested at the spiteful reasons for the persecution: ". . . For certain people it was a good opportunity to get rid of an author who was too successful . . . In the course of my underground work I heard people talk most unpleasantly about M. Sacha Guitry. As their remarks concerned the crime of intelligence with the enemy, I asked those who reported them to me to give dates, names, facts. All I got was tittle-tattle. I refused to allow my network to spread such stuff. I have been able to verify, on the other hand, that M. Sacha Guitry constantly turned down pressing offers from the German propaganda departments. Unlike certain persons who have been exonerated, he refused to go to Germany and he refused to make films for the Germans."

When Sacha's enemies found that they could not blacken his name with charges of collaboration, they fell back on accusations that he was unpatriotic because he had continued to produce plays during the Occupation. This was not very logical. Even the great incorruptible himself, Jean-Paul Sartre, had committed the same dreadful crime. Perhaps the most flagrant case was that of Paul Claudel. The author of religious verse whose ranting incomprehensibility was hailed as mysticism, he doubled the part of bigot and hypocrite with ease. On the one hand a fiery Inquisitor calling down eternal fire upon unbelievers, on the other he kept a firm grasp of temporal matters by remaining a well-paid director of the Gnome et Rhône firm which supplied the Luftwaffe with aircraft engines. (He had a strict regard for titles. He had been French Ambassador in Tokyo, and an unwary admirer at the time respectfully addressed him as *"Maître."* Claudel bristled. *"Call me Excellency!"* he snapped.) The first night of his play, *le Soulier de satin,* was applauded by rows of Nazi generals in 1943. Earlier still, a keen admirer of Pétain, he had dedicated to him a fulsome ode entitled *Paroles au Maréchal*. This was for-givable in view of public opinion at the time. In any case the majority of the Académie Française was on Pétain's side.* Where Claudel surpassed himself was at the Liberation, when he re-issued the same piece, with suitable amendments, under the title *Au Général de Gaulle*. The cynical old pantaloon was rewarded with a state funeral.

Deserted by most of his friends, barred from the theater and so denied everything that made life meaningful, Sacha rarely ventured out of the house. He lived perpetually in one of his numerous dressing-gowns and even slept in one. He sat and played endless games of belote in the silent drawing room, or suddenly broke off to add yet another sheet of indignant argument to the mounds of documents that squatted everywhere on tables and chairs. As evening approached his restlessness became worse, and at nine o'clock, the time when the curtain usually rose, he would mournfully strike the *trois coups* on his inkwell. For two years his exile continued, and often when the telephone rang it was only because some anonymous imbecile wished to insult him.

On August 8, 1947, after a final interview with the Juge d'Instruction, Sacha was at last cleared of all charges against him. "During the four years of the Occupation," read the official verdict, "he wrote three plays, *N'écoutez pas, Mesdames!*, *Vive l'Empereur*, and *le Bien Aimé*, which are blameless. He never allowed any of them to be acted in Germany, just as he had for-bidden his plays to be acted there before and during the war. Neither did he offer screenplays to the German film company. He did not write a single offending article or lecture throughout the whole of the Occupation. His activity as a writer is, in the last resort, safe from criticisms: it might almost serve as a model for certain careers which have been allowed to continue."

* Just before his fall Pétain was acclaimed by deliriously enthusiastic crowds. A few weeks later equally huge crowds, shouting death to Pétain, hailed De Gaulle in the same public square. Comparing photographs of the two occasions, De Gaulle drily remarked: "Look, you can see the same faces among them."

Gradually he began to go into the world again. He went out to dinner with Lana and found himself opposite a woman who kept asking: "Is it true, *Maître*, that you saw Germans during the war?" "I did not know you were a Juge d'Instruction, Madame," he replied cuttingly. And, to his neighbor, in an undertone: "Who is that stupid bitch?" "My wife, Monsieur," said the man impassively.

At home he took out the files he had been amassing and shot off the first broadside in his battle for vindication. It was typical of him that he should give his self-defense a punning title, *Quatre Ans d'occupations,* and in its five hundred or so pages, with the aid of every document and every letter that related to the subject, he successfully demonstrated his innocence. Later came *60 Jours de prison,* a reproduction of the six-hundred page manuscript in which he told the story of his imprisonment. Then he began the long battle to reconquer the favor of his public. Refused a visa to shoot a film about Talleyrand, he made his script into a play and took the Théâtre Edouard VII to launch it.

Ever since childhood Sacha had been fascinated by the man whom he held to be the greatest diplomatist ever to have lived. His play was the result of reading everything that had been written about him, of collecting autograph material over the years, and of long reflection on the character of one whose diplomatic virtuosity had enabled him to prosper as the servant of the Revolution, of Napoleon, and of the King, all with the same aplomb. Did the secret lie in Talleyrand's comment, "The gift of speech was bestowed on man to enable him to conceal his thoughts"? Was it to be found in his Chesterfieldian handling of men, women, and money? Or did he give a clue to the enigma when he said to Napoleon, "Sire, there are three sorts of knowledge: knowledge proper, *savoir-faire,* and *savoir-vivre.* It has been given to me to observe that *savoir-faire* and *savoir-vivre* can very well do without knowledge proper"? Talleyrand's wiliness and his limp had made him known as *"le diable boiteux."* This was the title Sacha chose for his play. As a piece of stagecraft it is exemplary. The complexities of diplomatic history are clarified and utilized with brilliant dramatic effect. The living, breathing portrait of Talleyrand makes this one of Sacha's finest biographical plays.

Early in 1948 *le Diable boiteux* became the fourteenth play of Sacha's to be produced at the Théâtre Edouard VII. "Pictures from the private collection of M. Sacha Guitry . . ." read the program; ". . . Mademoiselle Lana Marconi's dresses by Maggy Rouff. . . . Antique furniture kindly lent by the Maison Jansen. . . ." The magic of a Sacha Guitry first night had returned and it seemed as if the awfulness of recent years was forgotten. Sacha marched nervously up and down in his dressing room. Would the huge audience greet him as a playwright or as the prisoner of Fresnes? The curtain rose. Off-stage the uneven rhythm of Talleyrand's step was heard. The tap-TAP became louder. Sacha appeared in cocked hat, lacy jabot, and flowered waistcoat. The police who had mingled with the audience in case of riots looked warily about them. Nobody moved. A derisive whistle pierced the stillness. And the play continued. At the end of the first scene a thunderous round of applause burst out.

"I do not count as unimportant the whistle that greeted me at my entry on the first night," wrote Sacha. "On the contrary that single whistle gave excellent proof, indeed, that there weren't two whistles." *Le Diable boiteux* played to full houses throughout the whole of its run. Having shown the authorities that there was no fear of disorder attending his appearance in public— rather, that he was receiving a warm welcome every night—Sacha was allowed to go ahead with his original idea of filming the life of Talleyrand. The critics were, as usual, divided in their opinions. One journalist acidly applied to Sacha the riposte which an angry Napoleon once made to Talleyrand: "Monsieur, you are nothing but *merde* in a silk stocking!" Another took the curious view that *le Diable boiteux* was an apologia for the Vichy regime. But the reviews, wounding though they often were, could not spoil Sacha's joy at finding an audience again. He had rediscovered his public and he was back once more in the only surroundings that mattered to him: the theater.

The silence of past years was made up for by several books he brought out in quick succession. One of them was *Toutes Réflexions faites,* a miscellany of thoughts and epigrams he had pondered during the long blank evenings. The memory of August 23 came back and he wrote ironically of the Liberation: "I was the first person to be told about it." His experience of human ingratitude was summed up in the formula: "Does So-and-So get on your nerves? Then do him a favor—you'll soon be rid of him." And the critics received a goodly share of bile: "A professional critic has just decided to publish four hundred pages on Molière— but in spite of his praises he doesn't succeed in belittling him." Even critics of a century before were not spared: "Musset escaped Sainte-Beuve—in the same way as a man escapes an accident." Yet gaiety kept breaking in and Sacha told his favorite story about Ernest Renan, the agnostic scholar whose classic life of Jesus is one of the most beautiful to have been written. Arrived at the gate of Paradise, Renan is greeted by the Lord: "Ah, Monsieur Renan, how anxious I was to see you!" "And I to see *you!*" replies Renan.

With the next, *Elles et toi,* Sacha was back on familiar ground. "Women love men as a whole—*we* adore them in detail," he observed. "We have a head—while they have eyes, nose, mouth, hair, and ears. We have a body—they have shoulders, breasts, arms, hips. And if we men have legs—they have thighs, knees, ankles, and feet." A woman need not always be beautiful, Sacha reasoned. There are, in fact, very clear advantages to be enjoyed by a plain woman: "When you love a plain woman there's no reason to stop. On the contrary, you'll love her more and more, since if beauty fades with time, plainness on the other hand increases." Yet, beautiful or plain, the nature of women does not change: "Treacherous, faithless, indiscreet and perverse, they are nonetheless pitiable—and therein lies their strength!" He listed the main types of women he had known in greater detail than had Leporello when he drew up the catalogue of Don Giovanni's conquests: "There are those who tell you they're not for sale and that they won't accept a penny from you—and they're usually the ones who ruin you"; and there are those who ". . . think all men are the same because they always carry on with men in the same way." Reveling in the lies women tell, savoring their deceit and their inconstancy with the joy of a true connoisseur, Sacha added the inevitable postscript to all his encounters: "She gave herself to me—and it was she who had me."

Other plays followed *le Diable boiteux*. Lana Marconi, suitably groomed and rehearsed, was now his leading lady, and familiar faces of the pre-war casts re-appeared at his side. Pauline Carton was there with her perky button nose and Olive Oyl hairstyle; Jeanne Fusier-Gir chattered away beneath her eternal fringe; Émile Drain, the years adding to the dignity of his seigneurial features, could always be relied on for the "heavy" parts. Things were not the same, though, and they never could be again. Sacha had always treated his audiences with a certain arrogance—it had been a game they entered into, willing to be surprised and asking to be conquered—but now he seemed to regard them with something not far short of contempt. On one occasion, during an interval that had already lasted half an hour, the stage-manager had to confront a restive house with the message that Monsieur Guitry had decided to go home for dinner but would soon be back. Neither had the ill-feeling of the Liberation period wholly died out. At Lyon, where Sacha had traveled with his wife for a film première, they were kidnapped by a gang of Communists and forced to kneel before a monument to the Resistance. Sacha was, to all appearance, unmoved by the humiliation. There was little else left capable of wounding him further. In a strange sort of way the ravaged and exhausted man had achieved tranquility: "I end by telling you how happy I am," he wrote to his previous wife,

Geneviève. "I don't exaggerate, believe me, and I'm happy at the thought that you aren't seeing the state I'm in now (imagine, my God!, what a state I shall be in a few years hence!). No, it would have been too painful for me to let you see me like this! No! To grow old beside you, to do *that* to you . . . never!"

He returned to his previous custom of filming a play as soon as he had produced it in the theater. In the next ten years he wrote and directed no less than sixteen films, sometimes at a rate of three a year. The best of them were conceived directly for the medium. By contrast, the plays he wrote after *le Diable boiteux* were carelessly thrown together and often fell back on reminiscences of his earlier work. With his doubtful health he no longer felt able to make the effort needed to dominate an audience afresh every night, for a serious stomach operation in 1951 left him weakened. One of the better plays of this period was *Tu m'as sauvé la vie,* in which a misanthropic baron is saved from accidental death by a tramp. His ill-nature temporarily improved, the baron takes the tramp into his house and treats him with kindness. Once recovered, his old misanthropy returns and he throws out the tramp—who marries a countess, for many years the baron's unrequited lover. The tramp was played by Fernandel, who repeated his performance in the subsequent film.

In 1953 Peter Daubeny, the English impresario, invited Sacha and his company to London. It was Coronation time, and the visit awoke nostalgic memories of the old Cochran days. For the occasion Sacha had cobbled up *Écoutez bien, Messieurs,* a rather absent-minded diversion on familiar themes. It did not benefit from its setting in the cavernous Winter Garden Theatre, where Sacha's confidential manner was lost in its wide open spaces, though his timing and elegance remained as crisp as ever. He was interviewed on television and deployed his charm with cunning, deliberately mispronouncing the occasional English word and turning a genuine cough into an excellent piece of "business." Why shouldn't he adore the English public? "After all," he said, with a touch of Talleyrand about him, "they're the nation who gave birth to the greatest dramatist of all time, Shakespeare." As for himself, he confessed: "I write plays as an apple-tree produces apples. The trouble comes when a cherry-tree tries to produce apricots. . . ."

In Paris he made his last stage appearance in *Palsambleu*. He tackled the problem with ingenuity. The part he wrote for himself was that of a centenarian, hard of hearing and condemned to a bathchair. Since his colleagues had to keep repeating their speeches to him he had thus guarded against possible lapses of memory; and the bathchair spared him undue physical exertion. After writing the first act he did not feel at all well, so he cut himself out of the second. He did the same with the third act. Then, a few days later, he suddenly felt better and wrote a fourth act in which he was again on the stage. Still, he could not ignore that this was the end of a career that had for half a century given him his happiest moments. He rang down the curtain firmly and without sentimentality. As a sign of retirement he grew a large beard. The very nature of an actor's profession, in which he has to wear a variety of different make-ups, forbids this indulgence, and no famous performer has ever permanently worn a beard. The gesture was irrevocable.

If the stage was physically beyond Sacha now, there was always the cinema. He threw himself into film-making with a frenzied vigor which betrayed his fear that time was getting short for him. After rising at nine in the morning and taking a quick breakfast, he would drive off to the studios where he spent the day, coming back home to edit the day's "rushes" and seldom going to bed before midnight. It was a regime of monkish devotion to his work. Nothing was allowed to come between him and the movieola which was now permanently installed in his workroom. He had resigned from the Académie Goncourt after the inevitable squabble over Occupation attitudes, and there were no other outside links to distract him. His life centered upon the small screen of the film-editor and upon the images that flitted across it, vanishing and re-appearing at his will and living their magic-lantern existence by virtue of their creator's whim.

One of the most striking of the films was *la Poison*. It was dedicated to Michel Simon, the leading player, to whom Sacha wrote: "I put you among the greatest actors: Frédérick Lemaître, Sarah Bernhardt, my Father, Zacconi, Chaliapin. Like them, you stand alone, voluntarily apart—like them, you possess that valuable quality which cannot be acquired and cannot be passed on, the innate sense of theater, in other words the ability of making other people experience emotions which you yourself do not feel. . . ." This is as good a summary as anyone has written of the art of acting in general and of the art of Michel Simon in particular. Since the late nineteen-twenties his tortured voice, blubber-lipped face, and shambling trunk have lurched through countless French films. Before coming to the cinema he had been a pedlar, a boxer, a dancer, a photographer, and a music-hall performer. His experience of these varied levels of society may have nurtured his gift for eccentric pathos and macabre undertones. Now in his early seventies, he is reported, when not filming, to divide his attention between the pet monkeys which roam freely through his house, and a collection of erotica which is said to be among the finest in private ownership.

"Sacha Guitry is one of the rare directors to have understood me," said Michel Simon, who is a sensitive and complicated personality. Before making the film he posed one condition: "I will only play a scene once and I will not rehearse," he told Sacha. "I don't believe a film should be made just for the pleasure of technicians. When you're on the set, first of all it's the camera-man who says the scene hasn't gone well for him; then it's the sound engineer; after that it's the lighting expert; and at the end of it all, when everything is at its worst for the actor, only then is the scene finally shot. Sacha accepted my conditions. We never re-shot a single scene. Filming lasted for eleven days, although we'd prepared for three weeks' work. *La Poison* may not be a technical masterpiece, but it's a film that won great success. . . ."

In *la Poison* Michel Simon sketched a profoundly guileful portrayal of the peasant married to a nagging old shrew of a wife. After years of perpetual bickering they both seek ways of getting rid of each other. The husband goes to see a famous barrister who has just brought off his hundredth acquittal. The barrister lets him into a few trade secrets and he returns to his village fortified with a plan for the perfect crime. He murders his wife (*"Je crève!"* she gasps; *"Crève donc,"* he replies equably), and gives himself up. Thanks to the barrister's defense he is acquitted and is carried back in triumph to the village on the shoulders of other suffering husbands. This amiable black comedy is enlivened by the witty *montage* typical of Sacha. A good example consisted in the quick cuts between the court room where the murder trial is being held and scenes of a gang of children "trying" one of their members for a similar crime.

The following year brought *la Vie d'un honnête homme*, another collaboration between Sacha and Michel Simon. This time it pointed out the disadvantages of honesty as shown in the case of twin brothers, one of whom is a thorough rascal while the other is an honest man who makes life hell for all those around him. It is, of course, the wayward brother who triumphs and who bears out the truth of Joseph de Maistre's remark which prefaces the film: "I don't know what the life of a rogue can be like, since I've never been one, but the life of an honest man is abominable." It is not surprising that Sacha always named as his favorite films *le Corbeau*, a scarifying study of poison-pen scandals in a small town; and the English *Kind Hearts and Coronets*, where Denis Price murders his way through all those members of his family who stand between him and a coronet. As one critic observed of the films Sacha made in the post-war years, they contained ". . . a curious mixture of light-hearted immorality, macabre humor, and cynical wisdom that did not exclude feeling. . . ."

Even more notable was the tribute paid him by a younger generation of film directors for whom his pre-war plays and illustrious
associations meant little. François Truffaut, a leader of the *nouvelle
vague,* wrote: "It was always 'Sacha' that he gave us. In other
words, taking as his excuse some generally comic idea, he embroidered on themes that were personal to him: the benefits of
inconstancy in love, the social usefulness of asocial people such
as burglars, murderers, gangsters' molls and gigolos. He always
showed the paradox of life, and it's because life is so terribly paradoxical that Sacha was a terribly realistic film-maker."

While *cinéastes* of the future will doubtless prefer these pessi-
mistic comedies, the general public flocked in hundreds of thousands to see the lavish historical films Sacha was also making at
the same time. The first of these was *Si Versailles m'était conté,*
a grandiose pageant which recounted the history of the royal
palace from its origin as a simple hunting box through its development into the wonder of Europe. "Who, in your opinion,
is the greatest historian?" Sacha once asked a man who was a very
distinguished historian himself. "The archives," came the answer.
And for his documentation Sacha was able to draw upon his own
collection of autograph material by the French kings and their
mistresses, their ministers, and all those who were associated with
Versailles. This he did with a free hand, to the alarm of professional
historians whose respect for fact sometimes made them forget that
Sacha was making a film and not a historical study. "I am keeping
you at Versailles and I banish you to the attic rooms," says Louis
XIV to Madame de Montespan. The Curator of Versailles uneasily
reminded Sacha that she had been banished to the apartments
which are on the ground-floor in the right wing of the palace.
Surely, Sacha argued, the original speech was more in character
than: "I am keeping you at Versailles and I banish you to the
apartments which are on the ground floor in the right wing of
the palace"?

With simple logic, Sacha resolved to make his film in the palace and gardens of Versailles itself. The occasional grubby finger marks on a door handle, the flaking gilt of a wooden cherub, only served to make the atmosphere more believable. The sweep of three hundred years' events was traced with an acute sense of history. In its three hours' running time the film presented a series of sharp little cameos and sketches which coalesced in a lofty panorama. The music was worthy of the care Sacha had taken to incise every detail. It was written by Jean Françaix who before the war had composed the score of *les Perles de la couronne*. Françaix has for so long been known as one of the younger prodigies among French musicians that it is slightly disturbing to realize that he was born in 1912. His music for *Si Versailles m'était conté* preserved the illusion one has of his youthfulness. The cuckolded husband of Madame de Montespan is represented by a suitably birdlike and absurd allegretto, while a long sinuous melody in a minor key does duty for the poisoner La Voisin. Marie-Antoinette's toy farm is evoked in a charmingly *faux-naïf* nursery tune. For the concluding scene, a procession down the famous steps at Versailles of all the characters who have appeared in the film—Louis XIV, Napoleon, Clemenceau, to mention but a few—the music throws off all sophistication and launches into a maestoso fanfare which becomes, inescapably, the *Marseillaise*. In cold print the idea seems banal. On the screen the effect is wonderfully moving.

It would be impossible for an Englishman to make such an unashamedly patriotic film as this. Yet the average Frenchman, however left-wing he may think himself, is highly susceptible to *la gloire*. Wherever the film was shown, in the super establishments of the Champs-Élysées or in modest local cinemas, intense interest was shown in Louis XIV, loud applause greeted Napoleon, and Clemenceau was hailed with cheers. The names of the cast were among the most famous in the French cinema. No sooner had the audience recognized Gérard Philippe as d'Artagnan, than they were being preached at by Jean-Louis Barrault as Fénelon.

Madame de Pompadour appeared as Micheline Presle and Molière took on the features of Fernand Gravey. Familiar faces swam into view and were swept away by the centuries—Gaby Morlay, Danielle Delorme, Brigitte Bardot, Charles Vanel, Gisèle Pascal—and Revolutionary songs were chanted by Edith Piaf and Tino Rossi. The greatest surprise of a surprising film was the vision of Orson Welles, "resembling," as someone said, "a haggis," in the part of Benjamin Franklin. The cleverest piece of casting was that of the beautiful Claudette Colbert as Madame de Montespan. Sacha himself, who linked the episodes with an exuberant commentary, was content with a brief appearance as the aging Louis XIV. His acting was, said Dilys Powell, ". . . a fragment of theatre, exquisite, ironic, beautifully subdued to the requirements of the screen."

Si Versailles m'était conté was filmed in the short space of two months, the company often working on until two or three in the morning under Sacha's urging. In December 1953, it had a gala première at the Opéra. Detachments of the Garde Républicaine lined the ceremonial stairway inside the Opéra, while in the streets a vast crowd surged excitedly against the barriers. Sacha returned home that evening covered with glory. "It's the crown of your career, *Maître*," somebody said to him, "and now you're repaid for all the injustices you've had to endure." Sacha stayed silent for a moment. Then, with a weary gesture, he replied: "No, it's not over. It'll never be over. It'll take another hundred years—and more . . ."

All the profits of the film went toward the reconstruction of Versailles. They were considerable, for it attracted huge audiences everywhere and had soon taken the highest box-office receipts of any French film in history. Sacha's only problem now was to deal with the numerous tycoons who clamored for his services and offered him unlimited finance. He did not waste time in wry reflection on this abrupt change of fortune, and he immediately started work on his next production, another Technicolor epic to be called *Napoléon*. Here he spread himself on elaborate battle scenes scripted with witty hindsight. At Waterloo an English general calls on the French to surrender. *"Merde!"* comes the reply. "Who said that?" barks Cambronne, turning round in surprise. "What a hypocrite he is!" mutters one of his soldiers.

Again the cast was spangled with famous names. Many of them were carried over from the Versailles film to be joined by Danielle Darrieux, Michèle Morgan, and Jean Gabin, with Patachou masquerading as "Madame Sans-Gêne." Napoleon's gaoler, Sir Hudson Lowe, came to life again in the glowering jowls of Orson Welles. Still more unnerving was the apparition of Eric von Stroheim, his close-cropped Junker cranium draped in a luxuriant wig as he impersonated Beethoven playing the "Eroica Symphony" in a piano arrangement. (The excuse, of course, was valid in that Beethoven, much given to bombast himself and usually gulled by it in others, had dedicated the "Eroica" to Napoleon. Although, as the writers of program notes never tire of informing us, he later withdrew it when his hero had the bad taste to proclaim himself Emperor.)

The campaigns of Italy and Austria were nobly refought by Sacha, who had spent many pleasant hours maneuvering the antique toy soldiers in his collection at home. The expedition into Egypt unwound to the jaunty strains of a march by Jean Françaix, whose music was again one of the pleasures of the film. Napoleon's generals took their social pleasure in ballrooms where orchestras played transpositions of Chopin into the idiom of the twentieth century. There was a shade more weight about the Austrian march, and a bare Satie-esque directness in the accompaniment to the entry of Louis XVIII. As one had hoped but hardly dared expect, the Congress of Vienna opened to a pastiche of Ravel's *la Valse,* which in turn had been a pastiche of the traditional Viennese waltz. As an example of the refinements of in-breeding the music was deliciously unparalleled.

Napoléon was launched with even more splendor than its

predecessor. Forty drummers in Napoleonic uniform saluted President Coty and the Diplomatic Corps as they ascended the steps of the Opéra. Yet Sacha made the best entrance, one that recalled the last days of Sarah Bernhardt, for his illness had begun to develop into paralysis and he was carried under the blazing chandeliers in a sedan chair. Bearded and gaunt, he looked around him with approval at the footmen in their red and gold Imperial livery, and at Napoleon's own campaign tent which had been brought out for the occasion, along with its simple camp bed and portable folding furniture. Officialdom had obviously forgiven Sacha for having inadvertently chipped a piece of the Arc de Triomphe while filming.*

It was fitting that Sacha's last big production should have been *Si Paris nous était conté.* In this long and lavish film he paid his tribute to the city that was his life. Paris had given him fame and riches. There he had exercised a profession "which for over fifty years has brought me a happiness unalloyed." He had never felt more privileged than when he researched his way through the books, the documents, and the archives to write his script. The problem was not to find material but, rather, what to leave out of the abundant history of the place with which he had had a lifelong love affair. No studio was big enough to accommodate the sets, and the Parc des Expositions was taken over to house the twelve gigantic décors which were built for the film. Its wide expanse appeared to shrink as it became filled with reconstructions of medieval streets, Renaissance palaces, and eighteenth-century mansions. A cast of five thousand performed complicated maneuvers, presenting themselves one day as the army of Henri IV and on the next as a Revolutionary mob.

The leading actors were Jean Marais and Gérard Philippe, ac-

* Orson Welles, rightly, prophesied to André Maurois that the film would be immensely triumphant. "There are very few sure-fire subjects," Welles told him. "Napoleon is one of them. You can always write a *Life of Napoleon* or a *Life of Jesus* and find a hundred thousand readers. An American publisher once told me: 'I only know two types of book that really sell: the life of Lincoln and the biography of a dog.' He got one of his authors to write *Lincoln's Dog.* It sold a million copies."

companied by a detachment from the Comédie-Française. The actresses included Danielle Darrieux, Michèle Morgan, and Françoise Arnoul. Strong though the cast may have been, it was overshadowed by the presence of a man whose name is linked with Paris in a unique manner, for he had shown it to the world in pictures that have made it a little his own creation. Maurice Utrillo was then in the last year of his life. His wife had just rescued him from alcoholism, and as if in a trance he painted, over and over again, his famous picture of the church of Sacré Cœur in Montmartre. His return to sobriety was unavailing, and a few weeks after Sacha had filmed him at work he was dead. The sequence gave *Si Paris nous était conté* a note of poignant authenticity. As Sacha, confined to his wheelchair, watched the pathetic fumblings of the artist's brush, he could sympathize with the feelings of a man who, although he knew he was doomed, could not stop himself from working, so devoted was he to his craft.

Chapter 16

I presumed to animadvert on his eulogy of Garrick in his Lives of the Poets. "You say, Sir, his death eclipsed the gaiety of nations." Johnson: *"I could not have said more nor less. It is the truth; eclipsed, not* extinguished; *and his* death *did eclipse; it was like a storm."* Boswell: *"But why nations? Did his gaiety extend farther than his own nation?"* Johnson: *"Why, Sir, some exaggeration must be allowed."*

BOSWELL
Life of Johnson

When Sacha entered his eighth decade on the 21 February, 1955, his birthday gave him cause for dark reflections. "Sometimes, when you're in your forties, you think you'll retire one day and give a farewell performance," he wrote. "At the age of fifty you no longer think about it, and when you're sixty you can't even bear it to be mentioned." His insurance company followed its usual rule for actors and withdrew its cover after the age of seventy was attained. As writer, director, and principal actor in *Si Paris nous était conté*, Sacha was irreplaceable. Distracted by the myriad harassments of his ambitious project, anxiously watched by the backers who feared for the hundreds of millions of francs they had invested, he reached the end of the film with thankful relief.

Five months to the day after his seventieth birthday, Sacha had his first injection of morphine. "Unable to cure our illnesses," Lucien once joked, "doctors have to content themselves with christening them." The malady which attacked Sacha had been christened polyneuritis. It may result from some chronic disease, which in his case was rheumatism, and has its origin at the base of the spine. The pain starts between the ribs and then it spreads to the legs inflaming many of the nerves. The number of daily injections was raised to two, then three, and within a week four became necessary. During the next twelve months, Sacha calculated, he received one thousand four hundred and twenty-nine injections. "I had a very clear impression that I continued to suffer but that I couldn't feel it," he remarked.

Though all movement was irksome to him and it was as much as he could do to drag his pencil over the paper, he started preparing another film. Under the influence of morphine he found it difficult to take seriously the characters he was creating. The crimes he recounted in *Assassins et voleurs* were told with a nonchalance that sharpened the irony of the telling. A burglar breaks into a house and finds a man about to commit suicide. The latter begs the intruder to shoot him. At the end of the film, such is the ingenuity of the tale, one nods approval when it is the householder who shoots the burglar. Sacha's next film, *les Trois font la paire*, was written in growing discomfort and was directed from his sickbed. It featured Michel Simon as a policeman embroiled with a gang of crooks who, by a fiendish twist of the plot, are forced to murder their own boss. This was Sacha's last appearance in a film. He introduced it with a stream of paradox and was faded out into the opening shot on the typical line: "Of course, I'm not in favor of murder, but after all people have to live." *Les Trois font la paire* had an acerb morality which the most righteous could not deny.

Sacha now could not move from his bed. His drawn features looked all the paler for the flamboyant dressing-gown he still insisted on wearing. Sometimes, with the aid of nurses and after agonizing effort, he struggled into the room where he kept most of his pictures and his art objects. There, surrounded by the reminders of a prodigious career, he would slump in a chair and silently contemplate the tokens of his success. At other times he watched television unblinkingly. At first he did not miss a single program, and he sat through the news bulletins with the same wondering enjoyment as he did the sporting events. "Above all, don't try and explain to me how it works!" he ordered. And not least of television's benefits was the sight it gave at last of "one of those vipers who do so much harm to people: I refer to a critic . . . I saw him with my own eyes—and straightaway I understood. The unfortunate fellow is horrible to see. . . . You ought to see critics in the flesh as well as read them. The ugly mugs they've got are enough to enlighten and soothe you."

The day after Sacha's seventy-first birthday in 1956 was marked by the death of the only critic he had ever numbered among his friends. In his eighty-fifth year Paul Léautaud had at last allowed himself to be parted from his animals and taken to a clinic. Until five years previously he had lived in obscure and penurious retirement. Most people had thought, indeed, that he was already dead. Then he had been persuaded to give a radio interview. His malicious wit and biting tongue made him a celebrity overnight. His broadcasts and gramophone records earned him what was, by his own modest standard, untold wealth. He decided that people must be even bigger fools than he thought to pay him so handsomely just for talking and being himself. His first action was to buy six pairs of shoes, six hats, two overcoats, an electric coffee mill, and the most expensive delicacies he could find for his cats. He received a postbag as large as a film star's and was pursued by young women. But it had all come too late. In the clinic a nurse brought him a drink. The aged misanthrope took it and snarled: *"Maintenant, foutez-moi la paix."* Then he turned his face to the wall and died. As a gesture of affection Sacha made sure he had a decent funeral and paid for the gravestone himself.

Only a few weeks afterward Sacha heard that Charlotte Lysès was no more. His first wife was then seventy-nine and had died at the house of friends in Saint-Jean Cap Ferrat. Once again he found himself meeting burial expenses. At other times her death would have been the occasion of a sentimental thought and little more. Coming in the midst of his own grave illness, it awoke a train of memories that could not be checked. He had known her when he was a young man, the gay and irrepressible son of the most famous actor in Paris. His unblushing egoism she accepted as the inevitable effect of the confidence which radiated from him and which made those around him agree that life was the most wonderful thing in the world; his volubility, tedious in a less witty man, was pleasant to her because it was tirelessly amusing. In return, for her experience of the stage was greater than his, she helped him to perfect his acting and to guide into useful channels the undisciplined talent which he might otherwise have frittered away. Although when married she was no more faithful to him than he was to her, she had always loved him dearly and continued to do so long after they parted.

There can have been few more successful careers in the theater than the one Charlotte launched him upon. From the very beginning all was in his favor. The friends of a youth spent in the Olympian presence of Lucien Guitry had been the leading playwrights, actors, and authors of France. For them, as for his adoring public of the later years, he remained an *enfant gâté* whose selfishness was forgotten because he never failed to charm and surprise. No one could dramatize the trifling events of his private life with such attractive gusto or make of them so absorbing a commentary on human nature. Yet despite himself he was a moralist and followed in the tradition of La Rochefoucauld, Rivarol, and Chamfort. He did not contradict La Rochefoucauld's assertion that: "Nothing is rarer than true goodness; even the people who think they possess it are usually confusing it with self-satisfaction or weakness." With Rivarol he agreed that visions have a happy knack of appearing only to those who will believe in them. And like Chamfort he maintained that the man who reaches the age of forty without becoming a misanthrope has never loved his fellow men.

He could look back on a sustained period of activity rivaled only by such prolific dramatists as Goldoni or Lope de Vega. He had no thought for posterity and wrote simply to please himself and the audience of an evening. It was obvious that not all of his production would survive. It was just as clear that much of it would continue to live, as revivals of his plays and films have already shown. His view of men and women had the worldly commonsense of a La Fontaine or a Molière. He expected little and was not disappointed when people turned out to be neither saints nor models of honesty. Life as it was gave him his subject and he chronicled it for what it was worth. There was no call to blame or to praise. Irony was his reaction, that irony which Anatole France has described as calming anger because it teaches us to laugh at fools and evildoers whom we might else have been weak enough to hate. Irony, Sacha explained, was skepticism to true advantage dressed. "It doesn't only mean doubting other people's insight. It means doubting one's own insight with regard to one's neighbors. Irony thus becomes the only form of modesty which is untainted by vanity." This is not perhaps the most exalted approach to the problems of humanity. It nevertheless provides a workable philosophy for day-to-day use.

As the morphine invaded his system Sacha drowsed uncomfortably in his bed. He stirred himself to read a Simenon novel and was enthralled. Simenon became as much of a drug as the morphine and he devoured novel after novel. "If I have had to wait until I'm ill to enjoy reading your books," he wrote to Simenon, "then it has certainly been worth it." An idea for a film came into his mind and he forced himself to scrawl a scenario. It was the story of an author who sets out to find a truly happily married couple. He fails, but eventually he comes across his own ex-wife living with a totally unsuitable husband. The author takes her back and together they live happily ever after. The star of *la Vie à deux* was the beautiful Lili Palmer, and though her colleagues were Fernandel, Edwige Feuillère, Danielle Darrieux, Jean Marais, and Gérard Philippe, she it was who easily dominated the film. Sacha was by then too ill to direct it himself and the task was confided to another. He did not live to see the result.

For ten days throughout the July of 1957 a scorching heat wave covered Europe. Temperatures in Paris reached well into the nineties. The silence that filled the house in the avenue Élisée-Reclus was broken only by the comings and goings of nurses, by the hushed consultations of doctors. To suppress possible seats of infection they extracted twenty-two teeth. They gave Sacha insulin to fight the diabetes that intervened. His nerve-endings were so tender that in the excessive heat it was torture for him to bear even the lightest covering on his legs. He felt, he said in response to enquiries, "a little worse than yesterday, a little better than tomorrow." Years ago Sacha had declared that when the time came for him to die he wished to do so as slowly as possible, because, never having had enough time to live, he at least wanted enough time for dying. The wish was cruelly fulfilled. "But I shouldn't complain," he murmured feebly to a visitor, "I've had such a wonderful life."

For one who loved human existence so greedily the idea of death was appalling. As he sank deeper into suffering his thoughts turned to religion. *"Bonjour, mon prêtre!"* he greeted the priest who came to see him. *"Bonjour, mon Dieu!"* replied the priest with a twinkle in his eye. Other callers at the house were not so divinely inspired. The income tax authorities dispatched one of their creatures to distrain a picture by Cézanne. With the delicacy for which those life-enhancing paragons are renowned, the emissary haggled over unpaid taxes while Sacha lay dying in the next room. Albert Willemetz looked in to see him. Sacha congratulated his old friend on the three-thousandth performance his latest operetta was about to achieve. "That's nothing compared to me, though. I'm celebrating my ten-thousandth," he added, referring to his injections. Willemetz pushed over to him the little red exercise book in which he noted down ideas for future plays. With his diaphanous hand, now so weak that it could no longer bear the weight of his rings, Sacha waved it away. "And now, Albert," he said, "I want to sleep."

His favorite pictures were brought in and hung before his dimming eyes. His mind began to wander and he spoke aloud about his past life. He was recalling the great moments he had known: the first night of *Nono* . . . his father in *Pasteur* . . . the triumph of *Mozart* . . . how he conceived *le Roman d'un tricheur*. He spoke of Alphonse Allais and his cold melancholy look, of Sarah Bernhardt's lilting voice, of Monet's peasant simplicity. By a merciful quirk of his failing brain he did not remember all the vileness, all the infamy of the post-war years.

Sacha had always been a collector of deathbed epigrams. "I'd stop dying for an instant if a witticism or a good idea came into my mind," Voltaire had said. Among the remarks Sacha liked to quote was one by Forain, who, assured by his doctor that his pulse, temperature, and blood pressure were all normal, had replied: "Thank you, doctor, I'm dying cured." Then there was the grammarian Vaugelas. Professional to the end, he said: *"Je m'en vais . . ."* Recollecting himself, he added: *"Ou je m'en vas . . ."* He explained: *"L'un et l'autre se dit . . ."* And with his last breath, making sure that no grammatical loophole was left: *"Ou se disent."* The comment that Sacha cherished most was Fontenelle's. He died at the age of a hundred and two, and his doctor, on asking whether he felt anything, was told: "Nothing much except a great difficulty in keeping alive." What was Sacha's last coherent remark? It would satisfy a feeling for symmetry to report that the man whose lifelong wit had been so acutely exercised on women had made some supreme epigram that would have finished the matter for once and all. He did not. He looked at his wife, her eyes ringed with the shadows of drawn-out vigils, and he looked at the nurses who had tended him throughout his agony. "Women," he said simply, "are darlings. They are miracles of devotion, intelligence, and courage."

On the 20 July he suddenly cried: "I'm going to die . . . you mustn't let it happen. I can't bear it any longer . . . I'm done for. Pray for me. I'm suffering too much. *Mon petit* . . . don't look at me. We're not at the theater." He lost consciousness. At twenty past three in the morning of Wednesday, July 24, he died. In evening dress and wearing the insignia of the Légion d'honneur, he was laid out upon his bed. At his side were a Renoir nude and a Utrillo picture of Montmartre. At the head there hung a Cézanne still-life of apples and a picture of his father whom in death he resembled uncannily. All around him were red roses. The heat wave broke and heavy rain teemed in the street where Parisians lined up to pay their last respects to the man who for fifty years had entertained them so prodigally. The line was very long and doubled round the corner of the block. Most of them were women. They had been waiting since six o'clock in the morning.

Marcel Achard paused at the deathbed and said it reminded him of Sacha's observation: "You should never look at somebody who's sleeping. It's as if you were opening a letter that isn't addressed to you." Michel Simon called and was driven away in his car weeping uncontrollably as his wife sought to comfort him. The funeral was held on the Friday at Montmartre cemetery. Before Sacha was buried in the same grave as his father, twelve thousand people filed past the coffin. The bitterness of the Liberation was temporarily forgotten by the leading figures from the theater and the cinema who came to his funeral. Those who had vilified him, or, worse still, betrayed him by their cowardly silence when he had most need of them, now granted the acknowledgment they had withheld during his lifetime. But it was not the presence of the famous which made his funeral so notable. It was the thousands of ordinary Parisians who, as they shuffled through the rain, testified to the place Sacha really held in the affections of his fellow-countrymen. For with him had died the spirit of the boulevard and Paris was no longer quite herself.

Baisser de rideau

*A*fter Sacha's death very few people called at the house in the avenue Élisée-Reclus. The rooms which daily had witnessed an excited flow of activity were quiet and deserted. The shutters remained permanently closed and weeds began to grow in the little garden. Sacha had once intended to bequeath his home with all its treasures to the Académie Goncourt as the meeting place they always lacked. The events of 1944 made him change his mind. The historic film of *Ceux de chez nous*, which deserved to be in the national archives, he firmly banished for ever to the vaults of his bank. The debts he had left were huge. Gradually they were paid off, and as his plays and films continued to draw royalties his estate became rich again. In 1962 his executors sold the German rights of his plays. It was something he had always refused to do in his lifetime.

In the autumn of 1963, when the trees on the Champ de Mars

stood bleak and leafless, boards were put up round the house and bulldozers moved in. The site had been sold to a real-estate company. The position and the size of the land commanded a price of startling dimensions. All through the cold autumn days the machines went noisily about their task of destruction. The little stone cherubs and the ivy-covered urns in the garden were the first to go. Then the demolition team attacked the facade, and before long the great stairway was bared. It tapered off sadly on high, mantled with rubbish and chips of plaster. Next to it Sacha's picture gallery hung crazily in the open air. Then it collapsed in a cloud of rubble.

They managed to rescue the bust of Lucien which for nearly thirty years had watched over the destiny of his beloved home from a corner of the garden. The walls fell to the ground and the debris was cleared away. Within a few months a gross and unlovely block of flats squatted on the site. The last physical trace of Sacha Guitry had been removed from the spot that had meant so much to him.

Published Works of Sacha Guitry

Many, though not all, of Sacha's plays have been published in book form at one time or another, notably in a luxury edition brought out by Raoul Solar, Paris, during the nineteen-fifties. His other works are as follows:

Des Connus et des inconnus (SKETCHES). No publisher. 1903.

La Correspondance de Paul Roulier-Davenel. Dorbon aîné, 1910.

Le Taureau, le Veau, le Maquereau, le Chat, le Lapin, la Bête à Bon Dieu, le Crapaud, la Vache, la Poule (SKETCHES). Dorbon aîné, 1910.

Jusqu'à nouvel ordre (ESSAYS). Brunhoff, 1913.

La Maladie (ESSAYS). Brunhoff, 1914.

Le Courrier de Monsieur Pic (PERIODICAL, 9 ISSUES). 1920–21.

L'Esprit de Sacha Guitry (ed., Léon Treich). Gallimard, 1926.

Lucien Guitry raconté par son fils. Gerschel, 1930.

La Maison de Loti. Paillart, 1931.

Mes Médecins. Cortial, 1932.

Si j'ai bonne mémoire. Tome 1er (MEMOIRS). Plon, 1934.

Mémoires d'un tricheur (NOVEL). Gallimard, 1935.

Des Goûts et des couleurs (POETRY). No publisher. 1943.

De Jeanne d'Arc à Philippe Pétain. Éd. Sant'Andrea & Raoul Solar, 1944.

Toutes Réflexions faites (MAXIMS). Éd. de l'Élan, 1947.

Elles et toi (MAXIMS). Raoul Solar, 1947.

4 Ans d'occupations. Éd. de l'Élan, 1947.

Vers de Bohème. Raoul Solar, 1948.

60 Jours de prison. Éd. de l'Élan, 1949.

18, avenue Élisée-Reclus. Raoul Solar, 1952.

Et puis voici des vers. Raoul Solar, 1954.

Cent Merveilles. Raoul Solar, 1954.

Et Versailles vous est conté. Raoul Solar, 1954.

Théâtre, je t'adore! Hachette, 1958.

Les Femmes et l'amour. Le Livre Contemporain, 1959.

L'Esprit. Librairie Académique Perrin, 1962.

TITLE	FIRST PERFORMANCE
Le Page. Opéra-bouffe. (Music: LUDO RATZ)	Mathurins, 4.15.1902
Yves le fou.	Casino de Pont Aven., 8.25.1902
Nono.	Mathurins, 12.6.1905
Le Cocu qui faillit tout gâter.	Odéon, 12.21.1905
Le Kwtz.	Mathurins, 12.13.1905
Un Étrange Point d'honneur.	Théâtre Royal, 3.30.1906
Chez les Zoaques.	Théâtre Antoine, 11.5.1906
Les Nuées.	Théâtre des Arts, 12.29.1906
L'Escalier de service. (With ALFRED ATHIS)	Casino de Monte Carlo, 2.25.1907
La Clef.	Théâtre Réjane, 5.4.1907
La Partie de domino. (With ALPHONSE ALLAIS)	Tréteau Royal, 10.1.1907
Petite Hollande.	Odéon, 3.25.1908

TITLE	FIRST PERFORMANCE
Le Scandale de Monte Carlo.	Théâtre du Gymnase, 4.22.1908
Le Mufle.	Théâtre Antoine, 11.25.1908
Après . . . sorte de revue en un acte.	Théâtre Michel, 12.3.1908
Tell père, Tell fils. (Music: TIARKO RICHEPIN)	Théâtre Mévisto, 4.17.1909
La 33e.	? 1909
C'te Pucelle d'Adèle.	Gaietés-Rochechouart, 11.19.1909
Tout est sauvé fors l'honneur.	? 1910
Une Mésaventure amoureuse.	? 1911
Le Veilleur de nuit.	Théâtre Michel, 2.2.1911
Un Beau Mariage.	Théâtre de la Renaissance, 10.17.1911
Jean III . . .	Comédie Royale, 3.7.1912
Pas complet!	Théâtre Marigny, 9.1.1912
La Prise de Berg-op-Zoom.	Théâtre du Vaudeville, 10.4.1912
Le Pelèrine écossaise.	Bouffes-Parisiens, 1.15.1914
Deux Couverts.	Comédie-Française, 3.30.1914
La Jalousie.	Bouffes-Parisiens, 4.8.1915
Il faut l'avoir. Revue. (With ALBERT WILLEMETZ)	Palais-Royal, 11.6.1915
Une Vilaine Femme brune.	Théâtre des Variétés, 11.22.1915
Faisons un rêve.	Bouffes-Parisiens, 10.3.1916
Jean de la Fontaine.	Bouffes-Parisiens, 12.17.1916
Un Soir quand on est seul.	Bouffes-Parisiens, 6.2.1917
Un Type dans la genre de Napoléon.	Bouffes-Parisiens, 6.2.1917
Chez la reine Ysabeau.	Bouffes-Parisiens, 6.2.1917
L'Illusionniste.	Bouffes-Parisiens, 8.28.1917
Deburau. (Music: ANDRÉ MESSAGER)	Théâtre du Vaudeville, 12.9.1918
La Revue de Paris. (With ALBERT WILLEMETZ)	Théâtre du Vaudeville, 1918

TITLE	FIRST PERFORMANCE
Pasteur.	Théâtre du Vaudeville, 1.23.1919
Le Mari, la femme et l'amant.	Théâtre du Vaudeville, 4.19.1919
Mon Père avait raison.	Théâtre de la Porte Ste-Martin, 10.8.1919
Béranger.	Théâtre de la Porte Ste-Martin, 1.21.1920
Je t'aime.	Théâtre Édouard VII, 10.12.1920
Comment on écrit l'histoire.	Théâtre Sarah-Bernhardt, 11.4.1920
Le Comédien.	Théâtre Édouard VII, 1.21.1921
Le Grand Duc.	Théâtre Édouard VII, 4.12.1921
Jacqueline.	Théâtre Édouard VII, 11.5.1921
Chez Jean de la Fontaine.	Opéra, 1.17.1922
Une Petite Main qui se place.	Théâtre Édouard VII, 5.4.1922
Le Blanc et le noir.	Théâtre des Variétés, 11.9.1922
Un Sujet de roman.	Théâtre Édouard VII, 1.4.1923
L'Amour masqué. (Music: ANDRÉ MESSAGER)	Théâtre Édouard VII, 2.15.1923
On passe dans huit jours.	Théâtre des Variétés, 11.11.1923
Le Lion et la poule.	Théâtre Édouard VII, 11.25.1923
L'Accroche-coeur.	Théâtre de l'Étoile, 12.21.1923
Un Phénomène.	Alhambra, 8.24.1923
La Revue de Printemps. (With ALBERT WILLEMETZ)	Théâtre de l'Étoile, 5.5.1924
Une Étoile nouvelle.	Théâtre Édouard VII, 12.6.1924
On ne joue pas pour s'amuser.	Théâtre Édouard VII, 3.26.1925
Mozart. (Music: REYNALDO HAHN)	Théâtre Édouard VII, 12.2.1925
Vive la République! (With ALBERT WILLEMETZ)	Théâtre Marigny, 5.1.1926
Était-ce un rêve?	Théâtre Sarah-Bernhardt, 1926
À Vol d'oiseau. Revue. (With ALBERT WILLEMETZ)	Théâtre Édouard VII, 11.11.1926
Désiré.	Théâtre Édouard VII, 3.27.1927
Un Miracle.	Théâtre des Variétés, 12.6.1927

TITLE	FIRST PERFORMANCE
Mariette. (Music: OSCAR STRAUS)	Théâtre Édouard VII, 10.1.1928
Charles Lindbergh. "Féerie en 3 actes."	Théâtre du Châtelet, 11.29.1928
Histoires de France. (Music: HENRI BUSSER)	Théâtre Pigalle, 10.7.1929
La IIIe chambre. (With ALBERT WILLEMETZ)	Théâtre de la Madeleine, 10.30.1929
Chez Georges Washington. (Music: HENRI BUSSER)	Théâtre des Champs-Élysées, 3.12.1930
Un Homme d'hier et une femme d'aujourd'hui.	Théâtre de la Madeleine, 3.24.1930
Et vive le théâtre! Revue. (With ALBERT WILLEMETZ)	Théâtre de la Madeleine, 3.24.1930
Frans Hals.	Théâtre de la Madeleine, 3.28.1931
Sa Dernière Volonté.	Théâtre de la Madeleine, 6.3.1931
Revue-exposition de noirs.	Théâtre de la Madeleine, 6.3.1931
Monsieur Prudhomme a-t-il vécu?	Théâtre de la Madeleine, 11.4.1931
Villa à vendre.	Théâtre de la Madeleine, 11.4.1931
Chagrin d'amour.	Théâtre de la Madeleine, 11.4.1931
La S.A.D.M.P.	Théâtre de la Madeleine, 11.4.1931
Tout commence par des chansons.	Moulin de la Chanson, 12.22.1931
Mon Double et ma moitié.	Théâtre de la Madeleine, 12.28.1931
Le Voyage de Tchong Li.	Théâtre de la Madeleine, 3.15.1932
Les Desseins de la providence.	Théâtre de la Madeleine, 3.15.1932
Françoise.	Théâtre de la Madeleine, 3.15.1932
La nuit d'avril.	? 1932
Châteaux en Espagne.	Théâtre des Variétés, 4.5.1933
Adam et Ève.	Comédie-Française, 5.9.1933
Maîtresses de rois.	Casino de Paris, 1933
O mon bel inconnu. (Music: REYNALDO HAHN)	Bouffes-Parisiens, 10.5.1933
Un Tour au paradis.	Michodière, 11.6.1933

TITLE	FIRST PERFORMANCE
Le Renard et la grenouille.	Michodière, 11.6.1933
L'École des philosophes.	Palais des Beaux-Arts, Brussels, 12.20.1933
Son Père et lui.	Théâtre des Célestins, Lyon, 3.10.1934
Le Nouveau Testament.	Théâtre de la Madeleine, 10.3.1934
Mon Ami Pierrot.	Opéra-Comique, 1.11.1935
Quand jouons-nous la comédie?	Théâtre de Paris, 9.21.1935
La Fin du monde.	Théâtre de la Madeleine, 10.2.1935
Geneviève.	Théâtre de la Madeleine, 10.2.1936
Le Mot de Cambronne.	Théâtre de la Madeleine, 10.2.1936
Le Saut périlleux.	? 1936
Le Gala des ambassadeurs.	? 1937
Crions-le sur les toits.	? 6.10.1937
Quadrille.	Théâtre de la Madeleine, 9.23.1937
Dieu sauve le roy.	Palais de l'Élysée, 7.19.1938
Un Monde fou.	? 11.1938
You're telling me!	London Coliseum, 4.1939
Une Paire de gifles.	Théâtre de la Madeleine, 10.24.1939
Fausse alerte.	Théâtre de la Madeleine, 10.24.1939
Une Lettre bien tapée.	Théâtre de la Madeleine, 10.24.1939
Florence.	Théâtre de la Madeleine, 11.17.1939
L'École du mensonge.	Opéra, 2.8.1940
Cigales et fourmis.	? 1940
Le Bien-aimé.	Théâtre de la Madeleine, 10.30.1940
Vive l'Empereur!	Théâtre de la Madeleine, 5.9.1941
N'écoutez pas, Mesdames!	Théâtre de la Madeleine, 5.19.1942
Courteline au travail.	Comédie-Française, 5.19.1943

TITLE	FIRST PERFORMANCE
Pour un oui, pour un non.	? 1946
Le Diable boiteux.	Théâtre Édouard VII, 1948
Aux Deux Colombes.	Théâtre Édouard VII, 1948
Tôa.	Théâtre du Gymnase, 5.6.1949
Tu m'as sauvé la vie.	Théâtre des Variétés, 1950
Une Folie.	Théâtre des Variétés, 5.26.1951
Palsambleu.	Théâtre des Variétés, 4.1953
Écoutez bien, Messieurs.	Winter Garden Theatre, London, 6.1.1953

PLAYS PUBLISHED BUT UNPRODUCED:

Beaumarchais (Raoul Solar, 1950)

Madame Bergeret (Livre Contemporain, 1960)

༅ Films of Sacha Guitry

WITH PRINCIPAL PLAYERS

1914–15   *Ceux de chez nous.* Sacha Guitry, Sarah Bernhardt, Anatole France, Edgar Degas, Auguste Rodin, Saint-Saëns, Auguste Renoir, Henri Robert, Edmond Rostand, André Antoine, Claude Monet, Octave Mirbeau, Lucien Guitry.

1935   *Pasteur.* Sacha Guitry, Gaston Dubosc.

1935   *Bonne Chance.* Sacha Guitry, Jacqueline Delubac, Pauline Carton.

1936   *Le Nouveau Testament.* Sacha Guitry, Jacqueline Delubac, Pauline Carton.

1936   *Le Roman d'un tricheur.* Sacha Guitry, Jacqueline Delubac, Marguerite Moreno, Pauline Carton.

1936   *Mon Père avait raison.* Sacha Guitry, Jacqueline Delubac, Gaston Dubosc, Pauline Carton.

1936   *Faisons un rêve.* Sacha Guitry, Jacqueline Delubac, Raimu, with Arletty, Baron *fils*, Pierre Bertin, Victor Boucher, Jean Coquelin, Claude Dauphin, Yvette Guilbert, André Lefaur, Marguerite Moreno, Michel Simon.

1936   *Le Mot de Cambronne.* Sacha Guitry, Jacqueline Delubac, Marguerite Moreno, Pauline Carton.

1937   *Les Perles de la couronne.* Sacha Guitry, Raimu, Jacqueline Delubac, Lynn Harding, Arletty, Dalio, Claude Dauphin, Cécile Sorel, Renée Saint-Cyr, Marguerite Moreno, Jean-Louis Barrault, Pauline Carton.

1937   *Désiré.* Sacha Guitry, Jacqueline Delubac, Arletty, Saturnin Fabre, Pauline Carton.

1937   *Quadrille.* Sacha Guitry, Jacqueline Delubac, Gaby Morlay, Pauline Carton.

1938   *Remontons les Champs-Élysées.* Sacha Guitry, Jacqueline Delubac, Jean Périer, René Fauchois, Pauline Carton.

1939   *Ils étaient neuf célibataires.* Sacha Guitry, Elvire Popesco, Geneviève Guitry, Victor Boucher, Marguerite Moreno, Max Dearly, Saturnin Fabre, Gaston Dubosc, Pauline Carton.

1941   *Le Destin fabuleux de Désirée Clary.* Sacha Guitry, Geneviève Guitry, Jean-Louis Barrault, Gaby Morlay, Aimé Clariond, Jeanne Fusier-Gir.

1943   *Donne-moi tes yeux.* Sacha Guitry, Geneviève Guitry, Marguerite Moreno, Aimé Clariond, Dunoyer de Segonzac, Othon Friesz, Derain, Raoul Dufy, Touchagues, Vlaminck, Utrillo.

1943   *La Malibran.* Sacha Guitry, Geneviève Guitry, Jean Cocteau, Géori Boué, Suzy Prim, Jeanne Fusier-Gir.

1947   *Le Comédien.* Sacha Guitry, Lana Marconi, José Noguero, Pauline Carton.

1948   *Le Diable boiteux.* Sacha Guitry, Lana Marconi, Jean Debucourt, Pauline Carton.

1949   *Aux Deux Colombes.* Sacha Guitry, Lana Marconi, Jeanne Fusier-Gir.

1950   *Le Trésor de Cantenac.* Sacha Guitry, Lana Marconi, Jeanne Fusier-Gir, Pauline Carton.

1950   *Tu m'as sauvé la vie.* Sacha Guitry, Fernandel, Lana Marconi, Jeanne Fusier-Gir.

1950   *Deburau.* Sacha Guitry, Lana Marconi, Jeanne Fusier-Gir.

1951   *Adhémar, ou le jouet de la fatalité.* Fernandel, José Noguero.

1951   *La Poison.* Michel Simon, Jean Debucourt, Jeanne Fusier-Gir, Pauline Carton, Louis de Funès.

1952   *La Vie d'un honnête homme.* Michel Simon, Lana Marconi, Louis de Funès, Pauline Carton.

1952   *Je l'ai été trois fois.* Sacha Guitry, Lana Marconi, Bernard Blier, Louis de Funès.

1953   *Si Versailles m'était conté.* Sacha Guitry, Lana Marconi, Jean-Pierre Aumont, Jean-Louis Barrault, Claudette Colbert, Nicole Courcel, Danielle Delorme, Daniel Gelin, Fernand Gravey, Jean Marais, Gaby Morlay, Gérard Philippe, Tino Rossi, Charles Vanel, Orson Welles, Pauline Carton, Brigitte Bardot, Jeanne Fusier-Gir, Nicole Maurey.

1954   *Napoléon.* Sacha Guitry, Jean-Pierre Aumont, Pierre Brasseur, Pauline Carton, Danielle Darrieux, Jean Gabin, Yves Montand, Daniel Gelin, Jean Marais, Michèle Morgan, Patachou, Dany Robin, Nicole Maurey, Orson Welles, Eric von Stroheim, O. W. Fischer, Serge Reggiani, Lana Marconi, Luis Mariano.

1955   *Si Paris nous était conté.* Sacha Guitry, Françoise Arnoul, Danielle Darrieux, Jean Marais, Lana Marconi, Michèle Morgan, Sophie Desmarets, Odette Joyeux, Gérard Philippe, Pauline Carton, Aimé Clariond, Jean Debucourt, Jeanne Fusier-Gir, Utrillo.

1956   *Assassins et voleurs.* Magali Noël, Darry Cowl, Pauline Carton.

1957   *Les Trois font la paire.* Michel Simon, Darry Cowl, Sophie Desmarets, Pauline Carton.

1957   *La Vie à deux.* Pierre Brasseur, Lili Palmer, Edwige Feuillère, Louis de Funès, Gérard Philippe, Jean Marais, Danielle Darrieux, Fernandel, Pauline Carton, Pierre Larquey.

ᴓ Bibliography

UNPUBLISHED SOURCES

The author's private collection of manuscripts, letters, correspondence, and documents by and concerning Sacha and Lucien Guitry, Jules Renard, Tristan Bernard, and their circle.

SELECTED PRINTED SOURCES

Agate, James. *Immoment Toys*. Jonathan Cape, 1945.

———. *Around Cinemas*. Home and van Thal, 1948.

Antoine, André. *Le Théâtre*. Édit. de France, 1933.

Bainville, Jacques. *Une Saison chez Thespis*. Édit. Prométhée, 1929.

Baring, Maurice. *Punch and Judy*. Heinemann, 1924.

Basch, Victor. *Études d'esthétique dramatique*. J. Vrin, 1929.

Béguin, A., and Thévenaz, P. *Henri Bergson*. Édit. de la Baconnière, 1943.

Benjamin, René, and others. *Sacha Guitry*. Édit. "Le Capitole," 1926.

———. *Sacha Guitry, roi du théâtre*. Plon, 1933.

———. *Le Galère des Goncourt*. L'Élan, 1948.

Bernard, Jean-Jacques. *Mon père Tristan Bernard*. Albin Michel, 1955.
266

Bernhardt, Sarah. *Ma Double Vie*. Charpentier, Fasquelle, 1907.

Bonmariage, Sylvain. *Willy, Collette et moi*. Frémanger, 1954.

Bordeaux, Henry. *La Vie au théâtre*. Plon, 1913, 1919, 1921.

Brisson, Adolphe. *Le Théâtre* (séries 1, 6, 9). Lib. des Annales, Hachette, 1918.

Brisson, Pierre. *Au Hasard des soirées*. Gallimard, 1935.

———. *Du Meilleur au pire*. Gallimard, 1937.

Buache, Freddy. *Michel Simon*. Édit. du Panorama, 1962.

Choisel, Fernande. *Sacha Guitry intime*. Édit. du Scorpion, 1957.

Cochran, C. B. *The Secrets of a Showman*. Heinemann, 1925.

———. *Cock-a-doodle-doo*. Dent, 1941.

———. *A Showman Looks On*. Dent, 1945.

Colette. *La Jumelle noire*. Ferenczi, 1934, 1935, 1937, 1938.

———. *Lettres à Marguerite Moreno*. Flammarion, 1959.

———. *Lettres de la vagabonde*. Flammarion, 1961.

Delattre, F. *Les Dernières Années d'Henri Bergson*. P.U.F., 1941.

Descaves, Lucien. *Souvenirs d'un ours*. Édit. de Paris, 1946.

Doniol-Valcroze, Jacques. "Guitry cinéaste de la dernière heure." *Cahiers du cinéma*, Août/sept. 1957, no. 74.

Galtier-Boissière, Jean. *Mon Journal depuis la Libération*. La Jeune Parque, 1945.

———. *Mon Journal dans la drôle de paix*. La Jeune Parque, 1947.

———. *Mon Journal dans la grande pagaïe*. La Jeune Parque, 1950.

———. *Mémoires d'un Parisien*. (3 vols.) Table Ronde, 1961.

Georges-Michel, Michel. *Gens de théâtre que j'ai connus*. Brentano's, n.d.

Grun, Bernard. *Prince of Vienna*. W. H. Allen, 1955.

Guitry, Lana. *Et Sacha vous est conté* . . . Livre Contemporain, 1960.

Guitry, Lucien. *Souvenirs* . . . Les Oeuvres Libres, juin 1923.

Henri-Bellier, P. *Sacha Guitry et Yvonne Printemps*. Moderne Imprimerie, 1926.

Hermant, Abel. *Essais de critique*. Grasset, 1912.

———. *Les Théâtres*. Sansot, 1914.

Lauwick, Hervé. *Le Merveilleux Humour de Lucien et Sacha Guitry*. Arthème Fayard, 1959.

———. *D'Alphonse Allais à Sacha Guitry*. Plon, 1963.

———. *Sacha Guitry et les femmes*. Plon, 1965.

Léautaud, Paul. *Le Théâtre de Maurice Boissard*. (2 vols.) Gallimard, 1958.

––––––. *Journal Littéraire*, vols. I, II, IV, VIII, IX, XII, XV, XVI, XVII, XVIII. Mercure de France, 1955–66.

MacCarthy, Desmond. *Drama*. Putnam, 1940.

Madis, Alex. *Sacha*. Édit. de l'Élan, 1950.

Marcorelles, Louis. "Sacha Guitry." *Sight and Sound*, Autumn, 1957.

Mars, François. "Citizen Sacha." *Cahiers du Cinéma*, Oct., 1958, no. 88.

Martin, Marcel. *Le Language cinématographique*. Édit. du Cerf, 1955.

Martin du Gard, Maurice. *Carte rouge*. Flammarion, 1930.

––––––. *Soirées de Paris*. Flammarion, 1932.

––––––. *Harmonies critiques*. Édit. du Sagittaire, 1936.

––––––. *Mon Ami Sacha Guitry*. Édit. de la Nouvelle Revue Critique, 1941.

––––––. *La Chronique de Vichy*. Flammarion, 1948.

Mauriac, François. *Dramaturges*. Cahiers d'occident, 2e série, 1928.

Maurois, André. *Choses nues*. Gallimard, 1963.

Moreno, Marguerite. *Souvenirs de ma vie*. Édit. de Flore, 1949.

Olivier, Paul. *Raimu*. Fournier-Valdès, 1947.

Perrin, Michel. *Arletty*. Calmann-Lévy, 1952.

Prince, Stéphane. *Sacha Guitry hors sa legende*. Presses de la Cité, 1959.

Renard, Jules. *Correspondance*. Flammarion, 1954.

––––––. *Lettres inédites*. Gallimard, 1957.

––––––. *Journal*. NRF, Pléaide, 1960.

Richardson, Joanna. *Sarah Bernhardt*. Max Reinhardt, 1959.

Sée, Edmond. *Le Mouvement dramatique*. Édit de France, 1932, 1933, 1935.

Séréville, Geneviève de. *Sacha Guitry, mon mari*. Flammarion, 1959.

Sherek, Henry. *Not in front of the children*. Heinemann, 1959.

Tailhade, Laurent. *Les Commérages de Tybalt*. Crès, 1914.

Terriss, Ellaline. *Just a Little Bit of String*. Hutchinson, 1955.

Thiebault, Marcel. *Le Grand Comédien*. Jouve, 1919.

Un vieux bibliophile. *Les Pièces et la bibliographie de Sacha Guitry*. Impr. Coulouma, 1931.

Vandérem, Felix. *Le Miroir des lettres* (séries 1, 3, 6, 7). Flammarion, 1919–29.

Whitridge, Arnold. *Sacha Guitry*. Édit. de la pensée latine, 1927.

Abélard, Pierre, theologian, (1079–1142), 144

Achard, Marcel, dramatist, (1899–), 169, 252

Agate, James Evershed, dramatic critic, (1877–1947), 154, 155, 158, 189

Agoult, Marie de Flavigny, comtesse d', writer, (1805–1876), 144

Alexander III, Tsar, (1845–1894), 18, 21–22

Allais, Alphonse, humorist, (1854–1905), 39, 43–44, 81, 251

Allégret, Marc, film director, (1900–), 177 and n.

Annunzio, Gabriele d', writer, (1863–1938), 138

Antoine, André, theatre producer, (1859–1953), 33, 60, 63, 77, 86, 98, 138, 157, 209, 213

Arc, Jeanne d', patron saint, (1412–1431), 214

Arlen, Michael, (Dikran Kuyumjian), writer, (1895–1956), 66

Arletty, (Léonie Bathiat), actress, (1898–), 175, 176, 179, 187, 189, 209, 225, 226

Arnoul, Françoise, actress, (1931–), 244

Ashcroft, Dame Peggy, actress, (1907–), 194

Bacon, Francis, philosopher, (1561–1626), 90

Baker, Joséphine, singer, (1907–), 136

Balzac, Honoré de, novelist, (1799–1850), 72, 90, 112, 126, 154, 203, 214

Bardot, Brigitte, actress, (1934–), 177, 241

Baring, Maurice, writer, (1874–1945), 15, 127–128

Barker, Harley Granville-, dramatist, (1877–1946), 114

Baron, fils, (Louis Bouchenez), actor, (1838–1920), 89, 90

Barrault, Jean-Louis, actor, (1910–), 240

Barrès, Maurice, writer, (1862–1923), 143

Baudelaire, Charles, poet, (1821–1867), 144, 168, 181

Beaumarchais, Pierre Augustin Caron de, dramatist, (1732–1799), 144, 154

Becque, Henri François, dramatist, (1837–1899), 54–55, 142

Beecham, Sir Thomas, conductor, (1879–1961), 153

Beethoven, Ludwig van, composer, (1770–1827), 144, 242

Benjamin, René, writer, (1885–1948), 203

Bennett, Enoch Arnold, writer, (1867–1931), 117

Benoit, Pierre, novelist, (1886–1962), 206, 214

Béranger, poet, 121–122

Béraud, Henri, writer, 219

Bergson, Henri, philosopher, (1859–1941), 167–168, 174, 206–207 and n.

Berlioz, Hector, composer, (1803–1869), 144

Bernadette, Saint, (1844–1879), 153

Bernard, Jean-Jacques, dramatist, (1888–), 40, 228

Bernard, Tristan, humorist, (1866–1947), 4, 39, 40–42, 43, 57, 58, 69–70, 76, 81, 89, 114–115, 119, 137, 189, 208–209

Bernhardt, Sarah, actress, (1845–1923), 4, 14–16, 23–24, 32–33, 37–38, 46, 86, 98, 99, 119, 126, 128–130, 132–133, 138, 143, 154, 156, 158, 208, 238, 243, 251

Birley, Sir Oswald, painter, 145

Björnson, Bjornstierne, dramatist, (1832–1910), 60

Bonnard, Abel, writer, (1883–), 221

Bossuet, Jacques Bénigne, preacher, (1672–1704), 7, 142

Boswell, James, biographer, (1740–1795), 139, 245

Boucher, Victor, actor, (1879–1942), 58, 179, 189, 205

Boué, Géori, singer, 213

Boulanger, Georges, General, (1837–1891), 41

Boulestin, Xavier Marcel, restaurateur and writer, (1878–1943), 75

Bovy, Berthe, actress, (1887–), 171

Boyer, Charles, actor, (1899–), 179

Brahms, Johannes, composer, (1833–1897), 114

Brandès, Marthe, (Brunschwig), actress, (1862–1930), 35

Braque, Georges, painter, (1882–1963), 146

Brasseur, actor, 12

Bruant, Aristide, chansonnier, (1851–1925), 45

Byron, George Gordon, Lord, poet, (1788–1824), 37

Cagliostro, Guiseppe Balsamo, charlatan, (1743–1795), 144

Cambronne, Pierre, General, (1770–1842), 180–181, 242

Camus, Alfred, writer, (1913–1960), 218–219

Capus, Alfred, dramatist, (1858–1922), 39, 40, 43, 57

Carco, Francis, (Carcopino), novelist, (1886–1958), 203

Carcopino, Jérôme, historian, (1881–), 220–221

Carpentier, Georges, boxer, 126, 216

Carton, Pauline, actress, (1884–), 186, 188, 234

Caryll, Ivan, (Félix Tilkin), composer, (1861–1921), 133, 134

Catherine II, Empress, (1729–1796), 144, 154

Céline, (Louis Ferdinand Destouches), novelist, (1894–1961), 216

Cézanne, Paul, painter, (1839–1906), 59, 146, 162, 225, 250, 252

Chack, Paul, writer, 219

Chaliapin, Fedor Ivanovitch, singer, (1873–1938), 199, 237

Chamfort, (Nicolas Sébastien Roch), moralist, (1741–1794), 248

Chaplin, Charles Spencer, actor, (1889–), 21, 97

Chénier, André, poet, (1762–1794), 222

Chevalier, Maurice, singer, (1888–), 108, 135–136, 216

Choisel, Madame Fernande, secretary to S.G., 222, 225, 228

Choisy, abbé de, (Françoise Timoléon), writer, (1644–1724), 7

Chopin, Frédéric, composer, (1810–1849), 144, 155, 242

Churchill, Lord, diplomatist, 193

Clary, Désirée, queen of Sweden, (1777–1860), 213

Claudel, Paul, poet, (1868–1966), 229–230

Clemenceau, Georges, politician, (1841–1929), 68–69, 135, 145, 162–163, 240

Cochran, Sir Charles Blake, impresario, (1873–1951), 45, 117–118, 124–125, 163, 193–194

Cocteau, Jean, poet, (1889–1963), 4, 42, 72–74, 108, 169, 213, 214, 222, 224, 225

Colbert, Claudette, (Lily Chauchoin), actress, (1905–   ), 241

Colette, Sidonie Gabrielle, writer, (1873–1954), 74–77, 92, 108, 131, 139, 152–153, 175, 181, 209, 214, 228

Coppée, François, writer, (1842–1908), 14

Coquelin, Constant, actor, (1841–1909), 12, 128

Corneille, Pierre, dramatist, (1606–1729), 10, 11, 52, 113, 168

Corot, Jean Baptiste, painter, (1796–1875), 146

Cortot, Alfred, pianist, (1877–1962), 209

Courbet, Gustave, painter, (1819–1877), 146

Courteline, Georges, (Moinaux), writer, (1861–1929), 39, 144, 150, 151, 203, 222

Courteline, Madame Georges, (1869–1967), 209

Coward, Noël, dramatist, (1899–   ), 58, 168, 179, 188

Cunard, Lady, society hostess, 126

Daladier, Édouard, politician, (1884–1967), 204

Darrieux, Danielle, actress, (1917–   ), 242, 244, 250

Daudet, Alphonse, writer, (1840–1897), 18, 130, 202

Daudet, Madame Alphonse, (née Julia Allard), (1847–1940), 130

Daudet, Léon, writer, (1868–1942), 130, 203

Daudet, Lucien, writer, (1879–1946), 130

Daumier, Honoré, painter, (1808–1879), 147, 150

Dauphin, Claude, actor, (1903–   ), 179

Davidoff, actor, 21

Dearly, Max, actor, 192

Deburau, Jean Gaspard, mime, (1796–1846), 111–113

Debussy, Claude Achille, composer, (1862–1918), 76, 120, 144

Degas, Edgar, (de Gas), painter, (1834–1917), 98, 146, 147, 217

Déjazet, Virginie, actress, (1797–1875), 141

Delaunay, Louis Arsène, actor, (1826–1903), 128

Delacroix, Eugène, painter, (1798–1875), 141, 146

Delorme, Danièle, actress, (1926–   ), 241

Delubac, Jacqueline, (3rd Madame Guitry), actress, (1910–   ), 172, 173, 175, 176, 177, 179, 186, 187, 195–196, 198, 217

Delysia, Alice, (Lapize), actress, (1889–   ), 126

Demolder, Eugène, writer, (1862–1919), 47–48

Denis, Louise, companion to Voltaire, (c. 1710–1790), 144

Derain, André, painter, (1880–1954), 213, 216

Derval, Paul, (Pitron), director of the Folies-Bergère, (1880–1967), 107

Descartes, René, philosopher, (1596–1650), 141, 168, 212, 214

Descaves, Lucien, writer, (1861–1949), 203–204

Deslys, Gabie, actress, (1884–1920), 126

Diderot, Denis, (1713–1784), 80, 154

Dieudonné, Alphonse Emile, actor, (1832–1923), 60, 89

Dolly Sisters, singers, (Jennie, 1891–1941), 125, 136

Dongen, Cornelius Kees van, painter, (1877–   ), 148

Dorgelès, Roland Lecavalé, writer, (1886–   ), 203

Douglas, Norman, writer, (1868–1952), 121

Douroff, clown, 21

Drain, Émile, actor, (1890–   ), 234

Dreyer, Carl, film director, (1889–1968), 123 footnote

Dreyfus, Alfred, scapegoat, (1859–1935), 76, 214

Drouet, Juliette, actress, (1806–1863), 144

Dubarry, Madame, (Jeanne Bécu), royal mistress, (1743–1793), 174

Dufrény, Paul, secretary to S.G., 133

Dufy, Raoul, painter, (1878–1953), 171, 213

Dumas, Alexandre, fils, writer, (1824–1895), 13, 144

Duncan, Isadora, dancer, (1878–1927), 95

Duplessis, Marie, courtesan, (1824–1847), 112–113, 144

Duse, Eleonora, actress, (1859–1924), 45, 126, 154

Dyck, Sir Anthony van, painter, (1599–1641), 146

Edward VII, King, (1841–1910), 14, 56
Edwards, Alfred, newspaper magnate, (?–1914), 68
Ellesmere, Lord Chancellor, (1540–1617), 90
Éon, chevalier Charles Beaumont d', transvestite, (1728–1810), 144
Épinay, Louise de la Live d', patroness, (1726–1783), 154, 157
Evans, Dame Edith, actress, (1888–), 194

Fabre, Saturnin, actor, (1883–1961), 192
Fabre-Luce, Alfred, writer, (1899–), 221–222
Falconetti, Renée, actress, (1901–1946), 123 and footnote
Fauchois, René, dramatist, (1882–1962), 46, 51, 222–223, 225
Fauré, Gabriel, composer, (1845–1924), 46, 134–135
Fénelon, Fr. Salignac de la Mothe, (1651–1715), 240
Fernandel, (Fernand Contandin), actor, (1903–), 177, 179, 235, 250
Feuillère, Edwigs, actress, (1907–), 160, 250
Feydeau, Georges, dramatist, (1862–1921), 41, 62–63, 119
Flaubert, Gustave, novelist, (1821–1880), 52, 130, 143, 145, 168, 202
Fontenelle, Bernard le Bovier de, writer, (1657–1757), 52, 251
Forain, Jean Louis, painter, (1852–1931), 45, 141, 251
Fould-Springer, Max, Baron, 198
Forbes-Robertson, Sir John, actor, (1835–1937), 127
Françaix, Jean, composer, (1912–), 240, 242
France, Anatole, (Thibault), (1844–1924), 45, 98, 105, 143, 249
François Ier, King, (1494–1547), 187
Franklin, Benjamin, politician, (1706–1790), 241
Fresnay, Pierre, (Laudenbach), actor, (1897–), 170–171, 179, 234
Fusier-Gir, Jeanne, actress, (1897–), 212

Gabin, Jean, (Alexandre, Moncorgé), actor, (1904–), 179, 242

Gamelin, General, (1872–1958), 204
Garrick, David, actor, (1717–1779), 245
Gauguin, Paul, painter, (1848–1903), 142, 146
Gaulle, Charles de, General, (1890–), 217, 222, 230
George VI, King, (1895–1952), 193, 195
Germain, André, writer and dandy, 130
Gide, André, writer, (1869–1951), 143, 177
Gielgud, Sir John, actor, (1904–), 194
Giraudoux, Jean, dramatist, (1882–1944), 182, 214
Gluck, Christoph Willibald, composer, (1714–1787), 153, 155
Goddeville, Madame, 144
Goethe, Johann Wolfgang von, writer, (1749–1832), 144
Goldoni, Carlo, dramatist, (1707–1793), 5, 249
Gogh, Vincent van, painter, (1853–1890), 59, 146, 217
Goldwyn, Sam, (Goldfisch), film producer, (1884–), 85
Goncourt, Edmond de, writer, (1822–1896), 130, 202
Goncourt, Jules de, writer, (1830–1870), 130, 202
Got, Edmond François Jules, actor, (1822–1901), 128
Goya, (Francisco de Goya y Lucientes), painter, (1746–1828), 146, 149
Granier, Jeanne, actress, (1852–1939), 56
Gravey, Fernand, (Mertens), actor, (1905–), 241
Grimm, Frédéric Melchior, Baron, writer, (1723–1807), 154, 156, 157
Grock, (Adrien Wettach), clown, (1880–1959), 21
Guardi, Francesco, painter, (1712–1793), 146
Guilbert, Yvette, diseuse, (1868–1944), 136, 179
Guimard, Madeleine, dancer, (1743–1816), 154, 156
Guines, duc de, patron, 153
Guitry, Adèle, (S.G.'s aunt), 9
Guitry, Edmond, (S.G.'s uncle), 9
Guitry, Jean, (S.G.'s brother), actor, (1884–1920), 18, 22, 23, 24, 36, 51, 67–68, 137
Guitry, Lucien, (S.G.'s father), actor, (1860–1925), 4, 8; youth and early

life, 8–14; marriage and fatherhood, 16–20; as favourite son, 23; technique as actor, 32–35; personal character, 35–36; his circle of friends, 36, 38–39, 40–44; quarrel with Sacha, 50, 59, 65, 114–115; appears in Sacha's plays, 115, 117–118, 120–121, 122–124, 127–128, 132; his versions of Molière, 124–125; death, 136–137; his house, 139–141

Guitry, Sacha, (Georges Alexandre Pierre), (1885–1957), Family, etc., see: Adèle, Edmond, Jean, Lucien and Valentine Guitry; René and Renée de Pont-Jest; and Delubac, J., "Henriette," Lysès, C., Marconi, L., "Mariette," Printemps, Y., Séréville, G. de
Books: le Taureau, le veau . . . , 45–46; Lucien Guitry raconté par son fils, 165; correspondance de Paul Roulier-Davenel, 81–82; la Maladie, 93–94; la Maison de Loti, 164–165; Quatre ans d'Occupations, 231; 60 jours de prison, 231; Toutes réflexions faites, 233; Elles et toi, 233–234
Films: Ceux de chez nous, 99–100, 205, 208, 253; le Blanc et le noir, 177; Pasteur, 178; Faisons un rêve, 179; Désiré, 179; Mon père avait raison, 179; le Nouveau testament, 179; le Mot de Cambronne, 181; le Roman d'un tricheur, 182–186, 187; les Perles de la Couronne, 187, 229; Remontons les Champs-Elysées, 187–188, 211; Ils étaient neuf célibataires, 189–192; Le Destin fabuleux de Désirée Clary, 213; Donne-moi tes yeux, 213; la Malibran, 213; la Poison, 237–238; la Vie d'un honnête homme, 238; Si Versailles m'était conté, 239–241; Napoléon, 242–243; Si Paris nous était conté, 243–244, 245; Assassins et voleurs, 246; Les Trois font la paire, 246; la Vie à deux, 249–250
Plays: le Page, 47, 55; le Kwtz, 55, 56, 58; Nono, 57–59, 60, 62, 153; Chez les Zoaques, 60–61, 62, 66; la Clef, 62, 64, 67, 77; C'te pucelle d'Adèle, 77; la Petite Hollande, 77; Tell père, Tell fils, 81; le Veilleur de nuit, 82–84; Un beau mariage, 84–86; la Prise de Berg-op-Zoom, 88–89; la Pèlerine écossaise, 90–91; les Deux couverts, 91–92; Faisons un rêve, 100–105; Jean de la Fontaine, 105–107; l'Illusionniste, 108–111; De-

burau, 110–114, 143; Pasteur, 114, 115–119, 120, 127–128, 208; Mon père avait raison, 121; Je t'aime, 123; le Comédien, 123–124; Comment on écrit l'histoire, 129–130; Un sujet de roman, 130–132; l'Amour masqué, 133–135, 165; la Revue de Printemps, 136; Mozart, 137, 153–157, 171; Mariette, 158; la Jalousie, 160–161; Désiré, 164; Frans Hals, 170; Châteaux en Espagne, 173; Maîtresses de Rois, 172–173; O mon bel inconnu, 174–175; le Nouveau testament, 175; le Mot de Cambronne, 180–181; Crions-le sur les toits, 189; Dieu sauve le Roy, 193; You're telling me!, 194, 195; Un monde fou, 195, 211; Quadrille, 188–189; Florence, 205; le Bien-aimé, 211–212, 230; Vive l'Empereur, 212, 230; N'écoutez pas, Mesdames, 212–213, 230; le Diable boiteux, 231–233; Écoutez bien, Messieurs, 235; Palsambleu, 236

Guitry, Valentine, (S.G.'s aunt), 9–10
Guitry, marquis de, Chaumont, Guy de, soldier, 8
Gulbenkian, Calouste, billionaire, 147

Hackenschmidt, George, wrestler, (1877–1968), 125
Hahn, Reynaldo, composer, (1874–1947), 46, 155–157, 175, 193
Hals, Frans, painter, (1580/5–1666), 137
Hauptmann, Gerhart, dramatist, (1862–1946), 60
Hawtrey, Sir Charles, actor, (1858–1923), 127
Héloïse, abbess, (1101–1164), 144
Henri IV, King, (1553–1610), 144, 243
"Henriette," actress, 225
Henry VIII, King, (1509–1547), 187
Hermant, Abel, writer, (1862–1950), 221
Hicks, Sir Edward Seymour, actor, (1871–1949), 127, 194–195
Hitchcock, Alfred, film director, (1899–), 179
Honegger, Arthur, composer, (1892–1955), 189
Houdetot, Élisabethe, comtesse de, Egeria, (1730–1813), 144
Houdini, escapologist, (1874–1929), 125
Houdon, Jean Antoine, sculptor, (1741–1828), 147
Howell, Bert, theatrical agent, 193–194

Hugo, Victor, writer, (1802–1885), 12, 15, 16, 18, 37, 40, 100, 113, 144, 145, 146, 214
Huysmans, Joris Karl, writer, (1848–1907), 202–203

Ibsen, Henrik, dramatist, (1828–1906), 60
Indy, Vincent d', composer, (1851–1931), 75
Irving, Sir Henry, (John Henry Brodribb), actor, (1838–1905), 16, 143, 154, 194

Jacob, Max, poet, (1876–1944), 209
Jarry, Alfred, writer, (1873–1907), 48–49, 72
Joffre, Joseph, maréchal de France, (1852–1931), 145
Joffre, Madame, 209
Johnson, Dr. Samuel, lexicographer, (1709–1784), 139, 245
Joséphine, Marie Josèphe Tascher de la Pagerie, empress (1763–1814), 144
Jouvet, Louis, actor, (1887–1951), 55

Kiepura, Jan, singer, (1902–1960), 108
Kipling, Rudyard, writer, (1865–1936), 7

La Fontaine, Jean de, poet, (1621–1695), 51, 52, 105–107, 149, 188, 249
Largillière, Nicolas de, painter, (1656–1746), 148
Larguier, Léo, poet, (1872–1950), 203
La Tour, Maurice Quentin de, painter, (1704–1788), 147, 212
Laval, Pierre, politician, (1883–1945), 210–211, 217
Léautaud, Paul, writer, (1872–1956), 77–81, 85–86, 90–91, 92, 109, 110, 113, 118–119, 210, 181, 224, 247
Lebrun, Albert, politician, (1871–1950), 194
Lemaître, Frédérick, actor, (1800–1876), 128, 238
Lifar, Serge, dancer, (1905–   ), 189
Ligne, Prince de, soldier, (1735–1814), 14
Lincoln, Abraham, politician, (1809–1865), 243n.
Liszt, Franz, composer, (1811–1886), 46, 144
"Little Tich," (Harry Relph), comedian, (1868–1928), 21, 126–127, 136

Loti, Pierre, (Viaud), writer, (1850–1923), 164–165
Louis XIV, King, (1638–1715), 7, 8, 36, 49, 140, 142, 148, 149, 193, 204, 211, 239, 240
Louis XV, King, (1710–1774), 188
Louis XVI, King, (1754–1793), 188
Louis XVIII, King, (1755–1824), 242
Lowe, Sir Hudson, General, (1769–1844), 242
Lowendal, Ulrich, comte de, soldier, (1700–1755), 88
Lully, Jean Baptiste, composer, (1632–1687), 107, 162, 193
Lutyens, Sir Edward, architect, (1869–1944), 194
Lysès, Charlotte, (1st Madame Guitry), actress, (1878–1957), 66–67, 71–72, 73, 89, 92, 96, 99–100, 103, 107–108, 118–119, 160, 179, 199, 222, 247–248.

Madrali, wrestler, 125
Maistre, Joseph de, writer, (1753–1821), 238
Mallarmé, Stéphane, poet, (1842–1898), 96, 181–182
Mandel, Georges, politician, 68, 69
Manet, Édouard, painter, (1832–1883), 146
Marais, Jean, actor, (1913–   ), 243, 250
Marat, Jean Paul, agitator, (1743–1793), 188
Marconi, Lana, (5th Madame Guitry), actress, (1917–   ), 226–227, 232, 234, 251
Marie-Antoinette, de Lorraine, archiduchesse d'Autriche, queen, (1755–1793), 145
"Mariette," actress, 217, 225
Marryat, Captain Frederick, writer, (1792–1848), 143
Mary, Queen, (1867–1953), 128
Masefield, John, poet, (1870–1967), 194
Massenet, Jules Émile Frédéric, composer, (1842–1912), 155
Matisse, Henri, painter, (1869–1954), 146
Matisse, Madame, 209
Maugham, William Somerset, writer, (1874–1965), 39, 120
Maupassant, Guy de, writer, (1850–1892), 168
Mauriac, François, writer, (1885–   ), 121, 215

Maurier, Sir George Hubert Edward du, actor, (1873–1934), 126, 127

Maurois, André, (Hertzog), writer, (1885–1968), 243

Maurras, Charles, writer, (1868–1952), 203, 219

Max, Édouard de, actor, (1869–1924), 32–33, 72, 73, 77

Médicis, Marie de, regent, (1573–1642), 144, 187

Méliès, Georges, film pioneer, (1861–1938), 100

Memling, Hans, painter, (1430?–1494), 47

Messager, André, composer, (1853–1929), 113–114, 134–135, 137, 153, 155, 156

Meyerbeer, Giacomo, (Jakob Liebmann Beer), composer, (1791–1864), 155

Mirbeau, Octave, writer, (1848–1917), 4, 39, 58, 59–60, 63, 82, 85, 98, 111, 143, 164, 203

Mistinguett, (Jeanne Bourgois), singer, (1875–1956), 126, 136, 189–190, 192, 216

Mitchell, Leslie, radio commentator, 190

Modigliani, Amedeo, painter, (1884–1920), 146, 151, 217

Molière, (Jean Baptiste Poquelin), dramatist, (1622–1673), 4, 5, 10, 11, 83, 89, 121, 124–125, 141, 142, 157, 162, 169, 212, 241, 249

Monet, Claude, painter, (1840–1926), 4, 59, 63–64, 98, 145, 161–162, 251

Monrose, actor, 11–12

Montespan, Françoise-Athenaïs de Rochechouart, marquise de, royal mistress, (1641–1707), 8, 239, 240, 241

Moreno, Marguerite, (Monceau), actress, (1871–1948), 181–182, 186, 187, 192

Morgan, Michèle, (Simone Roussel), actress, (1920–   ), 242, 244

Morlay, Gaby, (Blanche Fumoleau), actress, (1893–1964), 189, 205, 241

Morny, Charles duc de, politician, (1811–1865), 14, 136

Mounet-Sully, Jean, actor, (1841–1916), 12, 33

Mozart, Wolfgang Amadeus, composer, (1756–1791), 46, 137, 144, 150, 153–157, 199

Musset, Alfred de, poet, (1810–1857), 143, 144, 193, 213, 233

Napoleon I, tyrant, (1769–1821), 37, 121, 139, 143, 144, 145, 158, 168, 188, 231, 232, 240

Napoleon III, dictator, (1808–1873), 130, 149, 188

Noblet, Georges, actor, (1854–1930), 89–90

Orléans, Philippe duc de, (1869–1926), 89

Osiris, Daniel, philanthropist, 71

Ostade, Adriaen van, painter, (1610–1684), 170

Pagnol, Marcel, writer, (1896–   ), 169, 177, 216

Païva, marquise de, (Thérèse Lachmann), cocotte, (1819–1885), 136

Palmer, Lili, actress, (1917–   ), 203, 250

Pascal, Blaise, philosopher, (1623–1662), 174, 212

Pascal, Gisèle, actress, (1923–   ), 241

Pasteur, Louis, biologist, (1822–1895), 115, 116–119

Pasteur Vallery-Radot, Louis, doctor, (1886–   ), 116

Patachou, (Henriette Ragon), singer, (1918–   ), 242

Perrin, Émile, theatre manager, 13–14

Pétain, Philippe, maréchal de France, (1856–1951), 206, 209, 210–211, 212, 214, 220, 229–230

Philippe, Gérard, actor, (1922–1959), 240, 243, 250

Piaf, Édith, singer, (1915–1963), 241

Picasso, Pablo Ruiz y, painter, (1881–   ), 142

Pickford, Mary, actress, (1893–   ), 97

Pissarro, Camille, painter, (1831–1903), 64

Poiret, Paul, dressmaker, (?–1943), 72, 175

Poitiers, Diane de, royal mistress, (1499–1566), 136

Polaire, (Marie Émilie Bouchard Zouzé), singer, (1879–1939), 76

Pompadour, marquise de, (Antoinette Poisson), royal mistress, (1721–1764), 147, 211, 212, 241

Pont-Jest, René de, (S.G.'s grandfather), writer, 17–18, 19, 25–26, 30–31, 47

Pont-Jest, Renée de, (Madame Lucien Guitry, S.G.'s mother), actress, 16, 19, 22, 23, 35

Popesco, Elvire, actress, (1896–   ), 192, 195, 205, 206, 225

Porto-Riche, Georges de, dramatist, (1849-1930), 53-54, 55

Potemkin, Gregory Alexandrovitch, courtier, (1736-1791), 144

Poussin, Nicolas, painter, (1594-1665), 201

Powell, Dilys, film critic, 241

Presle, Micheline, (Chassagne), actress, (1922-   ), 241

Printemps, Yvonne, (Wignolle), (2nd Madame Guitry), actress, (1894-   ), 107-108, 110-111, 114, 115, 119, 120, 121, 122, 127, 130, 136, 137, 151, 152-153, 157, 158-159, 160, 161, 163, 169-171, 179, 198

Racine, Jean, dramatist, (1639-1699), 10, 11, 142

Raimu, (Jean Auguste César Muraire), actor, (1883-1946), 103-105, 108, 177, 179, 187, 221

Rattigan, Terence, dramatist, (1911-   ), 168

Ravel, Maurice, composer, (1875-1937), 149, 242

Reinhardt, Max, (Goldmann), theatre producer, (1873-1943), 125

Réjane, (Gabrielle Charlotte Réju), actress, (1857-1920), 33, 45, 62

Rembrandt van Ryn, painter, (1606-1669), 146, 149

"Rémy," (Gilbert Renault), secret agent and writer, (1904-   ), 229

Renan, Ernest, writer, (1823-1892), 143, 233

Renard, Jules, writer, (1864-1910), 4, 35, 38-40, 43, 44, 46, 52, 56-57, 58-59, 62, 77, 79, 84-85, 137, 141, 143, 181, 183, 203

Renoir Auguste, painter, (1841-1919), 64, 96, 97, 146, 149, 225, 252

Renoir, Jean, film director, (1894-   ), 46

Richelieu, Armand Jean du Plessis de, cardinal, (1585-1642), 144, 148

Rimbaud, Arthur, poet, (1854-1891), 168

Rivarol, Antoine de, moralist, (1753-1801), 248

Robert, Henri, barrister, 98-99

Robespierre, Maximilien de, politician, (1758-1794), 145

Rochefoucauld, François, duc de la, moralist, (1613-1680), 248

Rodin, Auguste, sculptor, (1840-1917), 59, 97-98, 145-146, 147

Ronsard, Pierre de, poet, (1524-1585), 47

Rossi, Tino, singer, (1907-   ), 241

Rostand, Edmond, dramatist, (1868-1918), 37, 38, 39, 46, 129, 180

Rouault, Georges, painter, (1871-1958), 142

Rouff, Maggy, dressmaker, 232

Rousseau, Jean Jacques, writer, (1712-1778), 79, 144, 154, 188

Ruskin, John, writer, (1819-1900), 146

Russell, Bertrand, (Earl), mathematician, (1872-   ), 168

Saint-Saëns, Charles Camille, composer, (1835-1921), 98

Saint-Simon, Louis de Rouvroy, duc de, memorialist, (1675-1755), 8, 144

Sainte-Beuve, Charles, critic, (1804-1869), 233

Sand, George, (Aurore Dudevant), writer, (1804-1876), 112, 144

Sartre, Jean Paul, writer, (1905-   ), 229

Satie, Erik, composer, (1866-1925), 76

Schopenhauer, Arthur, philosopher, (1788-1860), 144

Schubert, Franz, composer, (1797-1828), 157

Schumann, Robert, composer, (1810-1856), 107

Schwob, Marcel, writer, (1867-1905), 181

Scotto, Vincent, song writer, (1878-1952), 136

Segonzac, André Dunoyer de, painter, (1884-   ), 213

Séréville, Geneviève de, (4th Madame Guitry), actress, (1921-   ), 198-200, 205, 216-217, 227, 234-235

Seurat, Georges, painter, (1859-1891), 146

Shakespeare, William, dramatist, (1564-1616), 18, 170

Shaw, George Bernard, dramatist, (1856-1950), 93

Sherek, Henry, impresario, (1900-1967), 126

Simenon, Georges, writer, (1903-   ), 249

Simon, Michel, actor, (1895-   ), 46, 179, 237-238, 246, 252

Simon, Simone, actress, (1914-   ), 177n.

Sisley, Alfred, painter, (1839-1899), 64

Sorel, Cécile, (Seurre), actress, (1873–1966), 163, 173

Soubise, Charles de Rohan, Prince de, courtier, (1715–1787), 154

Stalin, Josef Visarionovitch, (Djugashvili), tyrant, (1879–1953), 168

Stanislavsky, Konstantin Sergeyevitch, (Alexeyev), theatre producer, (1865–1938), 179

Stendhal, (Henri Beyle), writer, (1783–1842), 143

Straus, Oscar, composer, (1869–1954), 157–158

Strindberg, August, dramatist, (1849–1912), 60

Stroheim, Eric von, film director and actor, (1885–1957), 242

Stulpnagel, General von, 215

Tailhade, Laurent, poet, 49–50, 52, 81

Talleyrand-Périgord, Charles Maurice de, Prince de Bénévent, diplomatist, (1754–1838), 144, 148, 204, 207, 231–233, 236

Temple, Shirley, actress and politician, (1928–   ), 198

Terry, Dame Alice Ellen, actress, (1847–1928), 16

Tiepolo, Giovanni Battista, (Giambattista), painter, (1696–1770), 146

Titheradge, Madge, actress, (1887–1961), 91

Toulouse-Lautrec, Henry de, painter, (1864–1901), 30, 145, 179, 212, 225

Trevor, Austin, actor, 193

Truffaut, François, film director, (1932–   ), 239

Twain, Mark, (Samuel Langhorne Clemens), writer, (1835–1910), 44

Utrillo, Maurice, painter, (1883–1955), 146, 213, 217, 244, 252

Vadim, Roger, (Vadim Peniakoff), film director, (1928–   ), 177n.

Valéry, Paul, poet, (1871–1945), 209, 214, 228

Vallette, Alfred, editor, (1859–1935), 78–79, 80

Vanel, Charles, actor, (1892–   ), 241

Vaugelas, C. F., Sieur de, grammarian, (1585–1650), 251

Vega, Felix Lope de, dramatist, (1562–1625), 5, 249

Verlaine, Paul, poet, (1844–1896), 49, 144, 168

Vestris, Gaetano Apollino Baldassare, dancer, (1729–1808), 156

Victoria, Queen, (1819–1901), 189

Vlaminck, Maurice de, painter, (1876–1958), 213

Voltaire, (François Marie Arouet), writer, (1694–1774), 142, 144, 155, 212, 251

Vuillard, Édouard, painter, (1868–1940), 145

Wagner, Richard, composer, (1813–1882), 144, 188

Watteau, Antoine, painter, (1684–1721), 112, 146, 147

Welles, Orson, producer and actor, (1915–   ), 177, 241, 242, 243n.

Wells, Billy, boxer, (?–1967), 126

Wesendonck, Mathilde, Wagner's mistress, 144

Whistler, James Abbott McNeill, painter, (1834–1903), 146

Whitehead, Alfred North, philosopher, (1861–   ), 168

Wilde, Oscar Fingal O'Flahertie Wills, writer, (1854–1900), 75, 172

Willemetz, Alfred, theatre producer and writer, (1887–   ), 134–135, 206, 207, 224, 250–251

Willy, (Henri Gauthier-Villars), writer, (1859–1931), 74–77

Woods, Al, impresario, (1871–1951), 163

Wyndham, Sir Charles, actor, (1837–1919), 127

Wyndham-Lewis, David Bevan, writer, 190

Zacconi, Ermete, actor, (1867–1948), 237

Zola, Émile, writer, (1840–1902), 18, 130, 143, 202, 203, 214